BUSINESS TENANCIES –
THE NEW LAW

BUSINESS TENANCIES – THE NEW LAW

A practical guide to the changes to the
Landlord and Tenant Act 1954 Part II

Jacqui Joyce of Lovells

LEGALEASE
PUBLISHING

ISBN: 1-903927-42-0

Published by Legalease Publishing, Kensington Square House, 12-14 Ansdell Street, London W8 5BN

Printed and bound in Great Britain by The Manson Group, St Albans.

www.legalease.co.uk

Preface

There have been many changes to the law relating to property in recent months (and there are several more in the pipeline). This book deals with one which will affect all practitioners who deal with business tenancies whether lawyer, surveyor or client, namely the reforms to the Landlord and Tenant Act 1954, which were brought about by the Regulatory Reform (Business Tenancies) (England and Wales) Order 2003. The reforms take effect from 1 June 2004 and this book represents my views and understanding as at that date.

This work seeks to be a practical guide to the changes and how they will affect day-to-day practice. There are several areas where the changes are not altogether lucid and I look forward to receiving judicial guidance as some point in the, probably, not too distant future. In the meantime, I have done my best to give you my guidance.

I would like to thank all those people who have assisted me in preparing this book by sharing their ideas and concerns about how the amended Act will work, and also their wisdom and experience of this area of the law. In particular, my colleagues at Lovells and the members of the London Property Support Lawyers Group and the Property Litigation Association's Law Reform Committee. (The latter also are to be thanked for allowing me to reproduce their Post-Action Protocol in this work.) Lovells will no doubt be pleased to hear that I will now be able to get on with my day job!

Three people deserve special mention. The first is Patrick Martin at the Office of the Deputy Prime Minister for answering, with extreme patience, what must have seemed like an endless stream of queries (no doubt there will be more to come). The others are Dellah Gilbert and Barry Moody, both of Lovells, for their primary editing skills.

Finally, but by no means least, a thank you to my family and friends for putting up with me whilst I was writing and for, as ever, keeping me sane.

Jacqui Joyce,
June 2004

ABOUT THE AUTHOR

Jacqui Joyce qualified as a solicitor in 1991 and since then has been an assistant in Lovells' property litigation department. She has extensive experience of all types of property disputes, including acting on several reported cases. Jacqui provides specialist advice to clients in relation to legislative developments and procedural reforms in the commercial property sector. Jacqui is a member of the London Property Support Lawyers Group and a member of the Property Litigation Association's Law Reform Committee. She is also an accredited mediator with the ADR Group and regularly contributes to property journals.

CONTENTS

TABLE OF CASES

TABLE OF STATUTES

TABLE OF STATUTORY INSTRUMENTS

1. INTRODUCTION

A brief history

The Landlord and Tenant Act 1954 ('the Act') came into operation on 1 October 1954. Whilst Part I of the Act contains provisions relating to tenants of certain leases of residential property at low rents, and other miscellaneous provisions, it is Part II of the Act, relating to business tenancies, with which this work is concerned.

The main object of the Act is to provide business tenants with security of tenure, enabling them to continue to occupy premises for the purposes of their business so long as they comply with their obligations as tenants. When the contractual tenancy comes to an end by effluxion of time or operation of a landlord's break clause, its provisions are continued by the Act as a statutory tenancy and the tenant is given a right to apply to the court for a new tenancy to be granted to it on essentially the same terms. If the terms of that new tenancy cannot be agreed between the parties, then the court will decide what they are. The Act does, however, make provision for the landlord to obtain a market rent for the continued occupation by the tenant, and for the court to return possession to the landlord in certain specified circumstances, eg if it wishes to occupy the premises for its own purposes, to redevelop the premises, or if the tenant has committed substantial breaches of the terms of the tenancy.

This work is not intended to be a detailed treatise on the current workings of the Act or the law which has grown up around it. There are many other learned texts which deal with these issues. The purpose of this work is instead to look at the reforms to the Act which are brought into effect by the Regulatory Reform (Business Tenancies) (England and Wales) Order 2003[1] and to provide practical guidance on how these reforms will affect the day-to-day practice of persons dealing with this area. Throughout this work, the author has expressed opinions on various matters which are uncertain. Reference has also been made to the Guidance Note produced by the Office of the Deputy Prime Minister

---

1 SI 2003/3096.

(ODPM) which is responsible for the reforms.[2] Obviously, these are only views and, as with all new legislation, ultimately where areas are uncertain or open to more than one interpretation, it will be for the courts to decide the correct approach.

The consultation process

The Act has been amended once before by the Law of Property Act 1969, following recommendations from the Law Commission.[3] In 1988, the Law Commission published a working paper[4] in which it highlighted 19 aspects of the legislation which might merit reform. A further report was issued in 1992[5] and a formal consultation paper was issued in March 2001.[6] The latter proposed that the amendments to the Act should be by regulatory reform order (RRO) rather than through a normal Parliamentary Bill. The Regulatory Reform Act 2001 allows ministers to use such RROs to reform primary legislation and, in particular, to remove burdensome regulations. These RROs must not, however, reduce or remove any necessary protection or prevent anyone from exercising an existing right or freedom which they might reasonably expect to continue to exercise. Also any burden imposed under an RRO must be proportionate to the benefits which are expected to result from its creation. It was against these background constraints that the reforms were drafted.

The Regulatory Reform (Business Tenancies) (England and Wales) Order 2003

The statutory instrument

Reforms to the Act were brought about by the Regulatory Reform (Business Tenancies) (England and Wales) Order 2003 ('the Order')[7] which was made on 1 December 2003.

---

2 Copies of the ODPM Guidance Note may be obtained free of charge from ODPM Free Literature, PO Box 236, Wetherby, West Yorkshire LS23 7NB (tel 0870 122 6236, fax 0870 122 6237, e-mail odpm@twoten.press.net). The Guidance Note is also available on the ODPM website: www.odpm.gov.uk.

3 Report on the Landlord and Tenant Act 1954 Part II (Law Com No 17, 1969).

4 Part II of the Landlord and Tenant Act 1954 (Working Paper No 111, 1988).

5 Business Tenancies: A Periodic Review of the Landlord and Tenant Act 1954 Part II (Law Com No 208, 1992).

6 Business Tenancies in England & Wales (Consultation Paper, March 2001).

7 SI 2003/3096.

When it comes into effect

The Order provides that it will come into force 'at the end of the period of six months beginning with the day on which it is made'. Therefore, the commencement date of the Order was 1 June 2004.

The documents to look at

The changes to the Act are made by direct amendment to the Act. When considering the Act in future, practitioners will need to refer to several separate documents. In summary, these are:

- The Act as amended. See **Appendix 1** which sets out a Keeling Schedule showing the amendments to the Act.

- Schedules 1 to 4 to the Order. These set out the forms and requirements for validly excluding a tenancy from the Act and for a valid agreement to surrender a business tenancy. See **Appendix 2**.

- Article 29 of the Order. This contains the transitional provisions. See **Appendix 3**.

- A separate statutory instrument prescribing the statutory notices – the Landlord and Tenant Act 1954 Part 2 (Notices) Regulations 2004.[8] Schedule 1 to these Regulations sets out the prescribed forms. **Appendix 4** lists the relevant forms, and those which are used most regularly are reproduced in appropriate places throughout this work.

- A separate statutory instrument dealing with the changes to the Civil Procedure Rules.[9] CPR56 and Practice Direction 56, as amended, are set out at **Appendix 5**.

Are the changes retrospective?

The short answer is 'no'. The transitional provisions are set out at Art 29 of the Order. This is at **Appendix 3** to this work. Each of these provisions is considered in more detail in the appropriate chapter, but the list is set out here for completeness.

The transitional provisions provide that nothing in the Order shall have effect in relation to:

---

8 SI 2004/1005.

9 Civil Procedure (Amendment) Rules 2004 (SI 2004/1306).

- a section 25 notice served by the landlord, or anything done in consequence of it, where the notice was given before the Order came into force (Art 29(1)(a));

- a section 26 request served by the tenant, or anything done in consequence of it, where the request was made before the Order came into force (Art 29(1)(b));

- an agreement for the surrender of a tenancy which was made before the Order came into force and which fell within s24(2)(b) of the Act – ie was made before the tenant had been in occupation in right of the tenancy for one month (Art 29(2)(a)(i));

- an agreement which was authorised by the court under s38(4) of the Act (a contracting-out order or an order authorising an agreement to surrender) before the Order came into force (Art 29(2)(a)(ii)); and

- a notice under s27(2) of the Act (ie a notice terminating a fixed-term tenancy which is continuing after the end of the fixed term) which was given by the tenant to the immediate landlord before the Order came into force (Art 29(2)(b)).

There are also transitional provisions relating to the contracting-out procedures in respect of agreements for contracted-out leases entered into before 1 June 2004 and requirements made before 1 June 2004 that subtenancies should be contracted out by court order. These are explained further in **Chapter 2** (Art 29(3) and (4)).

The new rules for compensation to the tenant where possession is obtained by misrepresentation do not have effect where the tenant quit the holding before the Order came into force (Art 29(5)). See **Chapter 13** for more detail.

The new rules as to duties to give information do not apply to a section 40 notice served before the Order came into force (Art 29(6)). See **Chapter 5** for more detail.

2. CONTRACTING OUT OF SECURITY OF TENURE

The reforms of the part of the 1954 Act relating to contracting out of security of tenure caused more difficulty than all the others. The whole reform process was held up until this was resolved.

The pre-June 2004 procedure – court orders

Before 1 June 2004, the proposed parties to a lease were able to contract out of the security of tenure provisions contained in ss24 to 28 of the Act by obtaining a court order authorising the agreement to do so as provided for by s38(4). This was done by way of a joint application by the proposed landlord and the proposed tenant to the county court where the premises were situated and, in practice, following the introduction of the Civil Procedure Rules, to whichever county court would turn the applications around the quickest. Applications could also be made to the High Court. Most parties regarded this as an expensive and time-consuming process.

The reforms

The proposal was to remove the need to obtain a court order and allow the parties to contract out using a notice procedure with specific 'health warnings' being given to the tenant (see below).

Before this change was approved by Parliament, it had to be approved by Standing Committees of both the House of Lords and the House of Commons. The House of Lords Standing Committee was very concerned that this notice procedure would deprive tenants of a 'necessary protection', ie having the contracting out approved by the court. As explained above, this would have been contrary to the spirit of changing the legislation by means of the regulatory reform procedure.

The government responded to these concerns by obtaining a research report from universities in Bristol and Sheffield into the number of contracting-out orders refused by the courts. The research concluded that, where contracting-out applications were rejected by the courts, this was virtually always due to minor technical errors and rarely had anything to do with the court scrutinising the actual merits of the application and interfering to protect the tenant's rights.

This research, together with the results of further consultation by the government with organisations representing small businesses, was presented to both the House of Commons and House of Lords Select Committees in the autumn of 2003.

On 8 October 2003, the House of Lords Select Committee published its report. This stated that, in the light of evidence concerning both the nature and the number of contracting-out application refusals, the Committee was satisfied that the new health warning system:

> … provided as effective a protection for tenants as that provided under the present arrangement involving the Court and that, therefore, no necessary protection was lost under the contracting-out provisions under the proposal.

Ongoing review

In a letter to the House of Commons Select Committee, the government undertook to review the new contracting-out procedures after they had been in force for a year. It intends to look at the impact of the new procedures and whether they affect the degree of contracting out. It will be interesting to see the results of this review although, as the government itself points out, the trend is growing towards shorter leases which are more likely to be contracted out in any case. This trend can only continue with the impact of stamp duty land tax on leases.

However, as observed by Baroness Hanham in the House of Lords debate on the Order, it is not entirely obvious how the government will carry out this review. It is easy to calculate how many contracting-out orders go through the courts, as records are kept, but less easy to assess how many 'health warning' notices are served.

From 1 June 2004 – the notice procedures

The provisions which provide for contracting out are in the new s38A of the Act and Schedules 1 and 2 to the Order. Section 38A(1) provides that the parties may contract out of the security of tenure provisions of the Act. Section 38A(3) provides that such an agreement will be void unless:

- the landlord has served on the tenant a notice in the form, or substantially in the form, set out in Schedule 1 to the Order; and
- the requirements of Schedule 2 to the Order are met.

The health warning notice

The form of the health warning notice as set out in Schedule 1 follows:

Figure 1

FORM OF NOTICE THAT SECTIONS 24 TO 28 OF THE LANDLORD AND TENANT ACT 1954 ARE NOT TO APPLY TO A BUSINESS TENANCY

To: [*Name and address of tenant*]

From: [*Name and address of landlord*]

IMPORTANT NOTICE

You are being offered a lease without security of tenure. Do not commit yourself to the lease unless you have read this message carefully and have discussed it with a professional adviser.

Business tenants normally have security of tenure – the right to stay in their business premises when the lease ends.

If you commit yourself to the lease you will be giving up these important legal rights.

- You will have **no right** to stay in the premises when the lease ends.

- Unless the landlord chooses to offer you another lease, you will need to leave the premises.

- You will be unable to claim compensation for the loss of your business premises, unless the lease specifically gives you this right.

- If the landlord offers you another lease, you will have no right to ask the court to fix the rent.

It is therefore important to get professional advice – from a qualified surveyor, lawyer or accountant – before agreeing to give up these rights.

If you want to ensure that you can stay in the same business premises when the lease ends, you should consult your adviser about another form of lease that does not exclude the protection of the Landlord and Tenant Act 1954.

If you receive this notice at least 14 days before committing yourself to the lease, you will need to sign a simple declaration that you have received this notice and have accepted its consequences, before signing the lease.

But if you do not receive at least 14 days notice, you will need to sign a 'statutory' declaration. To do so, you will need to visit an independent solicitor (or someone else empowered to administer oaths).

Unless there is a special reason for committing yourself to the lease sooner, you may want to ask the landlord to let you have at least 14 days to consider whether you wish to give up your statutory rights. If you then decided to go ahead with the agreement to exclude the protection of the Landlord and Tenant Act 1954, you would only need to make a simple declaration, and so you would not need to make a separate visit to an independent solicitor.

Contents of the notice

The health warning notifies the tenant that it will be giving up its right to security of tenure under the Act. The notice specifically informs the tenant that it is giving up legal rights, and the effect of so doing. In particular it states:

- the tenant will have no right to stay in the premises at the end of the lease;
- unless the landlord chooses to offer the tenant another lease, the tenant will have to leave the premises;
- the tenant will be unable to claim compensation for the loss of its business premises, unless the lease specifically gives it this right; and
- if the landlord offers the tenant another lease, the tenant will have no right to ask the court to fix the rent.

The notice informs the tenant of the importance of obtaining professional advice before agreeing to give up these rights, and also explains the simple declaration and statutory declaration procedures.

Completing the health warning notice

The landlord is only required to fill in the following to complete the health warning notice:

- the name and address of the tenant to which the notice is being sent; and
- the name and address of the landlord from whom the notice is sent.

There is no requirement to fill in the details of the property or the proposed lease to which the notice relates. There is also no requirement to sign or date the notice.

Whilst there is no requirement to refer to the premises, it would be advisable if a landlord were to put details of the premises on the notice, and the date it was sent, to avoid confusion later, particularly if several notices are being done at the same time and/or being sent to the same tenant for different premises. The landlord may also wish to attach a copy of the lease to the notice for the avoidance of any doubt as to which lease the notice relates to, although this is not required. See **p18** below as to when the health warning notice should be served.

The first requirement of Schedule 2 to the Order – the declarations

Section 38A(3)(b) provides that an agreement to exclude security of tenure will be void unless the requirements in Schedule 2 to the Order are met.[1]

---

1 Sch 2 is set out in full in **Appendix 2**.

The requirements vary slightly depending on when the health warning notice is served. It depends whether or not the notice is served 'not less than 14 days before the tenant enters into the tenancy to which it applies, or (if earlier) becomes contractually bound to do so'.

The simple declaration – where the health warning notice is served not less than 14 days before the tenant enters into the tenancy or becomes contractually bound to do so

If not less than 14 days' notice is given to the tenant paragraph 3 of Schedule 2 to the Order provides that:

> … the tenant, or a person duly authorised by him to do so, must, before the tenant enters into the tenancy to which the notice applies, or (if earlier) becomes contractually bound to do so, make a declaration in the form, or substantially in the form, set out in paragraph 7.

The form of this simple declaration is as follows:

Figure 2

I................................ (*name of declarant*) of..
.... (*address*) declare that –

1. I/................................ (*name of tenant*) propose(s) to enter into a tenancy of premises at.. (*address of premises*) for a term commencing on..

2. I/The tenant propose(s) to enter into an agreement with................................ (*name of landlord*) that the provisions of sections 24 to 28 of the Landlord and Tenant Act 1954 (security of tenure) shall be excluded in relation to the tenancy.

3. The landlord has, not less than 14 days before I/the tenant enter(s) into the tenancy, or (if earlier) become(s) contractually bound to do so served on me/the tenant a notice in the form, or substantially in the form, set out in Schedule 1 to the Regulatory Reform (Business Tenancies) (England and Wales) Order 2003. The form of notice set out in that Schedule is reproduced below.

4. I have/The tenant has read the notice referred to in paragraph 3 above and accept(s) the consequences of entering into the agreement referred to in paragraph 2 above.

5. (*as appropriate*) I am duly authorised by the tenant to make this declaration.

DECLARED this........................ day of............................

To: [*Name and address of tenant*]

From: [*Name and address of landlord*]

IMPORTANT NOTICE

You are being offered a lease without security of tenure. Do not commit yourself to the lease unless you have read this message carefully and have discussed it with a professional adviser.

Continued over

Figure 2 (continued)

Business tenants normally have security of tenure – the right to stay in their business premises when the lease ends.

If you commit yourself to the lease you will be giving up these important legal rights.

- You will have **no right** to stay in the premises when the lease ends.

- Unless the landlord chooses to offer you another lease, you will need to leave the premises.

- You will be unable to claim compensation for the loss of your business premises, unless the lease specifically gives you this right.

- If the landlord offers you another lease, you will have no right to ask the court to fix the rent.

It is therefore important to get professional advice – from a qualified surveyor, lawyer or accountant – before agreeing to give up these rights.

If you want to ensure that you can stay in the same business premises when the lease ends, you should consult your adviser about another form of lease that does not exclude the protection of the Landlord and Tenant Act 1954.

If you receive this notice at least 14 days before committing yourself to the lease, you will need to sign a simple declaration that you have received this notice and have accepted its consequences, before signing the lease.

But if you do not receive at least 14 days notice, you will need to sign a 'statutory' declaration. To do so, you will need to visit an independent solicitor (or someone else empowered to administer oaths).

Unless there is a special reason for committing yourself to the lease sooner, you may want to ask the landlord to let you have at least 14 days to consider whether you wish to give up your statutory rights. If you then decided to go ahead with the agreement to exclude the protection of the Landlord and Tenant Act 1954, you would only need to make a simple declaration, and so you would not need to make a separate visit to an independent solicitor.

Contents of the simple declaration

The simple declaration by the tenant needs to have the following information completed:

- the name and address of the person making the declaration;
- the name of the tenant;
- the premises in the proposed tenancy;
- details of when the term of the tenancy commences; and
- the name of the landlord.

The declaration records:

- that the tenant proposes to enter into a tenancy of the premises and details the commencement date of the term;

- that the tenant proposes to enter into an agreement with the landlord to exclude security of tenure in relation to the tenancy;

- that the landlord has, not less than 14 days before the tenant enters into the tenancy, or (if earlier) becomes contractually bound to do so, served the health warning notice;

- that the form of the health warning notice is set out in the declaration;

- that the tenant has read the notice and accepts the consequences of entering into the agreement to contract out of the Act; and

- if appropriate, confirms the declarant is duly authorised by the tenant to make the declaration.

The statutory declaration – if the health warning notice is served less than 14 days before the tenant enters into the tenancy or (if earlier) becomes contractually bound to do so

If less than 14 days' notice is given to the tenant paragraph 4 of Schedule 2 to the Order provides that:

> The tenant, or a person duly authorised by him to do so, must before that time [ie before the tenant enters into the tenancy, or (if earlier) becomes contractually bound to do so] make a statutory declaration in the form, or substantially in the form, set out in paragraph 8.

The form of the statutory declaration follows.

Figure 3

I........................ (*name of declarant*) of..
.... (*address*) do solemnly and sincerely declare that –

1. I/........................ (*name of tenant*) propose(s) to enter into a tenancy of premises at.. (*address of premises*) for a term commencing on........................

2. I/The tenant propose(s) to enter into an agreement with........................ (*name of landlord*) that the provisions of sections 24 to 28 of the Landlord and Tenant Act 1954 (security of tenure) shall be excluded in relation to the tenancy.

3. The landlord has served on me/the tenant a notice in the form, or substantially in the form, set out in Schedule 1 to the Regulatory Reform (Business Tenancies) (England and Wales) Order 2003. The form of notice set out in that Schedule is reproduced below.

4. I have/The tenant has read the notice referred to in paragraph 3 above and accept(s) the consequences of entering into the agreement referred to in paragraph 2 above.

5. (*as appropriate*) I am duly authorised by the tenant to make this declaration.

Continued over

Figure 3 (continued)

To: [*Name and address of tenant*]

From: [*Name and address of landlord*]

IMPORTANT NOTICE

You are being offered a lease without security of tenure. Do not commit yourself to the lease unless you have read this message carefully and have discussed it with a professional adviser.

Business tenants normally have security of tenure – the right to stay in their business premises when the lease ends.

If you commit yourself to the lease you will be giving up these important legal rights.

- You will have **no right** to stay in the premises when the lease ends.

- Unless the landlord chooses to offer you another lease, you will need to leave the premises.

- You will be unable to claim compensation for the loss of your business premises, unless the lease specifically gives you this right.

- If the landlord offers you another lease, you will have no right to ask the court to fix the rent.

It is therefore important to get professional advice – from a qualified surveyor, lawyer or accountant – before agreeing to give up these rights.

If you want to ensure that you can stay in the same business premises when the lease ends, you should consult your adviser about another form of lease that does not exclude the protection of the Landlord and Tenant Act 1954.

If you receive this notice at least 14 days before committing yourself to the lease, you will need to sign a simple declaration that you have received this notice and have accepted its consequences, before signing the lease.

But if you do not receive at least 14 days notice, you will need to sign a 'statutory' declaration. To do so, you will need to visit an independent solicitor (or someone else empowered to administer oaths).

Unless there is a special reason for committing yourself to the lease sooner, you may want to ask the landlord to let you have at least 14 days to consider whether you wish to give up your statutory rights. If you then decided to go ahead with the agreement to exclude the protection of the Landlord and Tenant Act 1954, you would only need to make a simple declaration, and so you would not need to make a separate visit to an independent solicitor.

AND I make this solemn declaration conscientiously believing the same to be true and by virtue of the Statutory Declarations Act 1835

DECLARED at........................ this......................... day of.........................

Before me.................................

(*signature of person before whom declaration is made*)

A commissioner for oaths *or*

A solicitor empowered to administer oaths or (*as appropriate*).

Contents of the statutory declaration

The contents of the statutory declaration, and the information which needs to be completed, are almost exactly the same as the simple declaration (see **p10** above).

The differences are:

- The statutory declaration records that the health warning notice was served, but does not say when, ie it does not state less than 14 days' notice was given.

- The deponent has to 'solemnly and sincerely declare' rather than just 'declare' and must make the statutory declaration within the meaning of the Statutory Declarations Act 1835. This means they must make the declaration before an independent solicitor (or other person qualified to administer oaths) and pay the prescribed fee, which was £5 at the date this book was published.

How to make a statutory declaration

The method of making a statutory declaration may seem obvious to most practitioners but bears repeating.

It will probably be noted that the form of statutory declaration in the Order does not have any specified place for the declarant to actually sign. There are references in the Statutory Declarations Act 1835 to declarations being 'made and subscribed' and it appears to be a moot point whether a declarant must actually sign a statutory declaration. There is no statutory form of words which must be recited. In its *Guide to Oaths and Affirmations*[2] the Law Society states that the Statutory Declarations Act 1835 does not specifically require the declarant to make any oral declaration but that the practice is frequently adopted of requiring them to do so. This is, it states: 'a convenient way of impressing on the declarant the nature of the declaration which he is making, and at the same time complying with the obligation upon the commissioner for oaths to satisfy himself that the person before him is the declarant named in the declaration.'

The commissioner for oaths would normally ask the declarant to sign the document and then to say:

> I solemnly and sincerely declare that this is my name and handwriting and that the contents of this my declaration are true.

---

2 By Robin Spon-Smith, published by The Law Society (ISBN 1 85328 359 2].

Alternatively, the commissioner could merely ask the declarant to confirm that they are in fact the declarant and that they solemnly and sincerely declared that the contents of the statutory declaration were true – to both questions the answer should be 'yes'. Personal attendance by the declarant before the commissioner is required, of course, in all cases. It is not the role of the commissioner to advise the declarant.

The second requirement of Schedule 2 to the Order – the endorsement

Paragraphs 5 and 6 of Schedule 2 to the Order provide that the lease (or other instrument creating the tenancy) must contain, or have endorsed on it:

- a reference to the health warning notice;

- a reference to the simple declaration or statutory declaration, as appropriate; and

- the agreement to exclude security of tenure, or a reference to the agreement.

Suggested wording for this endorsement is as follows (this may need to be varied depending on the individual circumstances of the case):

Exclusion of Tenant's Security of Tenure

1. In accordance with the provisions of s38A(1) of the Landlord and Tenant Act 1954, the parties have agreed that the provisions of ss24 to 28 of that Act (inclusive) shall be excluded in relation to the tenancy created by this Lease.

2. The landlord has served on the tenant a notice in the form, or substantially in the form, set out in Schedule 1 to the Regulatory Reform (Business Tenancies) (England and Wales) Order 2003 ('the Order').

3. The requirements specified in Schedule 2 to the Order have been met in that the tenant has made a [statutory*] declaration in the form, or substantially in the form, set out in paragraph [7*] [8*] of Schedule 2 to the Order.

* delete as appropriate

'Paragraph 7' should be retained (and reference to 'paragraph 8' and 'statutory' deleted) where the tenant has made a simple declaration, ie where the health warning notice was served not less than 14 days before the tenant entered into the lease, or became contractually bound to do so.

'Paragraph 8' and 'statutory' should be retained (and reference to 'paragraph 7' deleted) where the tenant has made a statutory declaration, ie where the health warning notice was served less than 14 days before the tenant entered into the lease, or became contractually bound to do so.

Where the parties do not know at the time of engrossing the lease whether more or less than 14 days' notice will be given, it is the author's view that they could use the following alternative wording for paragraph 3 above:

3. The requirements specified in Schedule 2 to the Order have been met in that the tenant has made the appropriate declaration in the form, or substantially in the form, set out in Schedule 2 to the Order.

Agreements for lease

The health warning notice has to be served before the tenant 'enters into the lease, or (if earlier) becomes contractually bound to do so'. Where there is an agreement for lease the tenant will be contractually bound to enter into it when the agreement for lease is exchanged. The health warning notice will therefore have to be served, and the tenant's declaration made, before then.

The endorsement required by Schedule 2 to the Order (see **p14** above), however, has to be on the 'instrument creating the tenancy'. This will be the lease, even if there is an agreement for lease.

It is probably also sensible to put the endorsement in the agreement for lease as well, with a slight adjustment to the wording at the end of paragraph 1 of the suggested wording above to refer to 'the tenancy which the parties have hereby agreed to enter into'. In effect, agreements for lease will no longer be conditional on obtaining authorisation for an exclusion of security of tenure as this will be done before the agreement for lease is entered into.

For agreements for lease entered into before 1 June 2004 requiring the lease to be contracted out and where such lease will be completed after 1 June 2004, see **p25** below.

Practical issues

Although the notice procedure appears straightforward there are several practical issues which need to be considered.

How exactly should the health warning notice be served?

Section 66(4) of the Act will apply to the service of the health warning notice. This provides that s23 of the Landlord and Tenant Act 1927 shall apply. Section 23 of the Landlord and Tenant Act 1927 states:

Any notice, request, demand, or other instrument under this Act shall be in writing and may be served on the person on whom it is to be served either personally, or by leaving it for him at his last known place of abode in England or Wales, or by sending it through the post in a registered letter addressed to him there, or, in the case of a local or public authority or a statutory or a public utility company, to the secretary or other proper officer at the principal office of such authority or company, and in the case of a notice to a landlord, the person on whom it is to be served shall include any agent of the landlord duly authorised in that behalf.

It is not clear exactly what is meant by 'last known place of abode' but commentaries seem to imply that, in the case of an individual it should be addressed to the subject premises if the individual is still trading there, otherwise to their last known residential address. In the case of a company, notices should be sent either to the subject premises (again if it continues to trade from those premises) or its registered office. It would be prudent to serve at the registered office with a copy to the trading premises.

Service by recorded delivery is now permitted under the provisions of the Recorded Delivery Service Act 1962. Registered Post has now been replaced by Special Delivery.

While s23 of the Landlord and Tenant Act 1927 makes it mandatory for a notice under this section to be in writing, the methods of service set out in this section are permissive. If, however, any method of service other than those prescribed is adopted, there could be issues as to proof of service (see **p17** below).

If the notice is served personally, the effective date of service will be the date the notice is served or left at the premises.

If the notice is served by recorded delivery, irrespective of whether the notice is returned or not, the date of service would be the date on which the recorded delivery letter was posted. The courts have held that there is no indication in s23 that there has to be some attempted or actual delivery.[3] The same will apply to Special Delivery.

Who should serve the health warning notice?

Section 38A(3)(a) of the Act refers to 'the landlord' serving the health warning notice on the tenant. There would not appear to be any reason why, as for other notices, the health warning notice cannot be served by the landlord, or its solicitor, or any other agent of the landlord on its behalf. This does not need to be recorded on the actual notice (but, in practice, if the solicitor is serving the notice as agent for the landlord they should say so in the covering letter). In all cases, however, it is the landlord's name which should go in the actual notice, not that of its agent.

---

3 *Webber (Transport) Ltd v Network Rail Infrastructure Ltd (formerly Railtrack Plc)* [2003] EWCA Civ 1167 (CA).

Joint landlords

Where there are joint landlords, the name and address of each one of the joint landlords should be put in the notice. One notice may, however, be served on behalf of all the joint landlords.

On whom should the health warning notice be served?

Section 38A(3)(a) of the Act and Schedule 2 to the Order provide that the health warning notice must be served 'on the tenant'. However, the normal rules of agency will apply.

The ideal would always be to serve the notice on the actual tenant, with a copy to any solicitor or other agent whom the landlord is aware is acting for the tenant in relation to that tenancy. This avoids any issues as to whether, if the notice were served on an agent, that agent was properly authorised, or whether 'the tenant' in fact did see and appreciate the consequences of the notice. In practice, however, if the notice is served on the agent, and the agent is specifically referred to as such in a covering letter, and the tenant itself (ie not the agent) makes the declaration, then it is extremely unlikely that the tenant could argue it was not properly served. The tenant will have stated in its declaration that it received the notice, read it and accepted its consequences, which must count as 'proof' of service. This will also avoid any arguments that the agent was not authorised to accept service as even if they were not, the declaration would ratify the acceptance of service by the agent. In this case though the landlord may wish to insist that the declaration is actually signed by the tenant (even though there is no requirement for it to do so).

Joint tenants

Where there are joint tenants the health warning notice should include the names and addresses of all the joint tenants, who will collectively be 'the tenant'. Identical notices should be served on each of the joint tenants individually.

Evidence of contracting out

The agreement to contract out will be void if the landlord has not served the health warning notice so the landlord, and any purchaser of the landlord's reversion, will want to have evidence that the notice was served. It would be prudent to retain with the property deeds a copy (maybe even a certified copy) of the notice and any covering letter.

The main proof of service of the notice is, however, the tenant's declaration which confirms it was served. Although there is no requirement for the declaration to be given to the landlord (it merely has to be 'made'), landlords may wish to insist on receiving the tenant's original declaration at completion or, at the very least, a certified copy to retain with the deeds.

When exactly should the health warning notice be served?

There has been a considerable amount of discussion in legal circles as to when precisely the health warning notice should be served. Can it be done at heads of terms stage, or should it be done when the final form of lease is known (as is the case now with contracting-out orders)?

The arguments for serving the health warning notice at heads of terms stage

1. The Act does not specifically state that the form of lease needs to be attached to the health warning notice. The purpose of the notice is merely to inform the tenant that the lease it will be entering into will not have security of tenure. The precise terms of that lease do not need to be known to enable the tenant to appreciate what it is giving up.

2. The reforms clearly envisage that more than 14 days' notice to the tenant will be the norm, with the statutory declaration route only being used in emergencies. However, it is unlikely that in practice the terms of many leases will be finally agreed more than 14 days before completion. If one has to wait until the lease terms are agreed before sending the notice then most of these would need the statutory declaration to be made by the tenant. What then would be the point of having the simple declaration procedure?

The arguments for serving the health warning notice when the terms of the lease are agreed

1. This is in effect what happened pre-June 2004 with the agreed lease being attached to the application to the court for the contracting-out order. There is nothing in the new provisions to suggest this should have changed.

2. The declaration refers to an agreement between the landlord and tenant that security of tenure shall be excluded in relation to the tenancy, ie it says 'the' tenancy rather than 'a' tenancy. The declaration also requires the commencement date of the term of the tenancy to be inserted, which tends to point to that date being agreed when the declaration is made. This could, however, be circumvented by inserting 'commencing on the date set out in the tenancy' in this part of the declaration.

3. The health warning notice itself refers to the tenant committing itself to 'the' lease. The argument is that if the terms of the tenancy change from when the notice is served to when the lease is granted, then the notice did not apply to 'the' lease but only 'a' lease. The tenant may be content to have the lease terms which were in play when the notice was served excluded from security of tenure, but may not be content to do so for the final terms of the lease which are agreed later.

Metropolitan Police District Receiver v Palacegate Properties Ltd[4]

Practitioners, no doubt, will want to take into consideration the decision of the Court of Appeal in the *Palacegate Properties*[5] case, above, when considering this issue. In this case, the Court of Appeal decided that, on the provisions of s38(4) of the Act in relation to contracting-out orders, the contracting-out order was not invalidated by a change in the lease terms between court authorisation and completion. The change in question was, in effect, a change from the rent being payable annually in arrears to quarterly in advance. The court decided that that change had no bearing on the court's function in determining whether the tenant had understood that it was giving up protection under the Act. However, it did say that a change in terms might be a relevant factor, depending on what that change was. It gave the example of a change in the length of term being a material consideration in the case of a lease which contemplated substantial capital expenditure by the tenant. Per Pill LJ:

> A court authorising an agreement excluding protection would be expected to make greater inquiry as to the proposed tenant's consent if the term is a short one than if the term is a long one and a change which substantially shortens the term would be material. A court may be expected to satisfy itself that the prospective tenant knows what he is giving up and the extent of the inquiry will depend on the terms proposed. It follows that a change in the terms may be a relevant factor for the purposes of s38(4)(a).

The author has two comments on this case:

*   It is based on the presumption that the court would know the effect of the change in terms on the tenant's liabilities. A tenant receiving a health warning notice, and without the benefit of the court's scrutiny, would not necessarily appreciate the effect of any changes made to the lease after that date.

---

4 [2000] 3 All ER 663 CA.

5 *Metropolitan Police District Receiver v Palacegate Properties Ltd* [2000] 3 All ER 663 CA.

- It presupposes that the courts actually do consider the terms of the lease when authorising the exclusion of protection.

The landlord's options

It would appear the landlord has, in effect, the following options:

1. To serve the health warning notice at heads of terms stage and not serve again, ie it takes the view that the notice is merely to warn the tenant that whatever the terms of the lease, it will be excluded from security of tenure.

2. To serve the notice at heads of terms stage, or when the draft lease is sent out, but if there is a fundamental change to the terms, eg different premises, term etc, then to serve another health warning notice just before completion. The problem with this is deciding what changes in terms would make such a difference and require a new notice (see *Palacegate* above). Any change to the length of the term of the lease, or the insertion of a landlord's break clause, would seem to fall within that category as they would have a fundamental effect on when the effects of the exclusion from security of tenure came into play, ie when the tenant would have to give up possession. Changes to other terms may not have so obvious an effect.

3. To serve the notice when the terms of the lease are finally agreed. This would probably mean that the notice would be served with the engrossment and the tenant would nearly always have to make a statutory declaration and not a simple declaration. This is the cautious approach and would leave no argument as to validity.

Ultimately, until the position has been clarified by Parliament or the courts, it is likely that landlords will take the cautious approach, especially if they know they will want possession at some point in the future. However, see the comments on the recent case of *Brighton & Hove City Council v Collinson & anr*[6], at **p26** below, as to the Court of Appeal's view that the Act should not be construed in an over-technical way.

The declaration

Similar issues to those discussed in the preceding paragraphs arise relating to the tenant's declaration, whether simple or statutory.

---

6 [2004] EWCA Civ 678.

When should it be made?

Schedule 2 to the Order does not set out any requirements as to when the tenant's declaration should be made. The declaration could be made by the tenant as soon as the health warning notice has been served. In practice, it will probably be made just before completion of the lease or, where appropriate, other document by which the tenant becomes contractually bound to enter into the lease (eg an agreement for lease).

Does the declaration have to be served?

There is no requirement that the declaration has to be served on the landlord, merely a requirement that it is 'made'. However, all landlords will want to see the declaration and at least have a certified copy of it before the lease is completed, if not the original. This should then be kept with the deeds as the court order would previously have been.

Who makes the declaration?

The declaration clearly envisages that the declarant will not necessarily be the tenant. This could be so that, if the tenant is a company, a person authorised by the company could make the declaration. It would also enable a solicitor, or other person, to make the declaration on behalf of the tenant, even if the tenant is an individual.

The declaration states specifically that the person making it is duly authorised by the tenant to do so. It is the author's view that a landlord is entitled to rely on this and does not have to check further to see if that authorisation has in fact been given (unless it has actual knowledge that it has not).

Solicitors, or other agents, will need to consider carefully whether they are prepared to make the declaration on behalf of their tenant clients. The declaration states that the tenant has read the health warning notice and accepts its consequences. The agent would want something in writing from their client confirming this is the case before signing on its behalf, in which case, it may be easier for the tenant client to make the declaration.

Joint tenants

Where there are joint tenants it would appear from the wording of the declaration that one of those joint tenants could make the declaration on behalf of 'the tenant'. Again, as above, the declaration specifically states that the declarant is duly authorised by 'the tenant' to do so. It would be very difficult for one of the joint tenants to argue at a later date that that authority had not been given, particularly if it has signed the lease which records that the notice was served. A cautious landlord, though, may want to see authorisation from the other joint tenants that they had received the health warning notice and understood its consequences, and therefore in practice, it would require a declaration from each of the joint tenants as a condition of the agreement.

If all joint tenants make a declaration they all could sign one declaration (ie one piece of paper). The form, however, does not lend itself to this and in practice they will each have to make a separate declaration on a separate form. In either case, the reference to the name of 'the tenant' should include the names of all the joint tenants.

What if the tenant has made a statutory declaration but then the lease is not entered into in less than 14 days from service of the health warning notice?

A situation may arise where the parties proceeded with the 'deal' as a matter of urgency and this necessitated the tenant making a statutory declaration. The urgency then disappeared and the lease was completed more than 14 days after the health warning notice was served. Does the tenant have to make a new, simple declaration or will the statutory declaration suffice? The author's view is that a new simple declaration will not be necessary. The statutory declaration which has already been made will be 'substantially in the same form' as the simple declaration required. It would be very bizarre indeed if the courts were to construe a declaration which confers a higher degree of protection on the tenant as not being 'substantially in the same form' as the simple declaration which is considered to offer a lower degree of protection to the tenant.

However, this would not work the other way around, ie if the health warning notice had been served more than 14 days before the anticipated completion date, and the tenant had made a simple declaration. If the completion date was then brought forward to be less than 14 days after the service of the health warning notice, a new statutory declaration would have to be made by the tenant. The whole purpose of the provisions is that in those situations, ie where the tenant has less than 14 days' notice, it has the extra protection of the extra requirements of the statutory declaration.

It is the author's view that the simple declaration would not be construed by the courts as being 'substantially in the same form' as the statutory declaration, as the one vital thing setting apart the statutory declaration is missing, ie the requirement for the formal declaration before a solicitor or commissioner for oaths.

Transitional provisions

Article 29 of the Order has transitional provisions about contracting out in relation to agreements for lease entered into before 1 June 2004 and provisions in tenancies requiring sub-tenancies to be contracted out. It also deals with contracting-out orders made before 1 June 2004.

Contracting-out orders made before 1 June 2004

Article 29(2)(a)(ii) of the Order provides that nothing in the Order shall have effect in relation to an agreement to contract out of the Act which was authorised by the court under s38(4) of the Act before the Order came into force. Those agreements will still be effective.

Covenants for sub-letting

It is common in leases for there to be a covenant providing that if the tenant wishes to sub-let the premises it must obtain the court's approval to an agreement between the parties for that sub-tenancy to be excluded from security of tenure. Clearly, as the provision for court approval was abolished after 1 June 2004, this is no longer possible.

Article 29(3) of the Order solves this problem by providing that any references to the existing s38(4) procedures (contracting out with court approval) in leases are to be construed as references to the use of the procedures specified in the new s38A (notices).

New wording

The transitional provision does not specifically state that it is confined to leases which had these provisions and which were entered into before 1 June 2004. So if, by error, a lease entered into after 1 June 2004 still included the requirement for a court order, it is the author's view that Art 29(3) would apply in that case too.

However, this should not be relied on and landlords will want to amend their documentation to make reference to the new procedures. Suggested wording is as follows (although, obviously, this may need to be varied depending on the individual circumstances of each case).

Exclusion of security of tenure

1. Prior to the grant of any underlease, or, if earlier, the parties to that underlease becoming contractually bound to enter into it, the parties to that underlease shall enter into an agreement to and shall exclude ss24 to 28 of the Landlord and Tenant Act 1954 ('the Act') in relation to that underlease.

2. In particular before the underlessee enters into the underlease, or (if earlier) becomes contractually bound to do so:

    (a) the tenant will serve on the underlessee a notice in the form, or substantially in the form, set out in Schedule 1 to the Regulatory Reform (Business Tenancies) (England and Wales) Order 2003 ('the Order'), and

    (b) the underlessee will comply with the requirements specified in Schedule 2 to the Order in that the underlessee shall make a declaration or a statutory declaration in the form, or substantially in the form, set out in paragraph 7 or 8 of Schedule 2 to the Order as appropriate; and

    (c) a reference to the above notice and declaration shall be contained in or endorsed on the instrument creating the underlease; and

    (d) the agreement under s38A(1) of the Act to exclude ss24 to 28 of the Act, or a reference to that agreement, shall be contained in or endorsed on the instrument creating the underlease.

An, alternative, shorter version could be:

Exclusion of security of tenure

Prior to the entering into of any underlease, or (if earlier) the parties to that underlease becoming contractually bound to enter into it, the parties to the underlease will enter into a valid agreement under s38A of the Landlord and Tenant Act 1954 ('the Act') to exclude the provisions of ss24 to 28 of the Act in relation to that underlease.

Agreements for leases

It is common for agreements for lease to provide that the landlord agrees to the future grant of the lease on the condition that the lease is first contracted out of security of tenure by obtaining a section 38 court order.

The transitional provisions at Art 29(4) of the Order provide that the existing arrangements for applications for a court order should continue to apply in relation to agreements for lease entered into before the new provisions came into force. This transitional provision will only apply until all such existing arrangements have come into effect, and will, therefore, be for a limited period. The transitional provisions in the Statutory Instrument dealing with changes to the Civil Procedure Rules specifically disapply those changes where this transitional provision applies. The changes remove CPR56.2(4) which deals with contracting-out applications to the court. Clearly, this will still be needed in the situation where such an order is still required under an agreement for lease.[7]

---

7 See r 20 of Supreme Court of England and Wales, County Courts, England and Wales, The Civil Procedure (Amendment) Rules 2004, SI 2004/1306.

After 1 June 2004, the contracting out will, in effect, have to be done before the agreement for lease, so there will be no need to include these type of provisions. Although, see **p15** above about the possibility of endorsements on the agreement for lease.

Other issues about agreements for lease

What if the terms of the lease change after the agreement for lease has been entered into?

The contracting out is done before the tenant enters into the lease or becomes contractually bound to so. Where there is an agreement for lease this is, therefore, done before the agreement is entered into. What happens if the terms of the lease are varied after that?

If the variation to the lease is one which is contemplated by the agreement for lease then no further notices/declarations are needed. The lease as varied would be contracted out. If the variations are not contemplated by the agreement and are such that they would amount to a surrender and re-grant then it is the author's view that a fresh notice/declaration should be made before the lease is completed as, in effect, the agreement for lease has been abandoned by the parties and a new form of lease entered into. If there are other changes, which do not amount to such a fundamental change then this will depend on the extent of those variations and will involve consideration of the *Palacegate*[8] issues as set out at **p19** above. The safest course may be to do a fresh notice/declaration in these circumstances.

What if the tenant who takes the lease is different from the party to the agreement for lease?

In effect, what is happening here is that the parties to the agreement for lease are choosing not to enforce it and instead the landlord is entering into a new lease with the new tenant. Therefore a new health warning notice will need to be served on that new tenant and the tenant will need to make the appropriate declaration before the lease is entered into or the tenant becomes contractually bound to do so.

What if the agreement for lease is assigned?

Two distinct views have emerged on the issue of an agreement for lease which is assigned. The first view is that once the agreement for lease has

---

[8] *Metropolitan Police District Receiver v Palacegate Properties Ltd* [2000] 3 All ER 663, CA

been exchanged (and the health warning notice served and declaration made before then) it is a binding agreement to take a contracted-out lease. If the agreement for lease is assigned by the prospective tenant what is being assigned is the benefit of the agreement to take a contracted-out lease. There is no need to serve a fresh notice on the assignee of the prospective tenant.

The contrary view is that the prospective tenant taking the assignment of the agreement for lease will be contractually bound to enter into the tenancy on completion of the assignment of the agreement for lease. The landlord will need to serve a fresh health warning notice on that new tenant and receive the new tenant's appropriate declaration, before completing that assignment. This is because it will be the tenant under the lease.

The author's view is that the first position is correct ie the agreement to contract out has already been validated and there is no need to serve any further notices. There is some support to this view from the recent Court of Appeal case of *Brighton & Hove City Council v Collinson & anr*[9]. In this case the lease was to be granted to a company tenant. The landlord had made it clear that he wanted to exclude security of tenure. An application was made to the Court to approve the contracting out in the names of the landlord, the proposed tenant company and its directors who were to be guarantors. The lease was, however, eventually executed with the directors as tenants. The company was not a named tenant. The Court of Appeal held the contracting out was valid. The landlord had argued that the contracting-out order related to 'the' tenant and that since the tenant to the lease had not been one for which the order was made, the order had no effect against their tenancy.

The Court of Appeal held that the argument was seeking to rely on technicalities. There was no need to construe the Act in an over-technical way. What was important was that the prospective tenants had understood that they were foregoing security of tenure. Whilst the facts are different to the situation we are discussing in that the actual tenant had been a party to the contracting-out order the principles of construction (ie do not be too technical) would certainly apply.

If a landlord adopts the second view, ie that a new notice is needed etc, then to avoid assignments of agreements for lease taking place without the landlord's knowledge, the landlord will probably want to provide in the agreement for lease for it to be unassignable (which is usual anyway).

---

9 [2004] EWCA Civ 678.

Alternatively, the landlord may allow an assignment of the agreement for lease on condition that the landlord be given sufficient notice of any proposed assignment to enable it to serve the health warning notice on the proposed assignee and that it be a condition precedent to any assignment that the proposed assignee must make the appropriate declaration and give it to the landlord.

Conditional agreements for lease

Where the agreement for lease is conditional on other conditions being satisfied eg the granting of landlord's consent, then it is the author's view that the health warning notice should still be served, and the tenant's declaration should still be made, before the agreement for lease is exchanged. The tenant is still contractually bound to enter into the tenancy when the agreement for lease is exchanged, rather than when the condition is satisfied. The satisfaction of the condition is merely the trigger for completion of the tenancy, the contractual obligation to do so, albeit conditional, arises when the agreement for lease is exchanged.

What if a contracted-out lease is assigned?

If a contracted-out lease is assigned there is no need to go through a fresh notice/declaration procedure with the assignee. The lease has already been validly contracted out and remains so. This is the same as under the pre-1 June 2004 rules where, similarly, there would have been no need to obtain a fresh contracting-out order with the assignee.

What if a contracted-out lease is varied?

Again, if a lease which is already contracted out is varied by agreement between the parties there will be no need to do a fresh notice/declaration. Care needs to be taken in these cases, however, that the variation does not amount to a surrender and re-grant, and in which case a fresh notice/ declaration would be required.

Options

Call options

Care needs to be taken when granting options to take contracted-out leases. The health warning notice and declaration must both happen before the tenant becomes contractually bound to take the lease, which, in the case of a call option, is when the tenant serves its notice of exercise of the option.

The author suggests that the landlord's health warning notice is served when the option is granted. The option agreement would contain, as a condition precedent to the exercise of the option, a requirement that the tenant makes (and gives to the landlord) its declaration. The form of the new lease is likely to be already fixed in the option agreement so there will not be any issues regarding the possibility of these changing if the notice is served well in advance of the option being exercised.

If the option for a new contracted-out lease is contained in a contracted-out tenancy then the landlord will in effect be serving two health warning notices – one for the immediate contracted out tenancy and one for the future contracted-out tenancy pursuant to the option. These should be clearly labelled so that there is no doubt in the future that both were served (otherwise it may be assumed they were just extra copies of the one notice).

What if the option is granted before 1 June 2004?

Obviously, if the option is granted before 1 June 2004 the route set out above (ie serving the health warning notice when the option is granted) could not be used as the parties cannot operate the health warning notice procedure as it will not be valid until 1 June 2004.

A way around this would be for the option agreement to provide that if the tenant wants to exercise the option before 1 June 2004 it must go through the court order procedure. If it wants to exercise the option after 1 June 2004, it must first serve a month's advance notice on the landlord (effectively warning the landlord that it plans to exercise the option). The landlord then has a month to serve its health warning notice. After the month has expired the tenant can serve notice exercising the option, but must, before doing so, make its appropriate declaration in response to the health warning notice (and give this to the landlord).

This method could be adopted for options entered into after 1 June 2004 but in light of the suggestion above it is the author's view that it would not be necessary in the normal case. It could, however, be relevant if the form of the lease could change, or the party exercising the option has an election to choose the terms in the lease. In the latter case, the option would provide that the tenant inform the landlord of its choice of terms (thereby crystallising the form of the lease) say one month before being entitled to exercise the option. The landlord then has a certain period to serve the health warning notice. After that period the tenant can serve notice exercising the option, but before doing so must make the appropriate declaration and give it to the landlord.

Another situation to consider is where the option was granted before the new procedures were known but is not available to be exercised until after 1 June 2004. It is too late to put any provisions in the option for the 'pre-notice' procedures mentioned above. The legislation does not cover this situation. It is the author's view that the new notice/declaration procedures will apply. The downside is that whereas the landlord can serve its notice at any time after 1 June 2004 before the option is exercisable, there is nothing to oblige the tenant to make the appropriate declaration before exercising the option. However, the tenant is only entitled to the option of taking a contracted-out lease and it is the author's view that if the tenant refused to make the declaration the courts would not impose a protected lease on the landlord.

Put options

Where the tenant is obliged to take a lease at the option of the landlord it is known as a 'put option'. The most common example is where a guarantor agrees in a lease that if the lease is disclaimed the guarantor will take a new lease if the landlord serves a notice requiring it to do so. In this situation the guarantor would be contractually bound to take the lease when the landlord served the notice or, on some arguments, when the original lease is entered into. If the guarantor's lease was to be contacted out the only certain way would be to serve the health warning notice and have the declaration made before the original lease is granted. If this is not done then after the original lease is granted there would be no way to force the guarantor to make the appropriate declaration and it is unlikely to choose to do so if it does not wish to take the lease.

However, before 1 June 2004, there were no provisions put into such guarantor covenants requiring guarantors to enter into court orders to contract out of the new lease. Again, it is the author's view that the courts would be unlikely to allow the guarantor to rely on its own recalcitrance to avoid the lease it takes being contracted out if that is what it has originally contracted to do. This problem is, however, unlikely to arise in practice. Where the lease is disclaimed the guarantor will still be liable under its guarantor obligations.[10] Unless there is some limitation on this in the lease, the landlord will be able to continue to enforce those covenants against the guarantor and will not need to enforce its put option. Indeed, it would be in the guarantor's interests to co-operate and take the new lease as at least then it would have some control over the lease and be able to assign or sub-let and offset some of its liability.

---

10 *Hindcastle v Barbara Attenborough Associates* [1997] AC 70

3. SURRENDERS

It is important to remember when looking at surrenders that there is a distinction between an actual surrender of a lease and an agreement to surrender a lease at some point in the future.

Pre-1 June 2004

Section 24(2)(b) of the Act provided that a lease could be surrendered, unless in the case of an instrument of surrender, that instrument 'was executed before, or was executed in pursuance of an agreement made before, the tenant had been in occupation in right of the tenancy for one month'.

The Law Commission pointed out that this led to most surrenders being valid except those where the tenant had been in occupation for less than a month. However, it also led to a degree of conflict or ambiguity between those provisions, which accepted the validity of a surrender made pursuant to an agreement reached after the tenant had been in occupation for one month, and s38(1) of the Act, which invalidates all agreements to surrender unless authorised by the court. Under s38(1) if the parties wanted to enter into a valid and enforceable agreement to surrender they had to obtain the approval of the court, as for contracting out.

From 1 June 2004

Section 24(2)(b) has been repealed and new procedures have been introduced for authorising agreements to surrender.

Actual surrenders

All actual surrenders (ie immediate surrenders without any prior agreement) are now valid. There is no longer any prohibition against surrenders during the first month of the tenancy.

Agreements to surrender

The ambiguity mentioned above has been removed following the repeal of s24(2)(b).

The provisions which deal with agreements to surrender are in the new s38A of the Act and Schedules 3 and 4 to the Order. Section 38A(2) provides that the parties may agree that the tenancy shall be surrendered 'on such date or in such circumstances as may be specified in the agreement and on such terms (if any) as may be so specified'.

Section 38A(4) provides that such an agreement will be void unless:

- the landlord has served on the tenant a notice in the form, or substantially in the form, set out in Schedule 3 to the Order (the 'health warning notice'); and

- the requirements of Schedule 4 to the Order are met.

The health warning notice

As mentioned above, the form of the health warning notice is set out in Schedule 3 to the Order. A copy of the form of notice is reproduced opposite (**Figure 4**).

Contents of the health warning notice

The health warning notice specifically informs the tenant that it is giving up legal rights, in particular it states:

- the tenant would normally have a right to renew its lease when it expires, but by agreeing to surrender it will give up this statutory right;

- the tenant will not be able to continue to occupy the premises beyond the date provided for under the agreement for surrender, unless the landlord chooses to offer a further term (in which case the tenant would lose the right to ask the court to determine the new rent);

- the tenant will need to leave the premises; and

- the tenant will be unable to claim compensation for the loss of the premises, unless the lease or agreement for surrender gives it this right.

The notice informs the tenant it is important to get professional advice before committing itself to the agreement to surrender. It also explains the simple declaration and statutory declaration procedures.

Completing the health warning notice

The landlord is required to fill in to complete the health warning notice only the following:

Figure 4

**FORM OF NOTICE THAT AN AGREEMENT TO SURRENDER A BUSINESS TENANCY
IS TO BE MADE**

To: [*Name and address of tenant*]

From: [*Name and address of landlord*]

IMPORTANT NOTICE FOR TENANT

**Do not commit yourself to any agreement to surrender your lease unless you have read this
message carefully and discussed it with a professional adviser.**

Normally, you have the right to renew your lease when it expires. By committing yourself to an
agreement to surrender, **you will be giving up this important statutory right**.

- You will **not** be able to continue occupying the premises beyond the date provided for
  under the agreement for surrender, **unless** the landlord chooses to offer you a further term
  (in which case you would lose the right to ask the court to determine the new rent). You will
  need to leave the premises.

- You will be unable to claim compensation for the loss of your premises, unless the lease or
  agreement for surrender gives you this right.

A qualified surveyor, lawyer or accountant would be able to offer you professional advice on
your options.

**You do not have to commit yourself to the agreement to surrender your lease unless you
want to.**

If you receive this notice at least 14 days before committing yourself to the agreement to surrender, you will need to sign a simple declaration that you have received this notice and have
accepted its consequences, before signing the agreement to surrender.

**But if you do not receive at least 14 days notice, you will need to sign a 'statutory' declara-
tion. To do so, you will need to visit an independent solicitor (or someone else empowered
to administer oaths).**

Unless there is a special reason for committing yourself to the agreement to surrender sooner,
you may want to ask the landlord to let you have at least 14 days to consider whether you wish
to give up your statutory rights. If you then decided to go ahead with the agreement to end your
lease, you would only need to make a simple declaration, and so you would not need to make a
separate visit to an independent solicitor.

- the name and address of the tenant to which the notice is being sent; and

- the name and address of the landlord from whom the notice is sent.

There is no requirement to fill in the details of the property, or the lease, or
the agreement to surrender to which the notice relates. There is also no
requirement to sign or date the notice.

As with contracting-out orders, whilst there is no requirement to refer to
the premises, a landlord may wish to put details of the premises on the

notice, and the date it was sent, to avoid confusion later. If the landlord is being very cautious he may wish to attach a copy of the agreement to surrender although this is not required.

The first requirement of Schedule 4 to the Order – the declarations

Section 38A(4)(b) provides that an agreement to surrender will be void unless the requirements in Schedule 4 to the Order are met.[1]

The requirements vary slightly depending on when the health warning notice is served. It depends whether or not the notice is served 'not less than 14 days before the tenant enters into the agreement under s38A(2)... [ie the agreement to surrender] or (if earlier) becomes contractually bound to do so'.

The simple declaration – where the health warning notice is served not less than 14 days before the tenant enters into the agreement to surrender or becomes contractually bound to do so

If not less than 14 days' notice is given to the tenant paragraph 3 of Schedule 4 to the Order provides that:

> The tenant or a person duly authorised by him to do so, must, before the tenant enters into the agreement under s38A(2) of the Act , or (if earlier) becomes contractually bound to do so, make a declaration in the form, or substantially in the form, set out in paragraph 6.

The form of this simple declaration is set out opposite (**Figure 5**).

Contents of the simple declaration

The simple declaration by the tenant needs to have the following completed:

• the name and address of the person making the declaration;

• the name of the tenant;

• the premises in the tenancy;

• the term commencement date of the tenancy; and

• the name of the landlord.

The declaration records:

• that the tenant has a tenancy of the premises and the date the term commenced;

---

1 Sch 4 to the Order is set out in full at **Appendix 2**.

Figure 5

I .... (*name of declarant*) of ....
.... (*address*) declare that –

1. I have/........................ (*name of tenant*) has a tenancy of premises at .... (*address of premises*) for a term commencing on ....

2. I/The tenant propose(s) to enter into an agreement with ....(name of landlord) to surrender the tenancy on a date or in circumstances specified in the agreement.

3. The landlord has not less than 14 days before I/the tenant enter(s) into the agreement referred to in paragraph 2 above, or (if earlier) become(s) contractually bound to do so, served on me/the tenant a notice in the form, or substantially in the form, set out in Schedule 3 to the Regulatory Reform (Business Tenancies) (England and Wales) Order 2003. The form of notice set out in that Schedule is reproduced below.

4. I have/The tenant has read the notice referred to in paragraph 3 above and accept(s) the consequences of entering into the agreement referred to in paragraph 2 above.

5. (*as appropriate*) I am duly authorised by the tenant to make this declaration.

DECLARED this ....day of ....

To: [*Name and address of tenant*]

From: [*Name and address of landlord*]

IMPORTANT NOTICE FOR TENANT

<u>**Do not commit yourself to any agreement to surrender your lease unless you have read this message carefully and discussed it with a professional adviser.**</u>

Normally, you have the right to renew your lease when it expires. By committing yourself to an agreement to surrender, **you will be giving up this important statutory right**.

- You will **not** be able to continue occupying the premises beyond the date provided for under the agreement for surrender, **unless** the landlord chooses to offer you a further term (in which case you would lose the right to ask the court to determine the new rent). You will need to leave the premises.

- You will be unable to claim compensation for the loss of your premises, unless the lease or agreement for surrender gives you this right.

A qualified surveyor, lawyer or accountant would be able to offer you professional advice on your options.

<u>**You do not have to commit yourself to the agreement to surrender your lease unless you want to.**</u>

If you receive this notice at least 14 days before committing yourself to the agreement to surrender, you will need to sign a simple declaration that you have received this notice and have accepted its consequences, before signing the agreement to surrender.

<u>**But if you do not receive at least 14 days notice, you will need to sign a 'statutory' declaration. To do so, you will need to visit an independent solicitor (or someone else empowered to administer oaths).**</u>

Unless there is a special reason for committing yourself to the agreement to surrender sooner, you may want to ask the landlord to let you have at least 14 days to consider whether you wish to give up your statutory rights. If you then decided to go ahead with the agreement to end your lease, you would only need to make a simple declaration, and so you would not need to make a separate visit to an independent solicitor.

- that the tenant proposes to enter into an agreement with the landlord to surrender the tenancy on a date or in circumstances specified in the agreement;

- that the landlord has, not less than 14 days before the tenant enters into the agreement or (if earlier) becomes contractually bound to do so, served the health warning notice;

- that the form of the health warning notice is set out in the declaration;

- that the tenant has read the notice and accepts the consequences of entering into the agreement to surrender; and

- if appropriate, confirms that the declarant is duly authorised by the tenant to make the declaration.

The statutory declaration – where the health warning notice is served less than 14 days before the tenant enters into the agreement to surrender or (if earlier) becomes contractually bound to do so

If less than 14 days' notice is given to the tenant paragraph 4 of Schedule 4 to the Order provides that:

> … the notice… must be served on the tenant before the tenant enters into the agreement [to surrender], or (if earlier) becomes contractually bound to do so, and the tenant, or a person duly authorised by him to do so, must before that time make a statutory declaration in the form, or substantially the form, set out in paragraph 7.

The form of statutory declaration is as follows:

Figure 6

I .... (*name of declarant*) of ....
.............................(*address*) do solemnly and sincerely declare that:

1. I have/.....................(*name of tenant*) has a tenancy of premises at ....
....(*address of premises*) for a term commencing on
....

2. I/The tenant propose(s) to enter into an agreement with ....(*name of landlord*) to surrender the tenancy on a date or in circumstances specified in the agreement.

3. The landlord has served on me/the tenant a notice in the form, or substantially in the form, set out in Schedule 3 to the Regulatory Reform (Business Tenancies) (England and Wales) Order 2003. The form of notice set out in that Schedule is reproduced below.

4. I have/The tenant has read the notice referred to in paragraph 3 above and accept(s) the consequences of entering into the agreement referred to in paragraph 2 above.

5. (*as appropriate*) I am duly authorised by the tenant to make this declaration.

To: [*Name and address of tenant*]

From: [*Name and address of landlord*]   (*continued opposite*)

Figure 6 (continued)
IMPORTANT NOTICE FOR TENANT

<u>**Do not commit yourself to any agreement to surrender your lease unless you have read this message carefully and discussed it with a professional adviser.**</u>

Normally, you have the right to renew your lease when it expires. By committing yourself to an agreement to surrender, <u>**you will be giving up this important statutory right.**</u>

- You will **not** be able to continue occupying the premises beyond the date provided for under the agreement for surrender, **unless** the landlord chooses to offer you a further term (in which case you would lose the right to ask the court to determine the new rent). You will need to leave the premises.

- You will be unable to claim compensation for the loss of your premises, unless the lease or agreement for surrender gives you this right.

A qualified surveyor, lawyer or accountant would be able to offer you professional advice on your options.

<u>**You do not have to commit yourself to the agreement to surrender your lease unless you want to.**</u>

If you receive this notice at least 14 days before committing yourself to the agreement to surrender, you will need to sign a simple declaration that you have received this notice and have accepted its consequences, before signing the agreement to surrender.

<u>**But if you do not receive at least 14 days notice, you will need to sign a 'statutory' declaration. To do so, you will need to visit an independent solicitor (or someone else empowered to administer oaths).**</u>

Unless there is a special reason for committing yourself to the agreement to surrender sooner, you may want to ask the landlord to let you have at least 14 days to consider whether you wish to give up your statutory rights. If you then decided to go ahead with the agreement to end your lease, you would only need to make a simple declaration, and so you would not need to make a separate visit to an independent solicitor.

AND I make this solemn declaration conscientiously believing the same to be true and by virtue of the Statutory Declarations Act 1835

DECLARED at ....this ....day of ....

Before me ....

(*signature of person before whom declaration is made*)

A commissioner for oaths *or*

A solicitor empowered to administer oaths or (*as appropriate*)

Contents of the statutory declaration

The contents of the statutory declaration, and the information which needs to be completed, are almost exactly the same as the simple declaration (see **p34** above).

The differences are:

- The declaration records that the health warning notice was served, but does not say when, ie it does not state less than 14 days' notice was given.

- The deponent has to 'solemnly and sincerely declare' rather than just 'declare'. The deponent must make the statutory declaration within the meaning of the Statutory Declaration Act 1835. They must make the declaration before an independent solicitor (or other person qualified to administer oaths) and pay the prescribed fee which is £5 at the date this book was published.

For the practical aspects of making the statutory declaration, see **Chapter 2, p13** above.

The second requirement of Schedule 4 to the Order

Paragraph 5 of Schedule 4 to the Order provides that the 'instrument creating the agreement to surrender' (ie the agreement to surrender) must contain or have endorsed on it:

- a reference to the health warning notice; and

- a reference to the simple declaration or statutory declaration as appropriate.

Suggested wording for this endorsement is as follows, (obviously this may need to be varied depending on the individual circumstances of the case):

1. This agreement to surrender has been authorised in accordance with the provisions of s38A(4) of the Landlord and Tenant Act 1954. In accordance with those provisions:

   (a) the landlord has served on the tenant a notice in the form, or substantially in the form, set out in Schedule 3 to the Regulatory Reform (Business Tenancies) (England and Wales) Order 2003 (the 'Order'); and

   (b) the requirements specified in Schedule 4 to the Order have been met in that the tenant has made a [statutory*] declaration in the form, or substantially in the form, set out in paragraph [6*] [7*] of Schedule 4 to the Order.

*delete as appropriate.

- Paragraph 6 is referred to where the tenant has made a simple declaration, ie where the health warning notice was served not less than 14 days before the tenant entered into the agreement to surrender or became contractually bound to do so. The words 'statutory' and 'paragraph 7' should be deleted.

- Paragraph 7 is referred to where the tenant has made a statutory declaration, ie where the health warning notice was served less than

14 days before the tenant entered into the agreement to surrender or became contractually bound to do so. References to 'paragraph 6' should be deleted.

Where the parties do not know at the time of engrossing the agreement to surrender whether more or less than 14 days' notice will be given it is the author's view that they could use the following alternative wording for paragraph (b) above:

> (b) The requirements specified in Schedule 4 to the Order have been met in that the tenant has made the appropriate declaration in the form, or substantially in the form, set out in Schedule 4 to the Order.

Note: These provisions only apply to agreements to surrender, they do not need to be complied with where the tenancy is just surrendered without a prior agreement.

Practical issues

The practical issues which arise in relation to agreements to surrender are more or less the same as those that arise in relation to contracting out of the security of tenure provisions – eg how to serve the notice, evidence of service, who should it be served on, who should make the declaration etc. For a detailed analysis of these issues, see **Chapter 2, pp15-22**.

What if the tenancy is contracted out of the Act

The new provisions do not change the law on this point. Section 38A(2) of the Act (as did s38(4) before it) applies only to tenancies 'to which this part of this Act (ie Part II) applies'.

Therefore, if the tenancy is not one to which Part II of the Act applies (eg because it has been contracted out), the provisions relating to agreements for surrender are of no effect, ie the parties may enter into a valid and binding agreement to surrender the tenancy without serving health warning notices, etc.

Transitional provisions

Article 29 of the Order sets out the transitional provisions. It specifically provides that nothing in the Order shall have effect in relation to an agreement for the surrender of a tenancy:

- which was made before 1 June 2004 fell within s24(2)(b) of the Act, ie was made before the tenant had been in occupation for one month (therefore, such agreements made before 1 June 2004 will still be invalid);[2] and

- which was authorised by the court under s38(4) of the Act before 1 June 2004. Such an agreement to surrender will still be valid.

---

2 Article 29(2)(a)(ii) of the Order.

4. To whom does the Act apply?

Pre-1 June 2004

The workings of the Act sometimes caused complications and anomalies as to who could operate the statutory procedures. For example, s23 of the Act gave details of the tenancies to which the Act applied. The general provision of s23 was that the Act applied to 'any tenancy where the property comprised in the tenancy is or includes premises which are *occupied by the tenant* and are so occupied for the purposes of *a business carried on by him* or for those or other purposes' (emphasis added).

If the same business entity claimed the right to renew (or, in the case of the landlord, the right to oppose renewal so that it could run a business at the premises (s30(1)(g))) there was no difficulty.

Complications arose where property and businesses were in separate ownerships although, through company shareholdings, they were in the control and beneficial ownership of the same person.

For example, where the tenant was an individual but it was their company carrying on the business, there was no right to renew the tenancy.[1]

Also, while s30(3) of the Act specifically allowed a landlord who had a controlling interest in a company to reclaim possession on the ground that that company would carry on a business there, it did not provide a ground for possession where a company landlord wanted possession of the property so that a controlling shareholder could trade from those premises.

There were also anomalies in that the definition of group companies only covered companies directly or indirectly owned by a holding company and not if an individual controlled each company.

---

1 *Nozari-Zodeh v Pearl Assurance Plc* [1987] 2 EGLR 91 CA.

From 1 June 2004

The tenant's interest

The introduction of a new s23(1A) of the Act clarifies the old s23 to make it clear that, for the purpose of Part II of the Act, an individual and any company they control will be treated as equivalent when assessing qualifications for the statutory procedures.

Therefore:

- occupation by a company in which the tenant has a controlling interest is treated as occupation by the tenant;

- where the tenant is a company, occupation by a person with a controlling interest is treated as occupation by the tenant company;

- the carrying on of a business by a company in which the tenant has a controlling interest is treated as the carrying on of a business by the tenant; and

- where the tenant is a company, the carrying on of a business by a person with a controlling interest is treated as the carrying on of a business by the tenant company.

For the meaning of 'controlling interest', see **p45** below.

The tenant does not change

It is important to realise that these provisions do not change the person (whether company or individual) entitled to the new lease.

Where the tenant is an individual and his company is in occupation, it is the individual tenant who will continue to be the tenant. A landlord will not be obliged to grant any new tenancy to the company in occupation. The occupation of the company merely allows the individual tenant to renew their lease in situations where they would not previously have had that right.

Calculating rent for new tenancy in licensed premises

Where the court is fixing the rent for a new tenancy under s34 and the premises are licensed, s34(1)(d) provides that any added value to the premises due to that licence is to be disregarded if the benefit of the licence belongs to the tenant.

A new s34(2A) provides that, where the provisions of the Act apply, because of the new definition of occupation and carrying on a business by a tenant in s23(1A), the same considerations apply to the meaning of tenant in s34(1)(d). In other words, tenant includes (i) a company in which the tenant has a controlling interest; or (ii) where the tenant is a company, a person with a controlling interest in that company.

The landlord's interest

Grounds of opposition – section 30(1)(g) of the Act

Section 30 of the Act deals with the grounds of opposition by a landlord to a new tenancy. Section 30(1)(g) is the ground that 'on the termination of the current tenancy, *the landlord* intends to occupy the holding for the purposes... of a business to be *carried on by him...*' (emphasis added).

As mentioned at **p41** above, before 1 June 2004, s30(3) of the Act caused problems where the landlord was a company but it was the controlling shareholder who wanted to trade from the premises. Section 30(3) has been repealed.

A new s30(1A) is added which states that where the landlord has a controlling interest in a company the reference in s30(1)(g) above to the landlord will be construed as a reference to the landlord or that company.

Similarly, a new s30(1B) is added which states that (subject to what is said below) where the landlord is a company and a person has a controlling interest in the company, the reference in s30(1)(g) to the landlord will be construed as a reference to the landlord company and that person with the controlling interest.

Ground (g) does not apply if the landlord acquired their interest five years before the end of the current tenancy. A new s30(2A) is added to extend this to cover the new provisions. It provides that the new s30(1B) will not apply if the controlling interest in the landlord company was acquired five years before the end of the current tenancy.

Split reversions

A split reversion arises where two or more different landlords own separate parts of the property but the tenant is occupying under one tenancy. This could happen, for example, where landlord A sold part of the reversion to landlord B.

The definition of 'landlord' in s44 of the Act is amended to include a new s44(1A) which provides that where there is a split reversion the reference to 'landlord' will be construed as a 'reference to all those persons collectively'.

Also, s35(1) is amended to provide that where the court orders the terms of the new tenancy when there is a split reversion those terms will include terms as to the apportionment of rent between the landlords.

The Law Commission's view was that although there may be different landlords for different parts of the property, so far as the tenant is concerned they are joint owners of the superior interest and 'they should collectively be entitled to operate the statutory procedure – or have it operated by their tenant – as it affects the totality of the property'.

Whilst the changes to the Act do not make it clear, it is the author's view that where there is a split reversion the landlords should together serve one notice on the tenant referring to both parts of the property and naming both landlords as 'the landlord'. Similarly, a tenant serving a section 26 request should serve each landlord separately with a copy of a request in identical form, which refers to the entirety of the split property and requests both the landlords to grant a new tenancy under the Act.[2]

The tenant should also bring one set of proceedings for one tenancy of both parts of the property with both landlords as joint defendants.

This is somewhat at odds with the ODPM's guidance on this issue, which states that:

> Landlords in such a position [ie split reversion] will need to take concerted action, but with separate notices for the individual parts of the premises. Similarly, a tenant will need to serve separate notices on all the landlords, taking proceedings against all of them separately (if proceedings are necessary), or naming them all as parties in a single set of proceedings.

The ODPM appear to be suggesting that there should be, for example, two separate section 25 notices each dealing with only one part of the property, served by the individual landlords. The author considers that the changes made to the Act do not require this and that the changes do not change the law as set out in the *M&P Enterprises* case.

Statutory compensation

There is one exception to this new rule where the tenant is entitled to statutory compensation for the refusal of a renewal where there is a split

---

2 See *M&P Enterprises (London) Ltd v Norfolk Square Hotels Ltd & others* [1994] 14 EG 128.

reversion. The compensation will be calculated separately for each part of the property in which the reversion is owned by a different landlord, and that sum should be recoverable exclusively from that reversioner,[3] ie the tenant cannot recover the whole sum from any one of the landlords.

Group companies and control of companies

Under s42 of the Act occupation and carrying on a business by a group company is taken to be occupation by the tenant company in the same group and there are similar provisions for landlords requiring possession under s30(1)(g) for occupation for a group company.

As mentioned at **p41** above, before 1 June 2004, the definition of a group of companies in s42(1) covered only the situation where those group companies were the subsidiaries of another holding company. Section 42 has now been expanded to cover the situation where the same individual (rather than a company) controls each company.

A new s46(2) is also added clarifying the meaning of control of a company. It provides that 'a person has a controlling interest in a company if, had he been a company, the other company would have been a subsidiary'. (Therefore, again, the definition is now the same whether the company is controlled by an individual or another company.)

'Company' is defined as having the meaning given by s735 of the Companies Act 1985 and 'subsidiary' is defined as having the meaning given by s736 of the Companies Act 1985.[4]

---

3 See s37(3B) of the Act.

4 These sections are reproduced in **Appendix 6**.

5. INFORMATION GATHERING – SECTION 40 NOTICES

Pre-1 June 2004

There has always been a provision in s40 of the Act for the parties to request information from each other. For example, to allow the tenant to ascertain who was the competent landlord and for the landlord to ascertain if there were any sub-tenancies. There was, however, no express method of enforcing compliance with this request if the information was not provided voluntarily.

From 1 June 2004

Section 40 notice served by landlord on tenant

The landlord's request for information about occupation and sub-tenancies is dealt with by new ss40(1) and (2). The new prescribed Form 4 is set out below (**Figure 7**).

Figure 7

LANDLORD'S REQUEST FOR INFORMATION ABOUT OCCUPATION AND SUB-TENANCIES

Section 40(1) of the Landlord and Tenant Act 1954

To: (*insert name and address of tenant*)

From: (*insert name and address of landlord*)

1. This notice relates to the following premises: (*insert address or description of premises*)

2. I give you notice under section 40(1) of the Landlord and Tenant Act 1954 that I require you to provide information –

   (a) by answering questions (1) to (3) in the Table below;

   (b) if you answer 'yes' to question (2), by giving me the name and address of the person or persons concerned;

   (c) if you answer 'yes' to question (3), by also answering questions (4) to (10) in the Table below;   (*continued over*)

Figure 7 (continued)

    (d)   if you answer 'no' to question (8), by giving me the name and address of the sub-tenant; and

    (e)   if you answer 'yes' to question (10), by giving me details of the notice or request.

TABLE

(1) Do you occupy the premises or any part of them wholly or partly for the purposes of a business that is carried on by you?
(2) To the best of your knowledge and belief, does any other person own an interest in reversion in any part of the premises?
(3) Does your tenancy have effect subject to any sub-tenancy on which your tenancy is immediately expectant?
(4) What premises are comprised in the sub-tenancy?
(5) For what term does it have effect or, if it is terminable by notice, by what notice can it be terminated?
(6) What is the rent payable under it?
(7) Who is the sub-tenant?
(8) To the best of your knowledge and belief, is the sub-tenant in occupation of the premises or of part of the premises comprised in the sub-tenancy?
(9) Is an agreement in force excluding, in relation to the sub-tenancy, the provisions of sections 24 to 28 of the Landlord and Tenant Act 1954?
(10) Has a notice been given under section 25 or 26(6) of that Act, or has a request been made under section 26 of that Act, in relation to the sub-tenancy?

  3.   You must give the information concerned in writing and within the period of one month beginning with the date of service of this notice.

  4.   Please send all correspondence about this notice to:

Name:

Address:

Signed:

Date:

˙[Landlord] ˙[on behalf of the landlord] ˙*delete whichever is inapplicable*

IMPORTANT NOTE FOR THE TENANT

This notice contains some words and phrases that you may not understand. The Notes below should help you, but it would be wise to seek professional advice, for example, from a solicitor or surveyor, before responding to this notice.

Once you have provided the information required by this notice, you must correct it if you realise that it is not, or is no longer, correct. This obligation lasts for six months from the date of service of this notice, but an exception is explained in the next paragraph. If you need to correct information already given, you must do so within one month of becoming aware that the information is incorrect.

The obligation will cease if, after transferring your tenancy, you notify the landlord of the transfer and of the name and address of the person to whom your tenancy has been transferred.

If you fail to comply with the requirements of this notice, or the obligation mentioned above, you may face civil proceedings for breach of the statutory duty that arises under section 40 of the Landlord and Tenant Act 1954. In any such proceedings a court may order you to comply with that duty and may make an award of damages.

<u>NOTES</u>

The sections mentioned below are sections of the Landlord and Tenant Act 1954, as amended, (most recently by the Regulatory Reform (Business Tenancies) (England and Wales) Order 2003).

Purpose of this notice

Your landlord (or, if he or she is a tenant, possibly your landlord's landlord) has sent you this notice in order to obtain information about your occupation and that of any sub-tenants. This information may be relevant to the taking of steps to end or renew your business tenancy.

Time limit for replying

You must provide the relevant information within one month of the date of service of this notice (section 40(1), (2) and (5)).

Information required

You do not have to give your answers on this form; you may use a separate sheet for this purpose. The notice requires you to provide, in writing, information in the form of answers to questions (1) to (3) in the Table above and, if you answer 'yes' to question (3), also to provide information in the form of answers to questions (4) to (10) in that Table. Depending on your answer to question (2) and, if applicable in your case, questions (8) and (10), you must also provide the information referred to in paragraph 2(b), (d) and (e) of this notice. Question (2) refers to a person who owns an interest in reversion. You should answer 'yes' to this question if you know or believe that there is a person who receives, or is entitled to receive, rent in respect of any part of the premises (other than the landlord who served this notice).

When you answer questions about sub-tenants, please bear in mind that, for these purposes, a sub-tenant includes a person retaining possession of premises by virtue of the Rent (Agriculture) Act 1976 or the Rent Act 1977 after the coming to an end of a sub-tenancy, and 'sub-tenancy' includes a right so to retain possession (section 40(8)).

You should keep a copy of your answers and of any other information provided in response to questions (2), (8) or (10) above.

If, once you have given this information, you realise that it is not, or is no longer, correct, you must give the correct information within one month of becoming aware that the previous information is incorrect. Subject to the next paragraph, <u>your duty to correct any information that you have already given continues for six months after you receive this notice</u> (section 40(5)). You should give the correct information to the landlord who gave you this notice unless you receive notice of the transfer of his or her interest, and of the name and address of the person to whom that interest has been transferred. In that case, the correct information must be given to that person.

If you transfer your tenancy within the period of six months referred to above, your duty to correct information already given will cease if you notify the landlord of the transfer and of the name and address of the person to whom your tenancy has been transferred.

If you do not provide the information requested, or fail to correct information that you have provided earlier, after realising that it is not, or is no longer, correct, proceedings may be taken against you and you may have to pay damages (section 40B).

If you are in any doubt about the information that you should give, get immediate advice from a solicitor or a surveyor.

Validity of this notice

The landlord who has given you this notice may not be the landlord to whom you pay your rent (sections 44 and 67). This does not necessarily mean that the notice is invalid.

If you have any doubts about whether this notice is valid, get advice immediately from a solicitor or a surveyor.

Further information

An explanation of the main points to consider when renewing or ending a business tenancy, 'Renewing and Ending Business Leases: a Guide for Tenants and Landlords', can be found at www.odpm.gov.uk. Printed copies of the explanation, but not of this form, are available from 1 June 2004 from Free Literature, PO Box 236, Wetherby, West Yorkshire, LS23 7NB (0870 1226 236).

Information the landlord needs to fill in on this notice

The landlord is required to insert in the form the following:

- to whom the notice is sent, ie name and address of the tenant;

- from whom the notice is sent, ie the name and address of the landlord;

- the address or description of the premises; and

- the name and address of the person to whom correspondence about the notice should be sent.

The notice should be signed and dated by the landlord, or a person on its behalf.

The information which the tenant must provide

The information which the tenant must provide is set out in s40(2) of the Act and is as follows:

1. Whether the tenant occupies the premises or any part of them wholly or partly for the purposes of a business carried on by it.

This is the same information as requested previously in s40 but is given the extended meaning brought about by the changes made to s23 to the meaning of occupation and carrying on a business, ie the tenant, if an individual, will have to say if a company in which they have a controlling interest is in occupation, etc. For more details about these changes see **Chapter 4**.

2. Whether the tenancy is subject to an immediate sub-tenancy.

3. If yes to question 2, details of the sub-tenancy will need to be provided, ie:

   (a) the premises comprised in the sub-tenancy;

   (b) the term of the sub-tenancy (or, if it is terminable by notice, by what notice it can be terminated);

   (c) the rent under the sub-tenancy;

   (d) who is the sub-tenant;

   (e) whether, to the best of the tenant's knowledge and belief, the sub-tenant is in occupation of the premises or part of the premises comprised in the sub-tenancy and, if not, what is the sub-tenant's address;

   (f) whether the sub-letting is contracted out of the Act. This is a new requirement; and

   (g) whether a section 25 notice or landlord's counternotice under s26(6) has been given under the Act and whether a section 26 request has been served in relation to the sub-tenancy and, if so, details of the notice or request – this is a new requirement.

4. To the best of the tenant's knowledge and belief, the name and address of any other person who owns an interest in reversion in any part of the premises. This is a new requirement. Where there is a split reversion ie where different landlords own different parts of the property but the tenant occupies the property under a single lease, the landlord may not necessarily know the reversioner of the other part of the property.

As of now, there is no prescribed form for responding to the notice, except that it must be in writing.[1]

At first glance it appears that the questions in the prescribed form of section 40 notice do not tally with the information which needs to be provided in s40(2). For example, question 2 in the table of questions asks if any other person owns an interest in the reversion, but does not ask for details of that person. However, the request for details is made in paragraph 2(b) of the main body of the section 40 notice. There is a cross-reference between this and the table of questions. The same is the case for questions 8 (sub-tenant's address) and 10 (details of section 25/26 notices) in the table of questions.

---

1 Section 40(1) of the Act.

Section 40 notice served by a tenant on a landlord

The notice for a tenant to serve on a landlord or other reversioner is dealt with by a new s40(3) and (4). There is a new prescribed form, Form 5, which is set out below (**Figure 8**).

Figure 8

TENANT'S REQUEST FOR INFORMATION FROM LANDLORD OR LANDLORD'S MORTGAGEE ABOUT LANDLORD'S INTEREST

Section 40(3) of the Landlord and Tenant Act 1954

To: (*insert name and address of reversioner or reversioner's mortgagee in possession [see the first note below]*)

From: (insert name and address of tenant)

1. This notice relates to the following premises: (*insert address or description of premises*)

2. In accordance with section 40(3) of the Landlord and Tenant Act 1954 I require you –

    (a) to state in writing whether you are the owner of the fee simple in respect of the premises or any part of them or the mortgagee in possession of such an owner,

    (b) if you answer 'no' to (a), to state in writing, to the best of your knowledge and belief –

        (i) the name and address of the person who is your or, as the case may be, your mortgagor's immediate landlord in respect of the premises or of the part in respect of which you are not, or your mortgagor is not, the owner in fee simple;

        (ii) for what term your or your mortgagor's tenancy has effect and what is the earliest date (if any) at which that tenancy is terminable by notice to quit given by the landlord; and

        (iii) whether a notice has been given under section 25 or 26(6) of the Landlord and Tenant Act 1954, or a request has been made under section 26 of that Act, in relation to the tenancy and, if so, details of the notice or request;

    (c) to state in writing, to the best of your knowledge and belief, the name and address of any other person who owns an interest in reversion in any part of the premises;

    (d) if you are a reversioner, to state in writing whether there is a mortgagee in possession of your interest in the premises; and

    (e) if you answer 'yes' to (d), to state in writing, to the best of your knowledge and belief, the name and address of the mortgagee in possession.

3. You must give the information concerned within the period of one month beginning with the date of service of this notice.

4. Please send all correspondence about this notice to:

Name:

Address:

Signed:

Date:

*[Tenant] *[on behalf of the tenant] (*delete whichever is inapplicable*)

IMPORTANT NOTE FOR LANDLORD OR LANDLORD'S MORTGAGEE

This notice contains some words and phrases that you may not understand. The Notes below should help you, but it would be wise to seek professional advice, for example, from a solicitor or surveyor, before responding to this notice.

Once you have provided the information required by this notice, you must correct it if you realise that it is not, or is no longer, correct. This obligation lasts for six months from the date of service of this notice, but an exception is explained in the next paragraph. If you need to correct information already given, you must do so within one month of becoming aware that the information is incorrect.

The obligation will cease if, after transferring your interest, you notify the tenant of the transfer and of the name and address of the person to whom your interest has been transferred.

If you fail to comply with the requirements of this notice, or the obligation mentioned above, you may face civil proceedings for breach of the statutory duty that arises under section 40 of the Landlord and Tenant Act 1954. In any such proceedings a court may order you to comply with that duty and may make an award of damages.

NOTES

The sections mentioned below are sections of the Landlord and Tenant Act 1954, as amended, (most recently by the Regulatory Reform (Business Tenancies) (England and Wales) Order 2003)

Terms used in this notice

The following terms, which are used in paragraph 2 of this notice, are defined in s40(8):

'mortgagee in possession' includes a receiver appointed by the mortgagee or by the court who is in receipt of the rents and profits;

'reversioner' means any person having an interest in the premises, being an interest in reversion expectant (whether immediately or not) on the tenancy; and

'reversioner's mortgagee in possession' means any person being a mortgagee in possession in respect of such an interest.

Section 40(8) requires the reference in paragraph 2(b) of this notice to your mortgagor to be read in the light of the definition of 'mortgagee in possession'.

A mortgagee (mortgage lender) will be 'in possession' if the mortgagor (the person who owes money to the mortgage lender) has failed to comply with the terms of the mortgage. The mortgagee may then be entitled to receive rent that would normally have been paid to the mortgagor.

The term 'the owner of the fee simple' means the freehold owner.

The term 'reversioner' includes the freehold owner and any intermediate landlord as well as the immediate landlord of the tenant who served this notice.

Purpose of this notice and information required

This notice requires you to provide, in writing, the information requested in paragraph 2(a) and (c) of the notice and, if applicable in your case, in paragraph 2(b), (d) and (e). You do not need to use a special form for this purpose.

If, once you have given this information, you realise that it is not, or is no longer, correct, you must give the correct information within one month of becoming aware that the previous information is incorrect. Subject to the last paragraph in this section of these Notes, your duty to correct any information that you have already given continues for six months after you receive this notice (section 40(5)).

You should give the correct information to the tenant who gave you this notice unless you receive notice of the transfer of his or her interest, and of the name and address of the person to whom that interest has been transferred. In that case, the correct information must be given to that person.

If you do not provide the information requested, or fail to correct information that you have provided earlier, after realising that it is not, or is no longer, correct, proceedings may be taken against you and you may have to pay damages (section 40B).

If you are in any doubt as to the information that you should give, get advice immediately from a solicitor or a surveyor.

If you transfer your interest within the period of six months referred to above, your duty to correct information already given will cease if you notify the tenant of that transfer and of the name and address of the person to whom your interest has been transferred.

Time limit for replying

You must provide the relevant information within one month of the date of service of this notice (section 40(3), (4) and (5)).

Validity of this notice

The tenant who has given you this notice may not be the person from whom you receive rent (sections 44 and 67). This does not necessarily mean that the notice is invalid.

If you have any doubts about the validity of the notice, get advice immediately from a solicitor or a surveyor.

Further information

An explanation of the main points to consider when renewing or ending a business tenancy, 'Renewing and Ending Business Leases: a Guide for Tenants and Landlords', can be found at www.odpm.gov.uk. Printed copies of the explanation, but not of this form, are available from 1 June 2004 from Free Literature, PO Box 236, Wetherby, West Yorkshire, LS23 7NB (0870 1226 236).

Information the tenant needs to fill in on the notice

The tenant is required to insert in the form the following:

- to whom the notice is sent, ie the name and address of the reversioner or the reversioner's mortgagee in possession;

- from whom the notice is sent, ie the name and address of the tenant;

- the address or description of the premises; and

- the name and address of the person to whom correspondence about the notice should be sent.

The notice should be signed and dated by the tenant, or a person on its behalf.

The information which the landlord or landlord's mortgagee must provide

The information which the recipient of the notice must provide is set out in s40(4) of the Act and is as follows:

1. Whether he is the owner of the fee simple of the premises (ie the freehold) or any part of them, or whether he is the mortgagee in possession of such an owner.

2. If not, then (to the best of his knowledge and belief):

    (a) the name and address of his (or, if it is the case, his mortgagor's) immediate landlord of the premises, or part thereof, of which he (his mortgagor) is not the freeholder;

    (b) the term of his, or his mortgagor's, tenancy (and the earliest date, if any, it is terminable by a notice to quit by the landlord); and

    (c) whether any section 25 notice or counternotice under s26(6) has been served or a section 26 request has been made in relation to the tenancy, and if so details of that notice – this is a new requirement.

3. To the best of his knowledge and belief, the name and address of any other person who owns an interest in reversion in any part of the premises. This is a new requirement to cover the situation where there is a split reversion and will enable the tenant to find out who the other reversioner is so that he can serve the appropriate section 26 request.

4. If the landlord is a reversioner, whether there is a mortgagee in possession of his interest in the premises and, if so, (to the best of his knowledge and belief) the names and addresses of the mortgagee.

Note: if there is a mortgagee in possession, he is the person with whom the tenant must conduct the renewal procedure (see s67 of the Act). 'Mortgagee in possession' is defined as including 'a receiver appointed by the mortgagee or by the court who is in receipt of the rents and profits'. Therefore, details of any such receivers need to be disclosed.

As now, there is no prescribed form for responding to the notice except that it must be in writing (s40(3)).

Miscellaneous amendments to section 40

As well as defining 'mortgagee in possession' as mentioned above, there are a few other small additions to the definitions in s40. The following new definitions are inserted:

- 'reversioner' – any person having an interest in the premises, being an interest in reversion expectant (whether immediately or not) on the tenancy;

- 'reversioner's mortgagee in possession' – any person being a mortgagee in possession in respect of such an interest; and

- 'sub-tenant' – the definition is extended to include a statutory tenant (ie after the end of the contractual term) under the Rent (Agricultural) Act 1979 as well as under the Rent Act 1977.

The explanatory notes on the prescribed form of tenant's section 40 notice also contain further definitions in lay terms of the various legal terms used in the notice.

Time for serving and responding to section 40 notices

The time for serving a section 40 notice has not changed. The section will not apply to notices served more than two years before the contractual term date (or the date it could be brought to an end by a landlord's notice to quit).[2]

However, there is a subtle difference in the time for responding to a section 40 notice. The person who is to respond to the notice (the 'information provider') is to do so 'within one month beginning with the date of service of the notice' (s40(5)(a)). The old s40 provided that a tenant was to respond 'within one month of service of the notice' and the landlord 'within one month after service of the notice'. In the author's view this brings forward by one day the time for the response. The case of *Zoan v Rouamba*[3] will apply. *Zoan* provided that where a time was to be calculated 'beginning with' a certain date you include that date in the calculations. Therefore, if a section 40 notice is served on 4 March, the response is due on or before 3 April, not 4 April.

This reasoning will also apply to time limits for updating information – see **p57**.

Service of section 40 notices

The section 40 notices should be served in accordance with s23 of the Landlord and Tenant Act 1927. For this and other practical issues as to service of notices, see **Chapter 2**.

---

2 Section 40(6) of the Act.

3 [2000]2 All ER 620 CA

A new continuing duty if any of the information changes

There were no provisions dealing with this pre-June 2004. The Law Commission considered that, although most people would act quickly upon receiving the information requested, there was a case for trying to ensure that the information was kept up to date. This did not, however, need to be done for any lengthy period as such an obligation would impose 'a heavy and unreasonably onerous burden' on the information provider. A short period would be appropriate.

The Act, therefore, now provides that where a party who has given information in response to a statutory notice, becomes aware, within the period of six months beginning with the date of service of the notice, that any information it gave is not, or is no longer, correct, that person must give 'the appropriate person' the correct information. This must be done within one month beginning with the date on which the information provider becomes aware (s40(5)). For calculating this period see comments at **p56** above as to the meaning of 'beginning with'.

To whom must the new/revised information be given?

The 'appropriate person' to whom the information must be given, will normally be the person who served the notice (s40(7)).

However, where:

- that person (the 'transferor'), ie the person who served the notice, has transferred its interest in the premises to some other person (the transferee); and

- the transferor or the transferee has given the information provider notice, in writing, of:

  1. the transfer; and

  2. the transferee's name and address,

the 'appropriate person' to whom the information is to be given is the transferee (s40A(2)).

If such a transfer has taken place, but no notice is given to the information provider, then any duty under s40 (ie the original duty to give information, or the s40(5)(b) duty to update that information) may be performed by the information provider by giving the information to either the transferee or the transferor (s40A(3)).

What happens if the 'information provider' transfers its interest?

If the information provider has transferred its interest, and it has informed the person who served the notice (or a transferee of that person's interest of which the information provider has been given notice) of:

- the transfer of his interest; and
- the name and addresses of the person to whom he transferred it,

then on giving such notice the information provider's duty under s40 ceases (s40A(1)).

Transfer of part of premises only

The Law Commission's intention was that where the information provider transfers his interest in part only of the property his duty will cease in relation to the part transferred, but the duty would continue in relation to the retained part. Section 40A(1) refers to the transfer of part only and, if the criteria are met, the duty ceasing in relation to that part.

Example 1:

L1 serves a section 40 notice on T1 on 3 July 2004. T1 has to provide the information within one month 'beginning with the date of service of the notice', ie by 2 August 2004. He does so. On 20 August 2004 T1 becomes aware some of the information was incorrect.

Scenario 1:

L1 still holds the freehold: T1 has to inform L1 of the change in the information 'within the period of one month beginning with the date on which he becomes aware' (ie by 19 September 2004).

Scenario 2:

L1 transferred his interest to L2 on 10 August 2004. L1 or L2 informed T1 of the transfer and of L2's name and address. T1 must provide the updating information to L2.

Scenario 3:

As Scenario 2, but T1 is not informed of the transfer from L1 to L2. T1 will satisfy his duty by giving the updating information to L1 or L2.

Example 2:

L1 serves a section 40 notice on T1 on 3 July 2004. As before, T1 has to provide the information by 2 August 2004. He does so. On 20 August T1 becomes aware some of the information is incorrect.

Scenario 1:

T1 is still the tenant. T1 has to inform L1 of the change in the information by 19 September 2004.

Scenario 2:

T1 transferred his interest in the premises to T2 on 10 August 2004. T1 informed L1, in writing, of the transfer and of T2's name and address. T1 has no duty to inform L1 of the change in the information. Neither has T2. L1 should consider serving a fresh notice on T2 whenever such a transfer takes place.

Note: if you are acting for a party and have served a section 40 notice, and if you are aware of a transfer of the other party's interest, you may wish to consider serving a fresh section 40 notice on that transferee, if you want to retain the benefit of the updating provisions.

What are the sanctions if a party does not comply with a section 40 notice?

Section 40B of the Act introduces a specific remedy against a person who has failed to comply with any duty imposed by s40. That person may be sued in civil proceedings for breach of statutory duty, and the court may:

- order that it complies with that duty; and

- make an award of damages.

Transitional provisions

Article 29(b) of the Order specifically provides that none of the above changes apply to a notice under s40 of the Act served before the Order came into force, ie before 1 June 2004.

6. THE RENEWAL PROCESS – NOTICES AND COUNTERNOTICES

The renewal process still starts with the service of a section 25 notice by the landlord or a section 26 request by the tenant. The amount of notice which has to be given, ie no less than six and no more than 12 months, has not changed.

Transitional provisions

The transitional provisions in Art 29(1) of the Order provide that where a section 25 notice was served or a section 26 request was made before the Order came into force (ie before 1 June 2004), then nothing in the Order has effect in relation to that notice or request or anything done in consequence of it.

Landlord's section 25 notice

Pre-June 2004

The landlord indicates in its section 25 notice whether or not it opposes the renewal, but does not set out details of its proposals for the new tenancy if it is not opposed. The first time the tenant may see these proposals is in the landlord's acknowledgment of service after proceedings have commenced.

From 1 June – unopposed renewal

There are now two separate prescribed forms of section 25 notice. The form for an unopposed renewal is Form 1 of Schedule 2 to the Landlord and Tenant Act 1954 Part 2 (Notices) Regulations 2004[1] and is set out overleaf (**Figure 9**).

The landlord must fill in the following details:

* to whom the notice is sent, ie the name and address of the tenant(s);

* from whom the notice is sent, ie the name and address of the landlord;

* the address or description of the property;

---

1 SI 2004/1005.

Figure 9

LANDLORD'S NOTICE ENDING A BUSINESS TENANCY WITH PROPOSALS FOR A NEW ONE

Section 25 of the Landlord and Tenant Act 1954

IMPORTANT NOTE FOR THE LANDLORD: If you are willing to grant a new tenancy, complete this form and send it to the tenant. If you wish to oppose the grant of a new tenancy, use form 2 in Schedule 2 to the Landlord and Tenant Act 1954, Part 2 (Notices) Regulations 2004 or, where the tenant may be entitled to acquire the freehold or an extended lease, form 7 in that Schedule, instead of this form.

To: (*insert name and address of tenant*)

From: (*insert name and address of landlord*)

1. This notice applies to the following property: (*insert address or description of property*).

2. I am giving you notice under section 25 of the Landlord and Tenant Act 1954 to end your tenancy on (*insert date*).

3. I am not opposed to granting you a new tenancy. You will find my proposals for the new tenancy, which we can discuss, in the Schedule to this notice.

4. If we cannot agree on all the terms of a new tenancy, either you or I may ask the court to order the grant of a new tenancy and settle the terms on which we cannot agree.

5. If you wish to ask the court for a new tenancy you must do so by the date in paragraph 2, unless we agree in writing to a later date and do so before the date in paragraph 2.

6. Please send all correspondence about this notice to:

Name:

Address:

Signed:

Date:

*[Landlord] *[On behalf of the landlord] *[Mortgagee] *[On behalf of the mortgagee]

*(*delete if inapplicable*)

SCHEDULE

LANDLORD'S PROPOSALS FOR A NEW TENANCY

(*attach or insert proposed terms of the new tenancy*)

IMPORTANT NOTE FOR THE TENANT

This Notice is intended to bring your tenancy to an end. If you want to continue to occupy your property after the date specified in paragraph 2 you must act quickly. If you are in any doubt about the action that you should take, get advice immediately from a solicitor or a surveyor.

The landlord is prepared to offer you a new tenancy and has set out proposed terms in the Schedule to this notice. You are not bound to accept these terms. They are merely suggestions as a basis for negotiation. In the event of disagreement, ultimately the court would settle the terms of the new tenancy.

It would be wise to seek professional advice before agreeing to accept the landlord's terms or putting forward your own proposals.

NOTES

The sections mentioned below are sections of the Landlord and Tenant Act 1954, as amended, (most recently by the Regulatory Reform (Business Tenancies) (England and Wales) Order 2003).

Ending of tenancy and grant of new tenancy

This notice is intended to bring your tenancy to an end on the date given in paragraph 2. Section 25 contains rules about the date that the landlord can put in that paragraph.

However, your landlord is prepared to offer you a new tenancy and has set out proposals for it in the Schedule to this notice (section 25(8)). You are not obliged to accept these proposals and may put forward your own.

If you and your landlord are unable to agree terms either one of you may apply to the court. You may not apply to the court if your landlord has already done so (section 24(2A)). If you wish to apply to the court you must do so by the date given in paragraph 2 of this notice, unless you and your landlord have agreed in writing to extend the deadline (sections 29A and 29B).

The court will settle the rent and other terms of the new tenancy or those on which you and your landlord cannot agree (sections 34 and 35). If you apply to the court your tenancy will continue after the date shown in paragraph 2 of this notice while your application is being considered (section 24).

If you are in any doubt about what action you should take, get advice immediately from a solicitor or a surveyor.

Negotiating a new tenancy

Most tenancies are renewed by negotiation. You and your landlord may agree in writing to extend the deadline for making an application to the court while negotiations continue. Either you or your landlord can ask the court to fix the rent that you will have to pay while the tenancy continues (sections 24A to 24D).

You may only stay in the property after the date in paragraph 2 (or if we have agreed in writing to a later date, that date), if by then you or the landlord has asked the court to order the grant of a new tenancy.

If you do try to agree a new tenancy with your landlord remember:

- that your present tenancy will not continue after the date in paragraph 2 of this notice without the agreement in writing mentioned above, unless you have applied to the court or your landlord has done so, and

- that you will lose your right to apply to the court once the deadline in paragraph 2 of this notice has passed, unless there is a written agreement extending the deadline.

Validity of this notice

The landlord who has given you this notice may not be the landlord to whom you pay your rent (sections 44 and 67). This does not necessarily mean that the notice is invalid.

If you have any doubts about whether this notice is valid, get advice immediately from a solicitor or a surveyor.

Further information

An explanation of the main points to consider when renewing or ending a business tenancy, "Renewing and Ending Business Leases: a Guide for Tenants and Landlords", can be found at www.odpm.gov.uk. Printed copies of the explanation, but not of this form, are available from 1 June 2004 from Free Literature, PO Box 236, Wetherby, West Yorkshire, LS23 7NB (0870 1226 236).

- the date the tenancy will end (ie six to 12 months from the date of service);

- the landlord's proposals for the new tenancy, which can be discussed (this is a new requirement – s25(8)). These are to be set out in the Schedule to the notice. Specifically, the landlord's proposals for the new tenancy must include details of:

  1. the property to be comprised in the new tenancy;

  2. the rent; and

  3. the other terms; and

- details of the person to whom correspondence about the notice should be sent.

The notice should be signed and dated by the landlord/its mortgagee or someone on its behalf.

The property to be comprised in the new tenancy

The new s25(8)(a) of the Act introduces the requirement that details of the property to be comprised in the new tenancy must be included. It states the landlord must set out its proposals as to the property to be comprised in the tenancy (being either the whole or part of the property comprised in the current tenancy).

The reference to the property being 'either the whole or the part of the property comprised in the current tenancy' means that the landlord must decide, at this stage, whether it wants the tenant to be tenant of the whole property. This will be relevant where the tenant has sublet part. The tenant is only entitled to renew the tenancy of the part he is occupying, but under s32(2) of the Act, the landlord can insist the tenant renews the whole lease. This saves the landlord having to deal direct with the sub-tenant and keeps the tenant liable under its lease for the whole property. Before the reforms, the landlord would have put its requirement that the tenant take a new lease of the whole in its acknowledgment of service.[2] Now it will also have to put it in its section 25 notice as well as in the acknowledgment of service[3] or its claim form if it makes the application for a new tenancy.[4]

---

2 Practice Direction 56 para 3.6(5).

3 See Practice Direction 56 paras 3.10 and 3.12.

4 See Practice Direction 56 para 3.7.

The rent payable under the new tenancy

The new s25(8)(b) of the Act introduces the requirement that details of the rent must be included. Again, this is to give the tenant as much notice as possible of the rent proposed. In practice, this may be not as easy as it sounds for landlords to provide. In a volatile market a landlord could have difficulty quoting a rent for 12 months in advance.

The other terms of the tenancy

The new s28(8)(c) of the Act introduces the requirement that other terms of the tenancy must be included. There is no guidance as to the amount of detail that the landlord has to provide.

Does he have to set out all the terms, ie attach a draft lease, or will heads of terms suffice? Alternatively, can the landlord be vague and state, eg 'as per landlord's standard terms for a unit in this centre' as they often currently do in an acknowledgment of service? The reason why this is so important is that s25(8) states that a section 25 notice 'shall not have effect' unless it sets out the landlord's proposals. Whilst this is not fatal, in that a fresh notice could be served, the landlord may lose valuable time and, in a rising market, uplifted interim rent.

The author considers that it is unlikely that a draft lease will be required at this stage as the purpose behind this amendment is merely to speed up the negotiating progress and provide the tenant with a starting point from which to work. Heads of terms should suffice and indeed reference to a standard from of lease should suffice if the rent is also quoted. The ODPM's Guidance Note enigmatically states

> … landlords are not required to sign a draft lease offered by way of a proposal.

Are these proposals binding?

Section 25 of the Act does not deal with the issue of whether the proposals are binding, but the prescribed form clearly states in its 'Important note for Tenant' that:

> The landlord is prepared to offer you a new tenancy and has set out proposed terms in the Schedule to this notice. You are not bound to accept these terms. They are merely suggestions as a basis for negotiation. In the event of disagreement, ultimately the court would settle the terms of the new tenancy.

This reflects the intention behind the amendments that the tenant is not bound to accept the terms offered. The idea is merely to speed up the renewal process.

The other side to this is whether the landlord is bound by the terms he has quoted, particularly if a draft lease is attached. Neither the Act nor the prescribed form of section 25 notice specifically deal with this point. One interpretation is that the landlord is being required to merely set out its 'proposals' not an 'offer'. The proposals are put forward for consideration and discussion and amount to no more than an invitation to treat.

It is conceivable though that, particularly if a draft lease is attached to the section 25 notice (and all the terms of the new lease are certain), a tenant could sign the notice and return it to the landlord accepting those terms and thereby argue that it has created a valid contract. (It is arguable that s2 of the Law of Property (Miscellaneous Provisions) Act 1989 will have been complied with if both parties have signed the section 25 notice.) The author suspects this is the reasoning behind the enigmatic quote from the ODPM's Guidance Note (**p65** above) about the landlord not having to sign any draft lease. However, in practice this is extremely unlikely. A tenant is almost certain to object to some of the terms put forward by the landlord, especially the rent!

It is clearly not the intention of the reforms that the landlord should be bound by its proposals and a late amendment to the ODPM's Guidance Note states: 'The proposals are not a legal offer capable of acceptance, unless otherwise stated.'

For case law as to whether proposals put forward in court documents were offers capable of acceptance, see *Lovely and Orchard Services Ltd v Dejan Investments (Grove Hall) Ltd*[5] and *Blair v Park Investments Ltd.*[6]

From 1 June 2004 – opposed renewal

The prescribed form of section 25 notice for an opposed renewal is Form 2 of Schedule 2 to the Landlord and Tenant Act 1954 Part 2 (Notices) Regulations 2004 set out opposite (**Figure 10**).

The landlord must fill in the following details:

- to who the notice is sent, ie the name and address of the tenant;
- from whom the notice is sent, ie the name and address of the landlord;
- the address or description of the property;
- the date the tenancy will end (ie six to 12 months from the date of service);

---

5 [1978] EGLR 44

6 1989, unreported, County Court.

Figure 10

LANDLORD'S NOTICE ENDING A BUSINESS TENANCY AND REASONS FOR REFUSING A NEW ONE

Section 25 of the Landlord and Tenant Act 1954

IMPORTANT NOTE FOR THE LANDLORD: If you wish to oppose the grant of a new tenancy on any of the grounds in s30(1) of the Landlord and Tenant Act 1954, complete this form and send it to the tenant. If the tenant may be entitled to acquire the freehold or an extended lease, use form 7 in Schedule 2 to the Landlord and Tenant Act 1954, Part 2 (Notices) Regulations 2004 instead of this form.

To: (*insert name and address of tenant*)

From: (*insert name and address of landlord*)

1. This notice relates to the following property: (*insert address or description of property*)

2. I am giving you notice under section 25 of the Landlord and Tenant Act 1954 to end your tenancy on (*insert date*).

3. I am opposed to the grant of a new tenancy.

4. You may ask the court to order the grant of a new tenancy. If you do, I will oppose your application on the ground(s) mentioned in paragraph(s)˙ of section 30(1) of that Act. I draw your attention to the Table in the Notes below, which sets out all the grounds of opposition.

   ˙(*insert letter(s) of the paragraph(s) relied on*)

5. If you wish to ask the court for a new tenancy you must do so before the date in paragraph 2 unless, before that date, we agree in writing to a later date.

6. I can ask the court to order the ending of your tenancy without granting you a new tenancy. I may have to pay you compensation if I have relied only on one or more of the grounds mentioned in paragraphs (e), (f) and (g) of section 30(1). If I ask the court to end your tenancy, you can challenge my application.

7. Please send all correspondence about this notice to:

Name:

Address:

Signed:

Date:

˙[Landlord] ˙[On behalf of the landlord] ˙[Mortgagee] ˙[On behalf of the mortgagee]
(˙*delete if inapplicable*)

IMPORTANT NOTE FOR THE TENANT

This notice is intended to bring your tenancy to an end on the date specified in paragraph 2.

Your landlord is not prepared to offer you a new tenancy. You will not get a new tenancy unless you successfully challenge in court the grounds on which your landlord opposes the grant of a new tenancy.

If you want to continue to occupy your property you must act quickly. The notes below should help you to decide what action you now need to take. If you want to challenge your landlord's refusal to renew your tenancy, get advice immediately from a solicitor or a surveyor.

NOTES

The sections mentioned below are sections of the Landlord and Tenant Act 1954, as amended, (most recently by the Regulatory Reform (Business Tenancies) (England and Wales) Order 2003)

Ending of your tenancy

This notice is intended to bring your tenancy to an end on the date given in paragraph 2. Section 25 contains rules about the date that the landlord can put in that paragraph.

Your landlord is not prepared to offer you a new tenancy. If you want a new tenancy you will need to apply to the court for a new tenancy and successfully challenge the landlord's grounds for opposition (see the section below headed '*Landlord's opposition to new tenancy*'). If you wish to apply to the court you must do so before the date given in paragraph 2 of this notice, unless you and your landlord have agreed in writing, before that date, to extend the deadline (sections 29A and 29B).

If you apply to the court your tenancy will continue after the date given in paragraph 2 of this notice while your application is being considered (section 24). You may not apply to the court if your landlord has already done so (sections 24(2A) and (2B)).

You may only stay in the property after the date given in paragraph 2 (or such later date as you and the landlord may have agreed in writing) if before that date you have asked the court to order the grant of a new tenancy or the landlord has asked the court to order the ending of your tenancy without granting you a new one.

If you are in any doubt about what action you should take, get advice immediately from a solicitor or a surveyor.

Landlord's opposition to new tenancy

If you apply to the court for a new tenancy, the landlord can only oppose your application on one or more of the grounds set out in section 30(1). If you match the letter(s) specified in paragraph 4 of this notice with those in the first column in the Table below, you can see from the second column the ground(s) on which the landlord relies.

Paragraph of section 30(1)	Grounds
(a)	Where under the current tenancy the tenant has any obligations as respects the repair and maintenance of the holding, that the tenant ought not to be granted a new tenancy in view of the state of repair of the holding, being a state resulting from the tenant's failure to comply with the said obligations.
(b)	That the tenant ought not to be granted a new tenancy in view of his persistent delay in paying rent which has become due.
(c)	That the tenant ought not to be granted a new tenancy in view of other substantial breaches by him of his obligations under the current tenancy, or for any other reason connected with the tenant's use or management of the holding.
(d)	That the landlord has offered and is willing to provide or secure the provision of alternative accommodation for the tenant, that the terms on which the alternative accommodation is available are reasonable having regard to the terms of the current tenancy and to all other relevant circumstances, and that the accommodation and the time at which it will be available are suitable for the tenant's requirements (including the requirement to preserve goodwill) having regard to the nature and class of his business and to the situation and extent of, and facilities afforded by, the holding.

(e)	Where the current tenancy was created by the sub-letting of part only of the property comprised in a superior tenancy and the landlord is the owner of an interest in reversion expectant on the termination of that superior tenancy, that the aggregate of the rents reasonably obtainable on separate lettings of the holding and the remainder of that property would be substantially less than the rent reasonably obtainable on a letting of that property as a whole, that on the termination of the current tenancy the landlord requires possession of the holding for the purposes of letting or otherwise disposing of the said property as a whole, and that in view thereof the tenant ought not to be granted a new tenancy.
(f)	That on the termination of the current tenancy the landlord intends to demolish or reconstruct the premises comprised in the holding or a substantial part of those premises or to carry out substantial work of construction on the holding or part thereof and that he could not reasonably do so without obtaining possession of the holding.
(g)	On the termination of the current tenancy the landlord intends to occupy the holding for the purposes, or partly for the purposes, of a business to be carried on by him therein, or as his residence.

In this Table 'the holding' means the property that is the subject of the tenancy.

In ground (e), 'the landlord is the owner an interest in reversion expectant on the termination of that superior tenancy' means that the landlord has an interest in the property that will entitle him or her, when your immediate landlord's tenancy comes to an end, to exercise certain rights and obligations in relation to the property that are currently exercisable by your immediate landlord.

If the landlord relies on ground (f), the court can sometimes still grant a new tenancy if certain conditions set out in section 31A are met.

If the landlord relies on ground (g), please note that 'the landlord' may have an extended meaning. Where a landlord has a controlling interest in a company then either the landlord or the company can rely on ground (g). Where the landlord is a company and a person has a controlling interest in that company then either of them can rely on ground (g) (s30(1A) and (1B)). A person has a 'controlling interest' in a company if, had he been a company, the other company would have been its subsidiary (section 46(2)).

The landlord must normally have been the landlord for at least five years before he or she can rely on ground (g).

Compensation

If you cannot get a new tenancy solely because one or more of grounds (e), (f) and (g) applies, you may be entitled to compensation under section 37. If your landlord has opposed your application on any of the other grounds as well as (e), (f) or (g) you can only get compensation if the court's refusal to grant a new tenancy is based solely on one or more of grounds (e), (f) and (g). In other words, you cannot get compensation under section 37 if the court has refused your tenancy on *other* grounds, even if one or more of grounds (e), (f) and (g) also applies.

If your landlord is an authority possessing compulsory purchase powers (such as a local authority) you may be entitled to a disturbance payment under Part 3 of the Land Compensation Act 1973.

Validity of this notice

The landlord who has given you this notice may not be the landlord to whom you pay your rent (sections 44 and 67). This does not necessarily mean that the notice is invalid.

If you have any doubts about whether this notice is valid, get advice immediately from a solicitor or a surveyor.

Further information

An explanation of the main points to consider when renewing or ending a business tenancy, 'Renewing and Ending Business Leases: a Guide for Tenants and Landlords', can be found at www.odpm.gov.uk. Printed copies of the explanation, but not of this form, are available from 1 June 2004 from Free Literature, PO Box 236, Wetherby, West Yorkshire, LS23 7NB (0870 1226 236).

- the ground(s) on which the landlord is opposing the renewal; and
- details of the person to whom correspondence about the notice should be sent.

The notice should be signed and dated by the landlord/its mortgagee or someone on its behalf.

Grounds of opposition

The grounds of opposition in s30(1) of the Act still apply. The original draft of the new notice had reproduced those grounds in the body of the notice so the landlord would have had to simply delete those that it did not wish to rely on. In the author's view, this would have saved simple errors occurring through the insertion of the wrong ground in the notice. Unfortunately, the form of the notice has now reverted to the old format where the landlord has to insert the letter of the paragraph in s30(1) on which it relies.

Withdrawal of landlord's section 25 notice

Paragraph 6 of Schedule 6 to the Act provides that where the competent landlord (as defined by s44 of the Act) has served a section 25 notice to terminate the relevant tenancy and, within two months after the giving of that section 25 notice a superior landlord:

- becomes the competent landlord, or
- serves a notice on the tenant in the prescribed form withdrawing the previous section 25 notice,

the original section 25 notice will cease to have effect.

There is a new prescribed form for withdrawing the section 25 notice which is Form 6, set out opposite (**Figure 11**).

Figure 11

LANDLORD'S WITHDRAWAL OF NOTICE TERMINATING TENANCY

Section 44 of, and paragraph 6 of Schedule 6 to, the Landlord and Tenant Act 1954

To: (*insert name and address of tenant*)

From: (*insert name and address of landlord*)

1.   This notice is given under section 44 of, and paragraph 6 of Schedule 6 to, the Landlord and Tenant Act 1954 ('the 1954 Act').

2.   It relates to the following property: (*insert address or description of property*)

3.   I have become your landlord for the purposes of the 1954 Act.

4.   I withdraw the notice given to you by (*insert name of former landlord*), terminating your tenancy on (*insert date*).

5.   Please send any correspondence about this notice to:

Name:

Address:

Signed:

Date:

˙[Landlord] ˙[on behalf of the landlord] (˙*delete whichever is inapplicable*)

IMPORTANT NOTE FOR THE TENANT

If you have any doubts about the validity of this notice, get advice immediately from a solicitor or a surveyor.

NOTES

The sections and Schedule mentioned below are sections of, and a Schedule to, the Landlord and Tenant Act 1954, as amended, (most recently by the Regulatory Reform (Business Tenancies) (England and Wales) Order 2003).

Purpose of this notice

You were earlier given a notice bringing your tenancy to an end, but there has now been a change of landlord. This new notice is given to you by your new landlord and withdraws the earlier notice, which now has no effect. However, the new landlord can, if he or she wishes, give you a fresh notice with the intention of bringing your tenancy to an end (section 44 and paragraph 6 of Schedule 6)

Validity of this notice

The landlord who has given you this notice may not be the landlord to whom you pay your rent (sections 44 and 67). This does not necessarily mean that the notice is invalid.

If you have any doubts about whether this notice is valid, get advice immediately from a solicitor or a surveyor. If this notice is *not* valid, the original notice will have effect. Your tenancy will end on the date given in that notice (stated in paragraph 4 of this notice).

Further information

An explanation of the main points to consider when renewing or ending a business tenancy, 'Renewing and Ending Business Leases: a Guide for Tenants and Landlords', can be found at **www.odpm.gov.uk**. Printed copies of the explanation, but not of this form, are available from 1 June 2004 from Free Literature, PO Box 236, Wetherby, West Yorkshire, LS23 7NB (0870 1226 236).

Tenant's section 26 request

From 1 June 2004

The details of the tenant's section 26 request have not changed but there is a new prescribed form, Form 3, which is set out opposite (**Figure 12**).

The tenant will need to fill in the following details:

- to whom the notice is sent, ie the name and address of the landlord;

- from whom the notice is sent, ie the name and address of the tenant;

- the address or description of the property;

- the date the tenant would like the new tenancy to begin;

- the tenant's proposals for the new tenancy – these are to go in the Schedule to the notice; and

- details of the person to whom correspondence about the notice should be sent.

The notice should be signed and dated by the tenant or someone on its behalf.

Tenant's proposed terms

Whereas the old prescribed form of section 26 request (and the first draft of the new forms) specifically provided for the tenant to state the property to be comprised in the new tenancy, the rent and its proposed 'other terms', the new prescribed form does not. This specific information must still, however, be provided as is made clear by s26(3) of the Act.

As with a landlord, if the tenancy is to start sometime in the future and the market is changing, the tenant may have difficulty quoting a rent, although this is no different from the pre June 2004 situation. As for the 'other terms', most tenants will probably do as they did pre-June 2004, ie insert 'as per terms of existing lease save for the following…'.

See the comments at **p77** below in respect of paragraph 6 of the section 26 request and the date by which the landlord is to serve any counternotice.

Forms where property is in Wales

It had originally been envisaged that there would be separate forms where the property is situated wholly or partially in Wales. This has now been

---

Figure 12

TENANT'S REQUEST FOR A NEW BUSINESS TENANCY

Section 26 of the Landlord and Tenant Act 1954

To: (*insert name and address of landlord*)

From: (*insert name and address of tenant*)

1. This notice relates to the following property: (*insert address or description of property*).

2. I am giving you notice under section 26 of the Landlord and Tenant Act 1954 that I request a new tenancy beginning on (*insert date*).

3. You will find my proposals for the new tenancy, which we can discuss, in the Schedule to this notice.

4. If we cannot agree on all the terms of a new tenancy, either you or I may ask the court to order the grant of a new tenancy and settle the terms on which we cannot agree.

5. If you wish to ask the court to order the grant of a new tenancy you must do so by the date in paragraph 2, unless we agree in writing to a later date and do so before the date in paragraph 2.

6. You may oppose my request for a new tenancy only on one or more of the grounds set out in section 30(1) of the Landlord and Tenant Act 1954. You must tell me what your grounds are within two months of receiving this notice. If you miss this deadline you will not be able to oppose renewal of my tenancy and you will have to grant me a new tenancy.

7. Please send all correspondence about this notice to:

Name:

Address:

Signed:

Date:

˙[Tenant] ˙[On behalf of the tenant] (˙*delete whichever is inapplicable*)

SCHEDULE

TENANT'S PROPOSALS FOR A NEW TENANCY

(*attach or insert proposed terms of the new tenancy*)

IMPORTANT NOTE FOR THE LANDLORD

This notice requests a new tenancy of your property or part of it. If you want to oppose this request you must act quickly.

Read the notice and all the Notes carefully. It would be wise to seek professional advice.

NOTES

The sections mentioned below are sections of the Landlord and Tenant Act 1954, as amended (most recently by the Regulatory Reform (Business Tenancies) (England and Wales) Order 2003)

Tenant's request for a new tenancy

This request by your tenant for a new tenancy brings his or her current tenancy to an end on the day before the date mentioned in paragraph 2 of this notice. Section 26 contains rules about the date that the tenant can put in paragraph 2 of this notice.

Your tenant can apply to the court under section 24 for a new tenancy. You may apply for a new tenancy yourself, under the same section, but not if your tenant has already served an application. Once an application has been made to the court, your tenant's current tenancy will continue after the date mentioned in paragraph 2 while the application is being considered by the court. Either you or your tenant can ask the court to fix the rent which your tenant will have to pay whilst the tenancy continues (sections 24A to 24D). The court will settle any terms of a new tenancy on which you and your tenant disagree (sections 34 and 35).

Time limit for opposing your tenant's request

If you do not want to grant a new tenancy, you have <u>two months from the making of your tenant's request</u> in which to notify him or her that you will oppose any application made to the court for a new tenancy. You do not need a special form to do this, but <u>the notice must be in writing and it must state on which of the grounds set out in section 30(1) you will oppose the application</u>. If you do not use the same wording of the ground (or grounds), as set out below, your notice may be ineffective.

If there has been any delay in your seeing this notice, you may need to act very quickly. If you are in any doubt about what action you should take, get advice immediately from a solicitor or a surveyor.

Grounds for opposing tenant's application

If you wish to oppose the renewal of the tenancy, you can do so by opposing your tenant's application to the court, or by making your own application to the court for termination without renewal. However, you can only oppose your tenant's application, or apply for termination without renewal, on one or more of the grounds set out in section 30(1). These grounds are set out below. You will only be able to rely on the ground(s) of opposition that you have mentioned in your written notice to your tenant.

In this Table 'the holding' means the property that is the subject of the tenancy.

Paragraph of section 30(1)	Grounds
(a)	Where under the current tenancy the tenant has any obligations as respects the repair and maintenance of the holding, that the tenant ought not to be granted a new tenancy in view of the state of repair of the holding, being a state resulting from the tenant's failure to comply with the said obligations.
(b)	That the tenant ought not to be granted a new tenancy in view of his persistent delay in paying rent which has become due.
(c)	That the tenant ought not to be granted a new tenancy in view of other substantial breaches by him of his obligations under the current tenancy, or for any other reason connected with the tenant's use or management of the holding.
(d)	That the landlord has offered and is willing to provide or secure the provision of alternative accommodation for the tenant, that the terms on which the alternative accommodation is available are reasonable having regard to the terms of the current tenancy and to all other relevant circumstances, and that the accommodation and the time at which it will be available are suitable for the tenant's requirements (including the requirement to preserve goodwill) having regard to the nature and class of his business and to the situation and extent of, and facilities afforded by, the holding.

(e)	Where the current tenancy was created by the sub-letting of part only of the property comprised in a superior tenancy and the landlord is the owner of an interest in reversion expectant on the termination of that superior tenancy, that the aggregate of the rents reasonably obtainable on separate lettings of the holding and the remainder of that property would be substantially less than the rent reasonably obtainable on a letting of that property as a whole, that on the termination of the current tenancy the landlord requires possession of the holding for the purposes of letting or otherwise disposing of the said property as a whole, and that in view thereof the tenant ought not to be granted a new tenancy.
(f)	That on the termination of the current tenancy the landlord intends to demolish or reconstruct the premises comprised in the holding or a substantial part of those premises or to carry out substantial work of construction on the holding or part thereof and that he could not reasonably do so without obtaining possession of the holding.
g)	On the termination of the current tenancy the landlord intends to occupy the holding for the purposes, or partly for the purposes, of a business to be carried on by him therein, or as his residence.

Compensation

If your tenant cannot get a new tenancy solely because one or more of grounds (e), (f) and (g) applies, he or she is entitled to compensation under section 37. If you have opposed your tenant's application on any of the other grounds mentioned in section 30(1), as well as on one or more of grounds (e), (f) and (g), your tenant can only get compensation if the court's refusal to grant a new tenancy is based solely on ground (e), (f) or (g). In other words, your tenant cannot get compensation under section 37 if the court has refused the tenancy on *other* grounds, even if one or more of grounds (e), (f) and (g) also applies.

If you are an authority possessing compulsory purchase powers (such as a local authority), your tenant may be entitled to a disturbance payment under Part 3 of the Land Compensation Act 1973.

Negotiating a new tenancy

Most tenancies are renewed by negotiation and your tenant has set out proposals for the new tenancy in paragraph 3 of this notice. You are not obliged to accept these proposals and may put forward your own. You and your tenant may agree in writing to extend the deadline for making an application to the court while negotiations continue. Your tenant may not apply to the court for a new tenancy until two months have passed from the date of the making of the request contained in this notice, unless you have already given notice opposing your tenant's request as mentioned in paragraph 6 of this notice (section 29A(3)).

If you try to agree a new tenancy with your tenant, remember:

- that one of you will need to apply to the court before the date in paragraph 2 of this notice, unless you both agree to extend the period for making an application; and

- that any such agreement must be in writing and must be made before the date in paragraph 2 (sections 29A and 29B).

Validity of this notice

The tenant who has given you this notice may not be the person from whom you receive rent (sections 44 and 67). This does not necessarily mean that the notice is invalid.

> If you have any doubts about whether this notice is valid, get advice immediately from a solicitor or a surveyor.
>
> *Further information*
>
> An explanation of the main points to consider when renewing or ending a business tenancy, 'Renewing and Ending Business Leases: a Guide for Tenants and Landlords', can be found at www.odpm.gov.uk. Printed copies of the explanation, but not of this form, are available from 1 June 2004 from Free Literature, PO Box 236, Wetherby, West Yorkshire, LS23 7NB (0870 1226 236).

dropped as joint regulations have been made with the Welsh Assembly. The same forms apply both to properties in England and/or Wales.

Special circumstances

There are new prescribed forms which deal with special situations, for example where the tenant may be entitled under the Leasehold Reform Act 1967 to buy the freehold or an extended lease, or where s57 of the Act applies (ie where a certificate is given by a government department etc, that the use or occupation of the property or part of it is to be changed by a specified date). A list of the relevant new forms is set out in **Appendix 3** to this work.

Counternotices

Pre-June 2004

There was no express obligation in the Act for a tenant to serve a counternotice to a landlord's section 25 notice, but if it did not do so it would lose its right to renew the lease. The old s29(2) provided that the court would not 'entertain' the tenant's application for a new tenancy if it had not served a counternotice. Similarly, a landlord wishing to oppose a renewal had to serve a counternotice to a tenant's section 26 request, otherwise it would lose its right to oppose the grant of a new tenancy.[6]

From 1 June 2004 – tenant's counternotice

The implied need for the tenant to serve a counternotice to a landlord's section 25 notice has been abolished. Accordingly, both s29(2) (see above) and s25(5) (a section 25 notice will not have effect unless it requires a tenant to serve a counternotice) of the Act have been repealed.

The rationale behind the abolition of the tenant's counternotice is that it is superfluous. The theory is that, even if a tenant serves a counternotice, it

---

6 Section 26(6).

does not necessarily mean it will go on to issue proceedings, and if it does, it still may discontinue those proceedings and even refuse any new lease ordered by the court. The only benefit of the tenant's counternotice is that, if it is not served, the landlord knows the tenant has lost its right to renew.

However, bearing in mind the change in time limits for issuing an application (see **Chapter 7**), the author's view is that retaining the counter-notice would have given the landlord some indication that a tenant was intending to renew. It is not to be.

From 1 June 2004 – landlord's counternotice

Requirement for service of a landlord's counternotice

Where a landlord wishes to oppose a renewal the requirement that it serve a counternotice setting out its grounds of opposition is retained. The rationale for this is that the landlord's grounds of opposition are set out at an early stage.[7]

Date for service of landlord's counternotice

The landlord's counternotice must still be served within two months of the making of the tenant's section 26 request.[8]

Paragraph 6 of the new prescribed form of section 26 request states that the landlord must tell the tenant of any grounds of opposition to the renewal 'within two months of receiving this notice'. This wording is misleading. As stated above, the Act (s26(6)) and indeed, the notes on the form, state that any counternotice must be served within two months of the 'making' of the tenant's request. The date that the request is 'made', ie formally served, is not necessarily the day it is actually 'received' by the landlord. For details of the effective date of service see **Chapter 2, p16**. The old prescribed form of section 26 request used to warn the landlord about this possible trap.

There is still no prescribed form for a landlord's counternotice.

Practical points

For practical issues as to the service of notices under the Act, see **Chapter 2** which deals with how notices should be served etc, and **Chapter 3** which sets out the new rules relating to service of notices where there are split reversions.

---

7 Section 26(6).
8 Section 26(6).

7. THE RENEWAL PROCESS – APPLICATIONS TO THE COURT FOR A NEW TENANCY

Transitional provisions

The new rules set out below apply only where the section 25 notice was served or the section 26 request was made after 1 June 2004.[1]

Who can make an application to court for a new tenancy?

Pre-1 June 2004

Only the tenant could apply to the court for a new tenancy.[2]

From 1 June 2004

Section 24(1) of the Act has been amended to provide that: 'either the tenant or the landlord... may apply to the court for an order for the grant of a new tenancy.' The rationale behind this is so that the parties are on equal footing, with either being able to bring negotiations to a head.

From 1 June 2004 – are there any circumstances where an application cannot be made?

Section 29(3) has been repealed. This was the section which set out the two-to-four month window from the giving of the section 25 notice/section 26 request for making applications to the court. The new s24(2A) of the Act provides that neither the tenant nor the landlord may make an application to the court for a new tenancy if the other party has already done so and has served that application. This is to prevent duplication. The requirement that the first application has to have been served was a late amendment to the Order, after it was pointed out that the other party may not know such an application had been made unless it had been served.

---

1 Art 29(1) of the Order.
2 Section 24(1) of the Act.

The new s24(2B) of the Act provides that neither the tenant nor the landlord may make an application for a new tenancy if the landlord has already made, and served, an application under s29(2) to terminate the tenancy.

For details of which application would take priority if both were served on the same day see **Chapter 9, p112**, which deals with the new Civil Procedure Rule 56.

As mentioned above, the requirement that a tenant must serve a counternotice before any application to the court for a new tenancy will be considered has been abolished.

From 1 June 2004 – withdrawal of application

The new s24(2C) of the Act specifically provides that a landlord may not withdraw its application to the court for a new tenancy unless the tenant consents to its withdrawal.

This is to prevent a landlord making and serving an application for a new tenancy (thereby preventing the tenant from doing so, see **p79** above) and then immediately discontinuing that application, and thereby precluding the tenant from renewing its tenancy.

There is no restriction on a tenant's ability to withdraw its application, as it could do pre June 2004. Indeed, the new s29(6) also provides that the court shall dismiss an application by a landlord under s24(1) for a tenancy to be renewed if the tenant informs the court that it does not want a new tenancy.

Time limits for renewal proceedings

Pre-1 June 2004

The time limits for the tenant to make an application to the court for a new tenancy were strict.[3] The tenant had to apply to the court at least two months, but not later than four months, after the service of the landlord's section 25 notice or the tenant's section 26 request. If the application was made either side of these time limits the proceedings would be invalid.

These strict time limits resulted in applications for new tenancies being made merely to preserve the tenant's rights to a new lease. Most

---

3 Old s29(3).

applications were abandoned on the parties reaching agreement as to the terms of the new lease. The time limits also resulted in cases of tenants being deprived of the right to renew because they, or their professional advisers, did not take action in time.

From 1 June 2004 – latest time for an application to the court for a new tenancy

Section 29(3) has been repealed. The new s29A(1)(a) of the Act provides that the court 'shall not entertain' an application to the court for a new tenancy under s24(1) by the landlord or the tenant if it is made after the end of the 'statutory period'.

The statutory period is defined in the new s29A(2) as being the period ending:

1. (where the landlord has served a section 25 notice) on the date specified in the notice as the date on which the tenancy will end; and

2. (where the tenant has served a section 26 request) immediately before the date specified in the request as being the date the new tenancy will begin.

Extending the latest date for making the application to the court for a new tenancy

The new s29B of the Act allows the parties to agree to extend the time limits for making an application to the court, either by the tenant or landlord, for a new tenancy (or by the landlord for termination of the tenancy, for which see **Chapter 8**).

The provisions provide that the time limit can be extended as follows:

1. the parties can make an initial agreement before the date specified in the landlord's notice or the tenant's request, ie before the end of the 'statutory period'; and

2. the parties can make one or more further agreements before the previous agreement expires.

How long can the extension be for?

There is no limit set out in the Act on how short or long the periods of extension may be.

How many extensions can be agreed?

There is no limit on the number of extensions which can be agreed.

Does the agreement to extend have to be in writing?

Section 29B does not specifically state that these agreements must be in writing. However, s69(2) of the Act will apply. This provides that any reference in the Act to an agreement between the landlord and the tenant (except in s17(1) and (2) and s38) shall be construed as a reference to an agreement in writing between them.

Suggested wording

A party wishing to extend the statutory period could write to the other side as follows:

> We propose that the time limit for making an application to the Court under s29A(1) of the Landlord and Tenant Act 1954 should be extended for a period of three months ie up to and including [*insert date for the avoidance of doubt*]. Please confirm your agreement by signing, dating and returning to us the duplicate of this letter attached.

Tactical considerations

Clearly, the ability to extend the time limit for making applications to court will remove unnecessary traps for tenants (and their solicitors). It will also save time and costs in abortive legal work. Care will need to be taken, however, to remember to keep extending the period if appropriate. Ultimately if the extension is not agreed before expiry of the statutory period or any previously agreed extension period, and the time for making the application to the court is missed, the tenant will lose its right to renew the tenancy.

How many extensions are agreed, and for what period(s), will, obviously, depend on the facts of each case. The parties may not want these extensions to be for too long a period in order to keep some pressure on the negotiations.

Can the parties agree a general extension of time?

It is the author's view that a general extension of time cannot be agreed. The wording of the Act does not lend itself to this interpretation. Section 29B(1) states the parties may agree that the application to court may be made 'before the end of a period specified in the agreement'. In the author's opinion this requires an actual specified period with a specific end date, not an open ended general extension.

Continuation of the tenancy during extended period

The new s29B(4) of the Act also provides that where an extension agreement is made, the section 25 notice or section 26 request shall be treated as terminating the tenancy at the end of this extended period specified in the agreement, In other words, the tenancy will continue during this period, enabling the tenant to continue in occupation and thereby protecting its right to renew. The tenant will, of course, be subject to the covenants within the tenancy for this period.

The parties may, therefore, want to think carefully about agreeing overly long extensions to the time limit for bringing proceedings for a new tenancy. The landlord will be tied to the tenancy being extended by this period (unless he has grounds to forfeit). The tenant will also be tied to the extension. If the tenant agrees a year's extension of time, and then decides it actually wants to vacate, it may be in difficulty if the landlord will not accept a surrender of the tenancy.

It is an unsettled area of law whether a tenant can serve a notice to terminate a tenancy under s27 of the Act, where a landlord has served a section 25 notice. (The author's view is that there is nothing in the Act or case law which precludes this.) What is clear, however, is that a tenant cannot serve a section 27 notice, where it has served an earlier section 26 request.[4] If the contractual term has not yet ended the tenant could just vacate the premises and thereby bring the tenancy to an end on the contractual term date. The tenancy would not be one to which the Act applies as the tenant is not in occupation.[5]

Application to court means what it says

Although it does not explicitly say so in the Act, the ODPM's Guidance Note states that it will be expected that parties still in negotiation will use the new facility to agree to extended deadlines for applications to the court. The ODPM states that:

> ... the presumption will be that if applications are made to the court, the parties have either failed to reach agreement, or one party wishes to expedite matters and that there will be no need to delay a court hearing.

---

4 See s26(4) of the Act.
5 *Esselte AB v Pearl Assurance Plc* [1997] EGLR 73, and the new s27(1), see **Chapter 10**.

The guidance goes on to state that:

> … amended Civil Procedure Rules will no longer automatically provide for a three months stay of proceedings at the request of the landlord.

For more details on the changes to the Civil Procedure Rules see **Chapter 9**.

The court will, however, retain a degree of flexibility in the handling of cases under its general case management powers and discretion. More time may be allowed in appropriate circumstances but the author considers the parties would need a very good reason to obtain a stay once proceedings have been commenced. So, do not apply to court unless you are ready to push ahead with the proceedings.

From 1 June 2004 – earliest time for an application to the court for a new tenancy

Where the tenant has made a section 26 request

The new s29A(3) of the Act provides that where a tenant has made a section 26 request for a new tenancy the court 'shall not entertain' an application for a new tenancy, by either party, which is made before the end of the period of two months beginning with the date of the making of the request, unless the application is made after the landlord has given a counternotice opposing the grant of a new tenancy.

This means, in practice, that if the landlord does not oppose the renewal (and, therefore, does not serve a counternotice, or serves a 'positive' counternotice saying he will not oppose) either party will have to wait two months from the making of the section 26 request before issuing the court application.

However, if the landlord is opposing the renewal, and serves its counternotice at any time within the two month window for doing so, either party (most likely the tenant in this scenario as the landlord would not want to issue proceedings for a new tenancy if it is opposing renewal) can issue the Court application straight after the service of the counternotice. It does not have to wait until the two month period has expired.

Where the landlord has served a section 25 notice

Where the landlord has served a section 25 notice (whether opposed or unopposed), by reason of the abolition of the requirement for service of a tenant's counternotice, either party (although, again, this is unlikely to be the landlord if the renewal is opposed) may apply to the court for a new

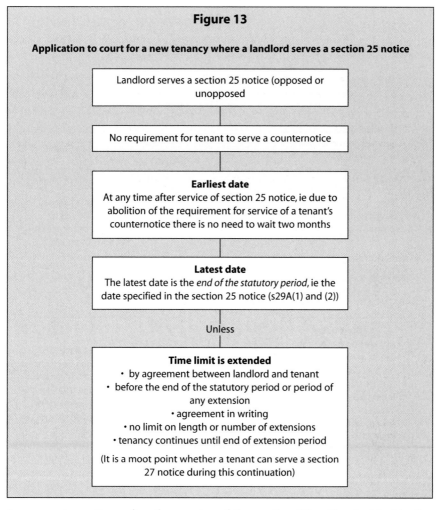

Figure 13

Application to court for a new tenancy where a landlord serves a section 25 notice

Landlord serves a section 25 notice (opposed or unopposed

No requirement for tenant to serve a counternotice

Earliest date
At any time after service of section 25 notice, ie due to abolition of the requirement for service of a tenant's counternotice there is no need to wait two months

Latest date
The latest date is the *end of the statutory period*, ie the date specified in the section 25 notice (s29A(1) and (2))

Unless

Time limit is extended
• by agreement between landlord and tenant
• before the end of the statutory period or period of any extension
• agreement in writing
• no limit on length or number of extensions
• tenancy continues until end of extension period

(It is a moot point whether a tenant can serve a section 27 notice during this continuation)

tenancy at any time after the service of the section 25 notice (subject to the latest date for applications, see **p81** above). There is no longer any need to wait two months.

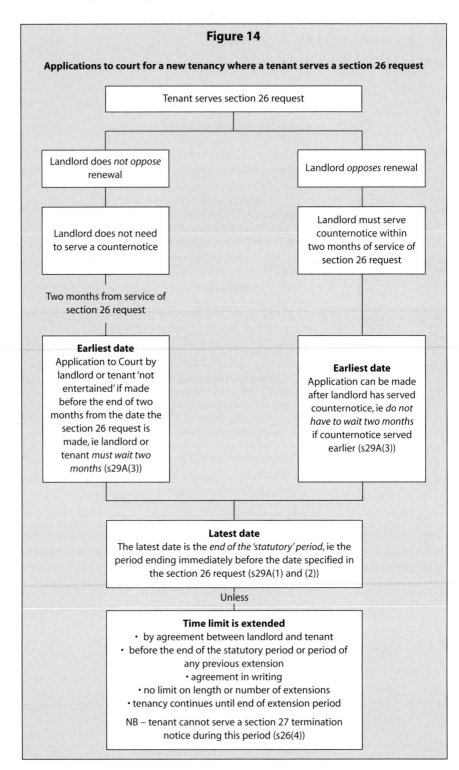

Figure 14

Applications to court for a new tenancy where a tenant serves a section 26 request

Tenant serves section 26 request

Landlord does *not oppose* renewal

Landlord *opposes* renewal

Landlord does not need to serve a counternotice

Landlord must serve counternotice within two months of service of section 26 request

Two months from service of section 26 request

Earliest date
Application to Court by landlord or tenant 'not entertained' if made before the end of two months from the date the section 26 request is made, ie landlord or tenant *must wait two months* (s29A(3))

Earliest date
Application can be made after landlord has served counternotice, ie *do not have to wait two months* if counternotice served earlier (s29A(3))

Latest date
The latest date is the *end of the 'statutory' period*, ie the period ending immediately before the date specified in the section 26 request (s29A(1) and (2))

Unless

Time limit is extended
• by agreement between landlord and tenant
• before the end of the statutory period or period of any previous extension
• agreement in writing
• no limit on length or number of extensions
• tenancy continues until end of extension period

NB – tenant cannot serve a section 27 termination notice during this period (s26(4))

8. Termination proceedings by a landlord

Pre-1 June 2004

If a landlord wished to oppose the renewal of a tenancy before 1 June 2004, it had to wait until the tenant had made an application to the court for a new tenancy and then oppose that application. The landlord still needed to deal with the tenant's proposals for a new tenancy, even though it was opposing the renewal.

From 1 June 2004

The landlord has a new right to start proceedings to terminate the tenancy without renewal. This new right is set out in the new s29(2) of the Act. The landlord must still prove his ground of opposition to a new tenancy under s30(1) of the Act. There are no changes to these save those to s30(1)(g) (landlord intends to occupy the premises itself) to accommodate the changes due to the new rules on ownership and control of a business (see **p43** above).

Note: the new rules apply only if the section 25 notice was served or the section 26 request was made after 1 June 2004.[1]

When does the new right arise?

The right applies if either:

- the landlord has served a section 25 notice stating its opposition to the grant of a new tenancy (s29(2)(a)); or

- the tenant has made a section 26 request for a new tenancy and the landlord has served a counternotice opposing the grant of a new tenancy (s29(2)(b)).

---

1 Art 29(1) of the Order.

When may the new right not be exercised?

The new s29(3) of the Act provides that the landlord may not make an application for termination of the tenancy if:

- the tenant has made an application to court for a new tenancy; or
- the landlord has made an application to court for a new tenancy.

From 1 June 2004 – latest time for application to the court for a termination order

The new s29A(1)(b) provides that the court 'shall not entertain' an application to the court by a landlord for an order for termination of the tenancy without renewal if it is made after the end of the 'statutory period'.

The statutory period is defined in the new s29A(2) as being the period ending:

1. where the landlord served a section 25 notice, on the date specified in the notice as the date on which the tenancy will end; and

2. where the tenant served a section 26 request, immediately before the date specified in the request as being the date the new tenancy will begin.

Extending the latest date for making the application to the court for a termination order

The new s29B of the Act deals with agreements to extend the time limits for making an application to the court by the landlord for a termination order (and by the landlord or tenant for an order for a new tenancy – see **Chapter 7**).

The provisions provide that the time limit can be extended as follows:

1. the parties can make an initial agreement before the date specified in the landlord's notice or the tenant's request, ie before the end of the 'statutory period'; and

2. the parties can make one or more further agreements before the previous agreement expires.

How long may the extension be for?

There is no limit set out in the Act on how short or long the periods of extension may be.

How many extensions may be agreed?

There is no limit on the number of extensions which can be agreed.

Does the agreement to extend have to be in writing?

Section 29B of the Act does not specifically state that these agreements must be in writing. However, s69(2) will apply. This provides that any reference in the Act to an agreement between the landlord and the tenant (except in s17(1) and (2) and s38) shall be construed as a reference to an agreement in writing between them.

Tactical considerations

For general comments regarding extensions of time and suggested wording see **p82** above.

What happens if the time limit passes without the landlord issuing proceedings to terminate?

If a landlord wishes to terminate the tenancy, it is very unlikely it will agree to extend its time for bringing proceedings to do so. It will normally want to push ahead so it can obtain possession as soon as possible. It is, however, possible to envisage circumstances where an agreement to extend time may be reached, eg if the tenant has said (probably on a without prejudice basis) it is considering moving out but needs time to relocate to other premises, or the landlord has not gathered all the evidence required to pursue the matter to court at that point in time.

The Act does not specifically spell out what happens if the extension expires without any court proceedings for termination being issued. Does the landlord lose its right to issue termination proceedings? Does the landlord lose its right to oppose the renewal? Or does the tenant, assuming it has not issued proceedings for a renewal within that time, lose its rights to renew? The author's view is that it is the latter. If no proceedings are issued (whether for renewal or termination) the section 25 notice or section 26 request would terminate the tenancy on the date specified (or at the end of any extension of the statutory period). If the tenant has not issued proceedings for a new tenancy in this time it would lose its rights to renew. Tenants will need to take care and bear this in mind. If a tenant does issue proceedings for a renewal in these circumstances it is the author's view that the landlord will still be able to oppose that renewal in the ordinary way.

From 1 June 2004 – earliest time for an application to the court for an order to terminate the tenancy without renewal

Where the tenant has made a section 26 request

Where a tenant has made a section 26 request for a new tenancy the Act still provides that the landlord must serve a counternotice if it wishes to oppose the renewal. Whilst s26(6) states that a landlord 'may' serve a counternotice opposing renewal, the new s29(2)(b) provides that the landlord may only apply to court to terminate the tenancy if it has first served a counternotice.

The landlord's counternotice has to be served within two months of the tenant making its section 26 request for a new tenancy. The landlord may then apply to the court for the order to terminate the tenancy without renewal at any time after service of that counternotice (subject to the latest date for applications set out at **p88** above). The landlord could, therefore, serve the counternotice on the day it receives the section 26 request and issue its termination proceedings immediately after service of that counternotice.

Where the landlord has served a section 25 notice opposing renewal

As there is no longer a requirement for the tenant to serve a counternotice in response to a section 25 notice, the landlord can apply to the court for an order to terminate the tenancy without renewal at any time after the service of the section 25 notice (subject to the latest date for applications set out at **p88** above). There is no longer any need to wait two months from the service of the section 25 notice.

Tactical considerations

Where a landlord wants to push ahead as quickly as possible he should aim to issue his proceedings as soon as possible after service of the section 25 notice. It would be in its interests to do this rather than allow time in between for a tenant to issue an application for a new tenancy. Although the landlord could oppose such an application he would probably prefer to be the claimant rather than the defendant.

What happens at the hearing

For changes to the Civil Procedure Rules see **Chapter 9**.

The court can order termination of the tenancy without renewal

At the hearing the court will, if the landlord has established its ground of opposition to the renewal, make an order for termination of the current tenancy without the grant of a new tenancy.[2] The tenancy will terminate in accordance with s64 of the Act at the expiration of three months beginning with the date on which the application is finally disposed of. The application is finally disposed of when it has been determined and any time for appealing or further appealing has expired (except that if the application is withdrawn or any appeal is abandoned the reference shall be construed as a reference to the date of the withdrawal or abandonment[3]). The normal period for appealing is within 14 days after the decision under appeal, unless the lower court (ie the one being appealed from) directs a different period.[4]

On a strict interpretation of s64, this three-month (plus) period only applies where otherwise, apart from s64, the effect of the section 25 notice or section 26 request would be to terminate the tenancy before the expiration of that three-month period.

Under the new provisions it is possible to envisage a situation where the landlord's proceedings for termination of the tenancy will be dealt with by the court before the date specified in the section 25 notice or section 26 request (especially if the tenant has already served a section 26 request that will end the tenancy in 12 months' time). The Act does not specifically deal with when the tenancy will end in that case. It is the author's view that it would be on the date specified in the section 25 notice or immediately before the date specified in the section 26 request, ie s64 would not come into play as the section 25 notice/section 26 request will not terminate the tenancy before the expiration of the three-month period.

Example 1:

The landlord serves a hostile section 25 notice on 1 December 2004 giving a termination date of 1 June 2005. The landlord issues termination proceedings on 1 February 2004. The court grants an order for termination on 1 July 2005. Assuming there is no appeal the tenancy will cease three months and 14 days after 1 July 2005, ie 14 October 2005.

Example 2:

The tenant serves a section 26 request on 1 December 2004 requesting a new tenancy to start on 2 November 2005. The landlord immediately serves a counternotice stating he requires possession and then issues proceedings straight away for termination without renewal. On 1 July 2005 the court makes an order for termination without renewal. Assuming there is no appeal against the termination order which extends time

---

2 Section 29(4)(a).

3 Section 64(2).

4 CPR 52.4.

> beyond 2 November 2005, the current tenancy will end on 1 November 2005, ie the day before the date specified in the section 26 request and not three months and 14 days after the court order.

It is, therefore, important for landlords who want to obtain a termination order to ensure they serve a section 25 notice as soon as possible to prevent the tenant serving a longer section 26 request.

If a termination order is not made

If the landlord does not establish its grounds of opposition the Court will make an order for the grant of a new tenancy and for the termination of the current tenancy immediately before the commencement of the new tenancy.[5] This provision is to make it clear that the tenant would not need to make a fresh application for a new tenancy.

In practice, what would probably happen is that, on making an order for a new tenancy, the court would fix directions for it to decide the terms of that new tenancy, ie directions for the parties to exchange a draft lease and expert valuation evidence. It would be open, of course, to the parties to agree the terms of the new tenancy without the court having to determine them.

Can the landlord withdraw his application?

The new s29(6) of the Act provides that a landlord may not withdraw its application for an order for termination of the tenancy unless the tenant consents to its withdrawal. This is to prevent landlords abusing their position by starting proceedings for a termination order and then immediately discontinuing them, so as to preclude the tenant from renewing his tenancy.

If the landlord does withdraw his proceedings, with the tenant's consent, the tenancy would terminate three months from the date of the withdrawal of the application.[6] Although, see points made at **p91**, above, as to where the withdrawal is before the date specified in the section 25 notice/section 26 request.

---

5 Section 29(4)(b).

6 Section 64(2).

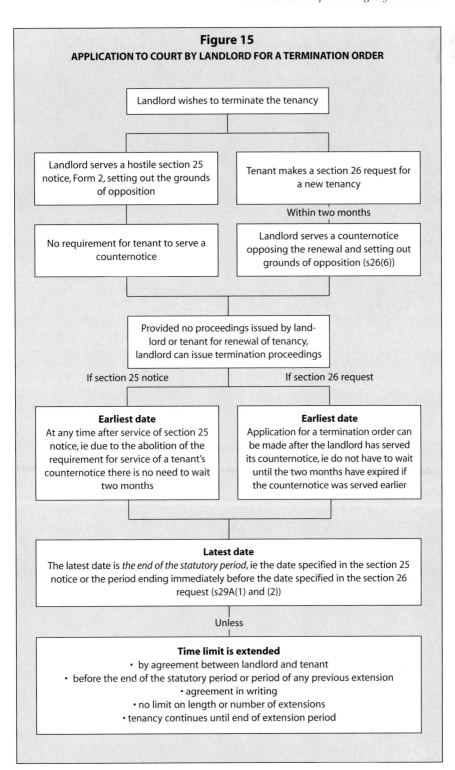

Figure 15
APPLICATION TO COURT BY LANDLORD FOR A TERMINATION ORDER

Landlord wishes to terminate the tenancy

Landlord serves a hostile section 25 notice, Form 2, setting out the grounds of opposition

Tenant makes a section 26 request for a new tenancy

Within two months

No requirement for tenant to serve a counternotice

Landlord serves a counternotice opposing the renewal and setting out grounds of opposition (s26(6))

Provided no proceedings issued by landlord or tenant for renewal of tenancy, landlord can issue termination proceedings

If section 25 notice

If section 26 request

Earliest date
At any time after service of section 25 notice, ie due to the abolition of the requirement for service of a tenant's counternotice there is no need to wait two months

Earliest date
Application for a termination order can be made after the landlord has served its counternotice, ie do not have to wait until the two months have expired if the counternotice was served earlier

Latest date
The latest date is *the end of the statutory period*, ie the date specified in the section 25 notice or the period ending immediately before the date specified in the section 26 request (s29A(1) and (2))

Unless

Time limit is extended
• by agreement between landlord and tenant
• before the end of the statutory period or period of any previous extension
• agreement in writing
• no limit on length or number of extensions
• tenancy continues until end of extension period

9. Changes to the Civil Procedure Rules

Where the section 25 notice is served or the section 26 request is made before 1 June 2004

The transitional provisions in the changes to the rules provide that where Art 29(1) of the Order applies, ie where the section 25 notice was served or the section 26 request was made before 1 June 2004, then the amendments to the Civil Procedure Rules 56 do not apply and the old versions of Part 56 and Practice Direction 56 will continue to apply. It is not intended to comment on those old provisions in this work, as practitioners will already be familiar with them. A summary of the old provisions is shown in the flowchart overleaf (**Figure 16**), and they are also shown in **Appendix 5**.

Where the section 25 notice is served or the section 26 request is made from 1 June 2004

CPR56 and Practice Direction 56 have been amended. The amended versions are set out in full at **Appendix 5** to this work. The provision for the three-month stay has been removed. As explained in **Chapter 7**, by reason of the new ability of the parties to postpone the time for making the application to the court, this 'automatic' stay is no longer required. The view is that if the parties apply to court they intend to push on with the proceedings. However, there is still a general discretion of the court to order a stay in any proceedings.[1]

Claims should still be started in the county court for the district in which the land is situated unless there are 'exceptional circumstances' justifying starting a claim in the High Court.[2]

The procedure to be adopted depends on whether the claim is an 'opposed claim' or an 'unopposed claim'.

---

1 See CPR3.1(2)(f).
2 CPR56.2 and Practice Direction 56 paras 2.2 – 2.6.

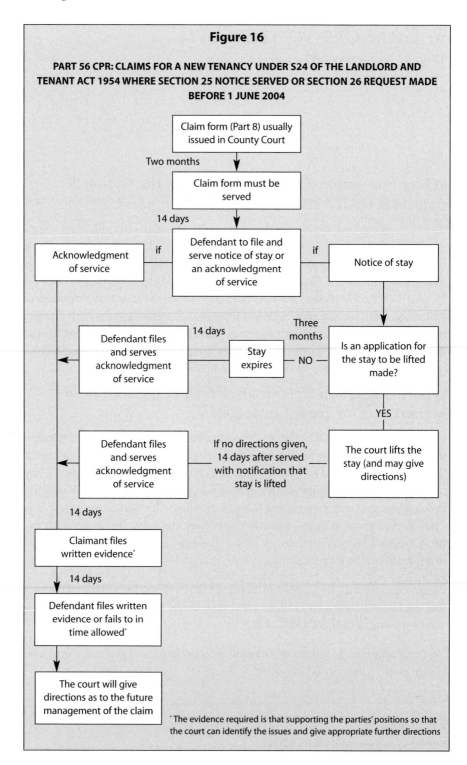

Figure 16

PART 56 CPR: CLAIMS FOR A NEW TENANCY UNDER S24 OF THE LANDLORD AND TENANT ACT 1954 WHERE SECTION 25 NOTICE SERVED OR SECTION 26 REQUEST MADE BEFORE 1 JUNE 2004

Claim form (Part 8) usually issued in County Court

Two months

Claim form must be served

14 days

Defendant to file and serve notice of stay or an acknowledgment of service

if — Acknowledgment of service

if — Notice of stay

14 days

Defendant files and serves acknowledgment of service

Stay expires

Three months

NO

Is an application for the stay to be lifted made?

YES

Defendant files and serves acknowledgment of service

If no directions given, 14 days after served with notification that stay is lifted

The court lifts the stay (and may give directions)

14 days

Claimant files written evidence*

14 days

Defendant files written evidence or fails to in time allowed*

The court will give directions as to the future management of the claim

*The evidence required is that supporting the parties' positions so that the court can identify the issues and give appropriate further directions

Unopposed claims for renewal

What is an unopposed claim?

CPR56.3(2)(b) and Practice Direction 56 paragraph 3.1(1) define an 'unopposed claim' as 'a claim for a new tenancy under s24 of the 1954 Act in circumstances where the grant of a new tenancy is not opposed'.

What procedure is to be used?

CPR56.3(3) provides that where the claim is an unopposed claim the procedure to be used is the Part 8 procedure. The claim form must be served within two months after the date of issue[3] and the general rules in CPR7.5 and 7.6 as to service of a claim form and extensions of time for service of a claim form are modified accordingly. CPR8.5 and 8.6 (which deal with the filing and service of evidence) do not apply.[4]

CPR56.3(3)(c) provides that the court will give directions about the future management of the claim following receipt of the acknowledgment of service. The time for filing the acknowledgment of service is not more than 14 days after service of the claim form.[5] The new Practice Direction 56 specifically provides that in an unopposed claim, 'no evidence needs to be filed unless and until the court directs it to be filed'.[6]

The contents of the claim form, acknowledgment of service etc will differ depending on whether it is the tenant or the landlord who is making the application for a new tenancy under s24 of the Act.

Unopposed application by the tenant for a new tenancy

Contents of the claim form

Practice Direction 56 paragraph 3.3 specifically provides that where the claim for a new tenancy is by the tenant, the person who is the 'landlord' as defined in s44 of the Act must be a defendant (ie the competent landlord).

Practice Direction 56 paragraphs 3.4 and 3.5 set out the contents of the tenant's claim form. The claim form must contain details of:

- the property to which the claim relates (*this is the same as previously*);

---

3 CPR56.3(3)(b).

4 CPR56.3(3)(a).

5 CPR8.3(1)(a).

6 Practice Direction 56 para 3.14.

- the particulars of the current tenancy, including:
    - (a) date;
    - (b) parties;
    - (c) duration;
    - (d) current rent (if not the original rent); and
    - (e) date and method of termination,

    (*this is the same as previously*);
- every notice or request given or made under s25 or s26 of the Act (*this is the same as before but reference to a counternotice has been removed*);
- the expiry of:
    - (a) the statutory period in s29A(2) (ie the date in s25 notice/s26 request by which proceedings must be brought); or
    - (b) any agreed extended period made under ss 29B(1) or 29B(2) of the Act (ie extensions of the above date or further extensions),

    (*this is new*);
- the nature of the business carried at the property (*this is the same as before*);
- whether the tenant relies on ss23(1A), 41 or 42 of the Act (ie occupation/carrying on of a business by company/controlling shareholder, trusts, group companies – see **Chapter 4**) and, if so, the basis on which he does so (*this is new*);
- whether the tenant relies on s31A of the Act (ie that landlord could carry out proposed works under s30(1)(f) without obtaining possession of the whole holding) and, if so the basis on which he does so (*this is new – it appears that this needs to go in the claim form even in an unopposed renewal application*);
- whether any, and if so what part, of the property comprised in the tenancy is occupied neither by the tenant claimant nor by a person employed by the tenant for the purpose of its business (*this is the same as before*);
- the tenant claimant's proposed terms of the new tenancy (*this is the same as before*);
- the name and address of:
    - (a) anyone known to the tenant claimant who has an interest in the reversion in the property (whether immediately or in not more

than 15 years) on the termination of the tenant's current tenancy and who is likely to be affected by the grant of a new tenancy (*this is the same as before*); or

(b) if the tenant claimant does not know of anyone specified by (a) above, anyone who has a freehold interest in the property (*this is new*).

The claim form must be served on the persons referred to in (a) or (b) as appropriate.

Acknowledgment of service by landlord in unopposed claim where claimant is the tenant

Practice Direction 56 paragraph 3.10 provides that where the claim for a new tenancy by the tenant is unopposed, the acknowledgement of service is to be in Form N210 and 'must state with particulars' the following:

- whether, if a new tenancy is granted, the landlord objects to any of the terms proposed by the tenant claimant and if so:

   (a) the terms to which he objects; and

   (b) the terms that he proposes in so far as they differ from those proposed by the tenant;

- whether the landlord is a tenant under a lease having less than 15 years unexpired at the date of the termination of the tenant's current tenancy and, if so, the name and address of any person who, to the knowledge of the landlord, has an interest in the reversion in the property expectant (whether immediately or in not more than 15 years from that date) on the termination of the landlord's tenancy;

- the name and address of any person having an interest in the property who is likely to be affected by the grant of a new tenancy; and

- if the tenant's current tenancy is one to which s32(2) of the Act applies (ie where the tenancy includes other property besides the holding), whether the landlord requires that any new tenancy shall be a tenancy of the whole of the property comprised in the tenant's current tenancy.

This is all information which was required under the old Rules.

A chart summarising the provisions is set out overleaf (**Figure 17**).

Figure 17

CPR 56: CLAIM BY TENANT FOR NEW TENANCY – UNOPPOSED

Claim form (Part 8) usually issued in county court

Contents of tenant's claim form (PD56 paras 3.3, 3.4 & 3.5)

NB: The competent landlord under s44 must be a defendant.

Must contain details of:

- the property;
- particulars of the current tenancy: date, parties, duration, current rent (if not the original rent), date and method of termination;
- every section 25 notice or section 26 request;
- the date by which proceedings had to be issued (s29A(2)) or any agreed extended period under s29B(1) or (2);
- nature of the business carried on at the property;
- whether the tenant relies on new rules for ownership/control of a business, trust or group companies, and, if so, the basis on which he does (ss23(1A), 41 or 42);
- whether the tenant relies on s31A and, if so, the basis on which he does (ie landlord could do works under s30(1)(f) without obtaining possession of the whole);
- whether, and if so what part of the property is occupied neither by tenant or its employee for purpose of the tenant's business;
- tenant's proposed terms for new tenancy; and
- name and address of anyone the tenant knows:

    (a) has an interest in the reversion in the property (whether immediately or in not more than 15 years) on the termination of the tenant's tenancy who will be affected by grant of new tenancy; or
    (b) if no one in (a), the freeholder.

NB Persons in (a) and (b) must be served with the claim form.

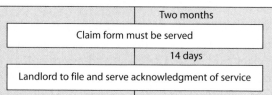

Two months

Claim form must be served

14 days

Landlord to file and serve acknowledgment of service

Contents of landlord's acknowledgement of service – (PD56 para 3.10) Form N210

The acknowledgment of service must state:

- whether the landlord objects to any of tenant's proposed terms for new tenancy and, if so, his counterproposals;
- whether the landlord is a tenant under a lease with less than 15 years unexpired at end of the tenant's tenancy and, if so, the name and address of the reversionary interest holder;
- the name and address of any person with an interest in the property who is likely to be affected by the grant of a new tenancy; and
- if s32(2) applies (ie where the tenancy includes other property besides the holding) whether the landlord requires any new tenancy to be a tenancy of the whole of the property in the current tenancy.

Evidence: No evidence need be filed unless and until the court directs it to be filed (PD56 para 3.14). Consider Property Litigation Association Post-Action Protocol.

Where the landlord makes the application for a new tenancy

Contents of the claim form

Practice Direction 56 paragraphs 3.4 and 3.7 set out the details which must be contained in the claim form. These are:

- the property to which the claim relates;
- the particulars of the current tenancy, including:

  (a) date;

  (b) parties;

  (c) duration;

  (d) the current rent (if not the original rent); and

  (e) the date and method of termination,

- every notice or request given or made under s25 or s26 of the Act;
- the expiry date of:

  (a) the statutory period in s29A(2) (ie the date in the s25 notice/s26 request by which proceedings must be brought); or

  (b) any agreed extended period made under s29B(1) or 29B(2) of the Act (ie extensions of the above date or further extensions);

- the landlord claimant's proposed terms of the new tenancy;
- whether the landlord is aware that the tenant's tenancy is one to which s32(2) of the Act applies (ie where the tenancy includes other property besides the holding) and if so, whether the landlord requires that any new tenancy shall be a tenancy of the whole of the property comprised in the current tenancy or just of the holding as defined in s23(3) of the Act; and
- the name and address of:

  (a) anyone known to the landlord who has an interest in the reversion of the property (whether immediate or in not more than 15 years) on the termination of the claimant's landlords current tenancy and who is likely to be affected by the grant of a new tenancy; or

  (b) if the landlord does not know of any one specified by (a) above, anyone who has a freehold interest in the property.

The claim form must be served on the persons referred to in (a) or (b) above as appropriate.

Acknowledgment of service by tenant in unopposed claim where claimant is the landlord

Practice Direction 56 para 3.11 provides that where the claim for a new tenancy by the landlord is unopposed the tenant's acknowledgment of service must be in Form N210 and 'state with particulars' the following:

- the nature of the business carried on at the property;
- if the tenant relies on ss23(1A), 41 or 42 of the Act (ie occupation/carrying on of a business by company/controlling shareholder, trusts, group companies, see **Chapter 4**), the basis on which he does so;
- whether any, and if so what part, of the property comprised in the tenancy is occupied neither by the tenant nor by a person employed by the tenant for the purposes of its business;
- the name and address of:

   (a) anyone known to the tenant who has an interest in the reversion in the property (whether immediate or in not more than 15 years) on the termination of the tenant's current tenancy and who is likely to be affected by the grant of a new tenancy; or

   (b) if the tenant does not know of any one specified in (a) above, anyone who has a freehold interest in the property.

- whether, if a new tenancy is granted, the tenant objects to any of the terms proposed by the landlord; and, if so:

   (a) the terms to which he objects; and

   (b) the terms that he proposes in so far as they differ from those proposed by the landlord.

A chart summarising the position is set out opposite (**Figure 18**).

Evidence in unopposed claims

This is dealt with in Practice Direction 56 para 3.14 which provides that 'no evidence need be filed unless and until the court directs it to be filed'. The requirement in the pre-1 June 2004 Rules[7] that the tenant was to serve his written evidence within 14 days of service on him of the acknowledgement of service, and for the landlord to serve his written evidence within 14 days of service on him of the tenant's evidence has been repealed where the

---

7 CPR56.3 (10) and (11).

Figure 18
CPR 56: CLAIM BY LANDLORD FOR NEW TENANCY – UNOPPOSED

Claim form (Part 8) usually issued in county court

Contents of claim form (PD56 paras 3.4 and 3.7)

Must contain details of:

- the property;
- particulars of the current tenancy: date, parties, duration, current rent (if not the original rent), date and method of termination;
- every section 25 notice or section 26 request;
- the date by which proceedings had to be issued (s29A(2)) or any agreed extended period under s29B(1) or (2);
- landlord's proposed terms for new tenancy;
- whether s32(2) applies (ie where the tenancy includes other property besides the holding) and, if so, whether the landlord requires the new tenancy to be of the whole of the property in the current tenancy or just the holding; and
- name and address of anyone the landlord knows:
  - (a) has an interest in the reversion of the property (whether immediately or in not more than 15 years) on the termination of the landlord's tenancy who will be affected by the grant of a new tenancy; or
  - (b) if no one in (a), the freeholder.

NB Persons in (a) and (b) must be served with the claim form.

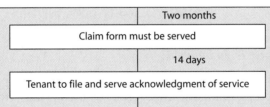

Two months

Claim form must be served

14 days

Tenant to file and serve acknowledgment of service

Contents of tenant's acknowledgement of service – (PD56 para 3.11) Form N210

The acknowledgment of service must state:

- nature of the business carried on at the property;
- whether the tenant relies on new rules for ownership/control of a business, trust or group companies, and if so the basis on which he does (ss23(1A), 41 or 42);
- whether, and if so what part of the property is occupied neither by tenant or its employee for purpose of the tenant's business;
- name and address of anyone the tenant knows:
  - (a) has an interest in the reversion in the property (whether immediately or in not more than 15 years) on the termination of the tenant's tenancy who will be affected by grant of new tenancy; or
  - (b) if no one in (a), the freeholder.
- whether the tenant objects to any of landlord's proposed terms for new tenancy and, if so, his counterproposals.

Evidence: No evidence need be filed unless and until the court directs it to be filed (PD56 para 3.14). Consider Property Litigation Association Post Action Protocol.

new CPR56 applies. This requirement was seen by most practitioners as a duplication of effort as the evidence to be served at that stage (so as to enable the court to identify the issues and give directions) was in most cases a repeat of what had been in the claim form or acknowledgement of service. Practitioners will welcome this change. The author suspects that after the claim form and acknowledgment of service have been exchanged the court will automatically fix a hearing to give directions. If it does not, either party could apply for one. For suggested directions see **p111** below which discusses the Property Litigation Association Post-Action Protocol.

Opposed claims

What is an opposed claim?

CPR56.3(2)(c) and Practice Direction 56 para 2.1A define an 'opposed claim' as:

> ... a claim for:
>
> (i) a new tenancy under s24 of the 1954 Act in circumstances where the grant of a new tenancy is opposed; or
>
> (ii) the termination of a tenancy under s29(2) of the 1954 Act.

What procedure is to be used?

CPR56.3(4) and Practice Direction 56 para 2.1A provide that where the claim is an opposed claim the procedure to be used is the Part 7 procedure, but the claim form must be served within two months after the date of issue and rules 7.5 (service of claim form) and 7.6 (extension of time for serving a claim form) are modified accordingly.

Where the tenant has made a claim for a new tenancy and the landlord opposes

The tenant's claim

The tenant will have made his claim in accordance with Practice Direction 56 paras 3.4 and 3.5 (see **p97** above). The contents of the tenant's claim form are the same whether the renewal is opposed or unopposed but unopposed is a Part 8 claim form and opposed is a Part 7 form.

Note: remember where Part 7 applies the tenant must serve on the defendant with the particulars of claim a form for defending the claim, a form for admitting the claim, together with a form for acknowledgement of service (The Defendant's Response Pack).

The landlord's acknowledgment of service

The landlord's acknowledgment of service is to be in Form N9[8] and should be served, under the Part 7 procedure, 14 days after service of the claim form (or service of the particulars of claim if later). In these cases as the requirement is, in effect, for the particulars of claim to be endorsed on the claim form the acknowledgment of service will be required 14 days after the service of the claim form.[9]

There is no extra prescribed information to be included in the acknowledgment of service. The landlord will, however, have to file a separate defence. Note: there is no requirement for the landlord to file an acknowledgment of service if it files its defence 14 days after service of the particulars of claim.[10]

The landlord's defence

The landlord's defence is to be filed 14 days after service of the particulars of claim or, if the landlord files an acknowledgment of service under CPR10, 28 days after service of the particulars of claim.

Practice Direction 56 paragraph 3.12 provides that in its defence the landlord must state with particulars:

- the landlord's grounds of opposition;
- full details of those grounds of opposition;
- whether, if a new tenancy is granted, the landlord objects to any of the terms proposed by the tenant and if so:

  (i) the terms to which he objects, and

  (ii) the terms that he proposes in so far as they differ from those proposed by the tenant;

- whether the landlord is a tenant under a lease having less than 15 years unexpired at the date of the termination of the tenant's current tenancy and, if so, the name and address of any person who, to the knowledge of the landlord, has an interest in the reversion in the property expectant (whether immediately or in not more than 15 years from that date) on the termination of the landlord's tenancy;

---

8 Practice Direction 56 para 3.12(1).

9 CPR10.3.

10 See CPR 10.1(3) and 15.4(1).

- the name and address of any person having an interest in the property who is likely to be affected by the grant of a new tenancy; and

- if the tenant's current tenancy is one to which s32(2) of the Act applies (ie where the tenancy includes other property besides the holding), whether the landlord requires that any new tenancy shall be a tenancy of the whole of the property comprised in the tenant's current tenancy.

'Grounds of opposition' is defined in Practice Direction 56 paragraph 3.1(3) as:

(i) the grounds specified in s30(1) of the 1954 Act on which a landlord may oppose an application for a new tenancy under s24(1) of the 1954 Act or make an application under s29(2) of the 1954 Act, ie the normal s30(1) grounds (a) to (g); or

(ii) any other basis on which the landlord asserts that a new tenancy ought not to be granted.

This later category would cover issues such as validity of applications to the court (eg were they made in time).

A chart summarising the position is set out opposite (**Figure 19**).

Where the landlord is making an application for the termination of a tenancy

Where the landlord is making an application for the termination of a tenancy this is again a Part 7 claim (see **p104** above).

Contents of the landlord's claim form

Where the landlord is making an application for the termination of a tenancy under s29(2) of the Act, Practice Direction 56 paragraphs 3.4 and 3.9 set out the details the claim form must contain. These are:

- the property to which the claim relates;

- the particulars of the current tenancy, including:

    (a) date;

    (b) parties;

    (c) duration;

    (d) the current rent (if not the original rent); and

    (e) the date and method of termination;

- every notice or request given or made under s25 or s26 of the Act;

Figure 19

CPR 56: CLAIM BY TENANT FOR NEW TENANCY – OPPOSED

Claim form (Part 7) usually issued in county court

Contents of tenant's claim form (PD56 paras 3.3, 3.4 and 3.5)

NB: The competent landlord under s44 must be a defendant

Must contain details of:

- the property;
- particulars of the current tenancy: date, parties, duration, current rent (if not the original rent), date and method of termination;
- every section 25 notice or section 26 request;
- the date by which proceedings had to be issued (s29A(2)) or any agreed extended period under s29B(1) or (2);
- nature of the business carried on at the property;
- whether the tenant relies on new rules for ownership/control of a business, trust or group companies, and, if so, the basis on which he does (ss23(1A), 41 or 42);
- whether the tenant relies on s31A and, if so, the basis on which he does so (ie landlord could do works under s30(1)(f) without obtaining possession of the whole);
- whether, and if so what part of the property is occupied neither by tenant or its employee for purpose of the tenant's business;
- the terms of the tenant's proposed tenancy; and
- name and address of anyone the tenant knows who:

  (a) has an interest in the reversion in the property (whether immediately or in not more than 15 years) on the termination of the tenant's tenancy who will be affected by grant of new tenancy; or

  (b) if no one in (a), the freeholder.

NB Persons in (a) and (b) must be served with the claim form.

Two months

Claim form must be served

14 days from service of particulars of claim

Landlord to file and serve acknowledgment of service in Fom N9 or defence. If acknowledgment of service is filed, landlord has 28 days after service of particulars of claim to file defence

Contents of landlord's defence – (PD56 para 3.12(2))

The defence must state:

- the landlord's grounds of opposition;
- full details of those grounds of opposition;
- whether, if a new tenancy is granted, the landlord objects to the tenant's proposed terms and, if so, his counterproposals;
- whether the landlord is a tenant under a lease with less than 15 years unexpired at the date of termination of the tenant's tenancy and, if so, the name and address of any person who to the landord's knowledge has an interest in the reversion (whether immediately or in not more than 15 years) on termination of the landlord's tenancy;
- the name and address of any person with an interest in the property who is likely to be affected by the grant of a new tenancy;
- if s32(2) applies (ie where the tenancy includes other property besides the holding) whether the landlord requires any new tenancy to be a tenancy of the whole of the property in the current tenancy.

Evidence: Evidence (including expert witness evidence) must be filed by the parties as the court directs and the landlord shall be required to file evidence first.

- the expiry date of:

    (a) the statutory period in 29A(2) of the Act (ie the date in the section 25 notice/section 26 request by which proceedings must be brought); or

    (b) any agreed extended period made under s29B(1) or 29B(2) of the Act (ie extension of the above date or further extensions)

- the landlord's grounds of opposition;
- full details of those grounds of opposition; and
- the terms of a new tenancy the landlord proposes in the event his claim fails.

'Grounds of opposition' are defined in Practice Direction 56 paragraph 3.1(3) as:

(a) 'the grounds specified in s30(1) of the 1954 Act on which a landlord may oppose an application for a new tenancy under s24(1) of the 1954 Act or make an application under s29(2) of the 1954 Act', ie the normal s30(1) grounds (a) to (g); or

(b) any other basis on which the landlord asserts that a new tenancy ought not to be granted.

This later category would cover issues such as validity of applications to the court (eg were they made in time).

Note: where Part 7 applies the landlord must serve on the defendant with the particulars of claim a form for defending the claim, a form for admitting the claim, together with a form for acknowledging service (the Defendant's Response Pack).

Acknowledgment of service and defence where the claimant is the landlord making an application for the termination of a tenancy under s29(2)

The requirements for the acknowledgment of the service and defence by a tenant where a landlord makes a claim for an order terminating the tenancy are dealt with in Practice Direction 56 paragraph 3.13 and CPR10. The acknowledgment of service is to be in Form N9 and should be served under the Part 7 procedure, 14 days after service of the claim form (or service of the particulars of claim if later). In these cases as the requirement is, in effect, for the particulars of claim to be endorsed on the claim form, the acknowledgment of service will be required 14 days after service of the claim form.[11]

---

11 CPR 10.3.

There is no extra prescribed information to go in the acknowledgment of service. The tenant will, however, have to file a separate defence. Note: there is no requirement for the tenant to file an acknowledgment of service if it files its defence 14 days after service of the particulars of claim.[12]

The tenant's defence is to be filed 14 days after service of the particulars of claim or, if the tenant has filed an acknowledgment of service under CPR10, 28 days after service of the particulars of claim.

Contents of the tenant's defence

In its defence, the tenant must state with particulars:

- whether the tenant relies on ss23(1A), 41 or 42 of the Act (ie occupation/carrying on of a business by company/controlling shareholder, trusts, group companies, see **Chapter 4**), and if so, the basis on which he does so;

- whether the tenant relies on s31A of the Act (ie that the landlord could carry out the proposed works under s30(1)(f) without obtaining possession of the whole holding) and, if so, the basis on which he does so; and

- the terms of the new tenancy that the tenant would propose in the event that the landlord's claim to terminate the current tenancy fails.

A chart summarising the positions is set out overleaf (**Figure 20**).

Judgment in default

The author can see no reason why the normal rules in Part 7 claims should not apply to these cases, thereby enabling a party to obtain judgment in default of service of an acknowledgment of service or a defence.[13]

Evidence in the opposed claims

The evidence requirements in an opposed claim (whether a claim by a tenant for a new lease which is opposed or a claim for a termination order by the landlord) are dealt with by Practice Direction 56 para 3.15. This states that:

> ... where the claim is an opposed claim, evidence (including expert evidence) must be filed by the parties as the court directs and the landlord shall file his evidence first.

For general comments as to the changes in CPR56 in respect of evidence, see **p102** above. It will probably be the case that after filing of the defence

---

12 See CPR10.1(3) and 15.4(4).
13 see CPR Part 12.

Figure 20

CPR 56: CLAIM BY LANDLORD FOR TERMINATION OF A TENANCY UNDER S29(2)

Claim form (Part 7) usually issued in county court

Contents of claim form (PD56 paras 3.4 and 3.9)

Must contain details of:

- the property;
- particulars of the current tenancy: date, parties, duration, current rent (if not the original rent), date and method of termination;
- every section 25 notice or section 26 request;
- the expiry date of the statutory period under s29A(2), ie the date by which proceedings had to be issued or any agreed extended period under s29B(1) or (2);
- the landlord's grounds of opposition;
- full details of those grounds of opposition; and
- the terms of a new tenancy the landlord proposes in the event its claim fails.

Two months

Claim form must be served

14 days after service of particulars of claim

Tenant to file and serve acknowledgment of service in Form N9 or defence. If acknowledgment of service is filed, tenant has 28 days after service of particulars of claim to file defence

Contents of tenant's defence – (PD56 para 3.13)

The defence must state:

- whether the tenant relies on the new rules for ownership/control of a business, trust or group companies, and, if so, the basis on which it does so (ss23(1A), 42 or 42)
- whether the tenant relies on s31A and, if so, the basis on which he does (ie landlord could do works under s30(1)(f) without obtaining possession of the whole; and
- the terms of the new tenancy that the tenant would propose in the event that the landlord's claim to terminate the current tenancy fails.

Evidence: Evidence (including expert witness evidence) must be filed by the parties as the court directs and the landlord shall be required to file evidence first (PD56 para 3.15).

the court will automatically fix a hearing to give directions (if it does not, either party could apply for one).

For suggested directions see the discussion of the Property Litigation Association's Post-Action Protocol below.

It is to be noted that in the case of opposed claims, whether they are instigated by the landlord or the tenant, it is the landlord who will be required to file his evidence first. This is entirely sensible, especially in cases such as opposition under ground 30(1)(f) (redevelopment) where the landlord will need to prove its intentions for the property. It would make no sense in such cases for the tenant to file evidence first.

Preliminary issues

Practice Direction 56 paragraph 3.16 specifically provides that, unless in the circumstances of the case it is unreasonable to do so, any grounds of opposition shall be tried as a preliminary case. For what is meant by 'grounds of opposition', see **p106** above.

Although it does not specifically say so, it is the author's view that the tenant could still, as before 1 June, raise issues as preliminary issue, for example the validity of a section 25 notice.

Property Litigation Association Post-Action Protocol

The Post-Action Protocol for business tenancy renewals was formulated by the Property Litigation Association with the aim of standardising the way lease renewals are dealt with by the courts. The Protocol has been running as a pilot in several London county courts and has been a great success. The protocol is reproduced in full at **Appendix 7**.[14]

Appendix A of the Protocol contains a set of standard directions for where the renewal is unopposed. Appendix C is a set of simple directions which can be used where the amount of rent in dispute is no greater than £10,000 per annum and the district judge considers that it is suitable to be in the fast track as opposed to the multi-track.

Appendix B of the Protocol is a set of standard directions for where the landlord opposes the grant of a new lease, under s30 of the Act or on a jurisdictional point (eg invalid notices).

---

14 See also the Association's website: www.pla.org.uk.

These suggested directions can still be applied fully to claims covered by the pre-1 June 2004 CPR56. The vast majority of the directions will also still be applicable to post-1 June 2004 CPR56, although there will need to be some variations dealing with service of evidence to accommodate the fact that CPR56.3(10) and (11) no longer apply, and the fact that in opposed renewals the landlord is to provide his evidence first. The author understands that these standard directions will be updated to take into account the changes to the rules and readers are advised to check the Property Litigation Association's website for updates.

Precedent of claims forms where there is more than one application to the court under s24(1) or s29(2)

Practice Direction 56 paragraph 3.2 deals with the situation where more than one application to the court is made under ss24(1) or 29(2).

One section 24(1) application served

Once an application under s24(1) for a new tenancy (by tenant or landlord) has been served on the defendant no further application to the court in respect of the same tenancy whether under s24(1) (for a new tenancy) or s29(2) (for a termination order) may be served by that defendant without the permission of the court.

Example 1:

If a tenant has served an application for a new tenancy on the landlord, the landlord cannot, without the court's permission, serve any application it has made for a new tenancy or for a termination order.

Example 2:

If a landlord has served an application for a new tenancy on the tenant, the tenant cannot, without the court's permission, serve any application it has made for a new tenancy.

Two applications for a new tenancy served on same day

If more than one application to the court is made under s24(1) for a new tenancy in respect of the same tenancy, and both applications are served on the same day, the landlord's application shall stand stayed until further order of the court. In effect, the same issues will be dealt with in the tenant's application as would be in the landlord's.

Application for new tenancy and application for termination order served on same day

If a landlord's application to the court for a termination order (s29(2)) is served on the same day as an application to the court (by implication by the tenant) for a new tenancy (in respect of the same tenancy) then the tenant's application for a new tenancy will stand stayed until further order by the court. This makes sense so that any grounds of opposition to the new tenancy can be dealt with first.

Application for termination order served before service of an application for a new tenancy which has already been issued

If a tenant has made an application for a new tenancy, but before he serves it, he is served by the landlord with an application for a termination order, the rules provide that the service of the landlord's application

> … shall be deemed to be a notice under rule 7.7 requiring service or discontinuance of the s24(1) application [for a new tenancy] within a period of 14 days after the service of the s29(2) application [for a termination order].

CPR7.7(3) goes on to provide that if the claimant (ie the tenant in this scenario) fails to comply with the notice to serve, then the court may on the application of the landlord: (a) dismiss the claim; or (b) make any other order it thinks fit.

However, unless the landlord knows the tenant has made an application for a new tenancy, it will not know that its application for a termination order is being treated as a notice to serve and will not, therefore, know if the tenant does not comply that it can apply to dismiss the tenant's claim.

The Rules do not make it clear what happens if the tenant does serve its application in accordance with the notice ie which set out proceedings will go ahead. It is implicit that it will be the tenant's (as the landlord's proceedings are to be treated as a notice to serve) but this does not necessarily make the most sense. It would make more sense to deal with any grounds of opposition first. If the tenant's proceedings are to be dealt with first there is no indication as to whether the landlord will have to serve a separate defence. The author's view is that the court may well order that the landlord's s29(2) application will stand as its defence in this scenario.

Interim rent

The new provisions for applications for interim rent are dealt with in Practice Direction 56 paragraphs 3.17-3.19.

The basic position is that if main proceedings have been commenced, either for a new tenancy or for the termination of an existing tenancy, the interim rent claim should be made in those proceedings by:

1. the claim form;

2. the acknowledgment of service or defence; or

3. an application on notice under Part 23.

Where no other proceedings have been commenced, or where such proceedings have been disposed of, an application for interim rent should be made by the Part 8 procedure. For more information as to what is to be included in the application, see **Chapter 11** on interim rent.

Where an application is made under s24D(3) of the Act the application should be on notice under Part 23 in the original proceedings. This is an application to re-calculate interim rent where interim rent was fixed as the rent under the new tenancy but the court has revoked the order for a new tenancy or the parties have agreed not to act on it. For more details see **Chapter 11, p130**.

10. TERMINATION OF FIXED-TERM TENANCIES BY A TENANT– SECTION 27

Termination by the tenant before end of the fixed term – section 27(1)

Pre-1 June 2004

Section 27(1) of the Act provided that a tenant could terminate a fixed term tenancy on the contractual expiry date by giving at least three months' prior written notice.

Confusion had arisen over whether the tenant was required to give such notice in order to avoid the tenancy continuing beyond the fixed term. The Court of Appeal in *Esselte AB v Pearl Assurance Plc*[1] made it clear, however, that a tenant who had vacated the premises by the end of the contractual fixed term had effectively ended the tenancy, and had no continuing obligation to pay rent.

From 1 June 2004

Section 27(1) of the Act has been amended to make it clear that a tenant wishing to end the tenancy at the end of the contractual term can do so by:

1. serving at least three months' notice before the end of the contractual term; or

2. not being in occupation of the premises by the end of the contractual term.

The result in 1 above has been achieved by the insertion of a new s27(1A) which provides that s24 of the Act (continuing the tenancy after the end of the contractual term unless terminated in accordance with the Act) shall not have effect where the tenant is not in occupation of the property at the end of the contractual term.

---

1 [1997] EGLR 73 CA

Where the tenant has moved out the tenancy will, therefore, end on the expiry of the contractual fixed term without the need for either party to serve any notices. This creates uncertainty for a landlord up to the end of the fixed term. It would be possible for a tenant who has vacated (without serving a section 27 notice) to move back in to the premises in the last few days of the term and thereby reactivate its protection under the Act.

Termination by tenant after the end of the fixed term – section 27(2)

Pre-1 June 2004

Section 27(2) required a tenant wanting to quit, where the tenancy had continued beyond the end of the contractual fixed term to give to the landlord three months' prior written notice ending on a quarter day.

This caused inconsistency in that a different number of days' notice had to be given depending on the quarter day in question. Also, it was another trap for tenants to ensure their notice expired on the correct day and was of a sufficient length.

From 1 June 2004

There have been three amendments to s27(2) of the Act.

When is the notice to end?

Section 27(2) has been amended to remove the requirement that the three months' notice must end on a quarter day. It may end now on any day.

What happens if the tenant moves out without serving a notice?

Section 27(2) has been amended to make it clear that a tenancy continuing after the end of the contractual expiry date 'shall not come to an end by reason only of the tenant ceasing to occupy the property comprised in the tenancy'. This is in contrast to the position before the end of the contractual fixed term (see **p115** above). To bring its tenancy to an end after the expiry of the contractual fixed term the tenant will have to serve a section 27(2) notice, ie it cannot just move out.

Apportionment of rent

Normally where a tenancy comes to an end midway through a rental period, rent (if payable in advance) will not be apportioned. So if a tenancy (where rent is payable quarterly) is brought to an end on 28 June, the tenant will still be obliged to pay the full amount for the June quarter, even though he is only occupying for four days of that quarter.

A new s27(3) of the Act provides for the apportionment of rent after a section 27(2) notice has been served. The tenant will pay rent up to the actual date for the ending of the tenancy, where the end of the notice period is not the same as the end of the rental period. Any excess rent already paid by the tenant in advance to the landlord will be recoverable by the tenant.

Example:

There is a five-year lease expiring on 25 December 2004. The tenant remains in occupation after the end of the fixed term. In April 2005 the tenant serves at least three months' notice under s27(2) of the Act ending on 25 July 2005. The tenancy will end on 25 July 2005 (and not the end of the quarter – 28 September 2005). Rent will only be payable until 25 July 2005. If the quarter's rent due on 24 June 2005 has already been paid then the tenant will be entitled to a refund for the apportioned amount for the period from 26 July 2005 to 28 September 2005.

Transitional provisions

The transitional provisions in Art 29(2)(b) of the Order provide that nothing in the Order has effect in relation to a notice under s27(2) of the Act (notice by tenant to terminate tenancy after the end of the fixed term) which was given by the tenant to the immediate landlord before the Order came into force, ie before 1 June 2004.

11. INTERIM RENT

A quick reminder

Interim rent is the rent which the court may order the tenant to pay while a protected tenancy continues by virtue of the provisions of s24 of the Act, ie after the expiry of the contractual fixed term. If the level of interim rent cannot be agreed by the parties it will be fixed by the court.

When do the new interim rent rules apply?

The new interim rent rules apply where the section 25 notice or section 26 request is served on or after 1 June 2004.

This is provided by the transitional provisions of the Order which state that:

> Where, before this Order came into force:
>
> (a)   the landlord gave the tenant notice under s25 of the Act; or
>
> (b)   the tenant made a request for a new tenancy in accordance with s26 of the Act,
>
> nothing in this Order has effect in relation to the notice or request or anything done in consequence of it.

Clearly, an application for interim rent is 'done in consequence' of a section 25 notice or section 26 request, and, therefore, if that notice is served before 1 June 2004 the interim rent provisions brought in by the Order will not apply.

Who can apply for interim rent?

Pre-June 2004

Section 24A(1) of the Act provided that only the landlord could apply for an interim rent.

Clearly, this provided scope for manipulation by landlords. If the market rent was lower than the passing rent under the old tenancy, then the landlord would simply not apply for an interim rent to be fixed, and the tenant would have had to continue to pay the passing rent.

From 1 June 2004

The whole of old s24A has been repealed and has been replaced by a new s24A. The new S24A provides that if a section 25 notice or section 26 request has been given then either the landlord or the tenant will be able to apply for interim rent, provided the other has not already made an application which has not been withdrawn.[1]

On a strict interpretation of the provisions, it could be argued that it is only the party who has served the notice or request who can make the application as the Act refers to either 'of them' being able to make the application (rather than 'either the landlord or the tenant under the said tenancy'). However, this is clearly not what was intended and it is the author's view that the courts would consider s24A as enabling either party to apply for interim rent, irrespective of who served notice on whom.

This change will be of great benefit to tenants in the situation where the market rent is lower than the passing rent. They can now take advantage of this by making their own application for interim rent if the landlord does not.

When can the interim rent application be made?

Pre-June 2004

There was no time limit (subject to limitation issues) on when the application could be made. In practice, in a rising market, applications would have been made by the landlord as soon as possible, as the interim rent was only payable from:

1. the date of the application; or

2. if later:

    (a) the day after the date in the section 25 notice that the tenancy was to end; or

    (b) the date in the section 26 request for the start of the new tenancy.

From 1 June 2004

Latest date for making an interim rent application

The new s24A(3) provides that an application for interim rent will not be entertained by the court if it is made more than six months after the

---

1 Section 24A(2).

termination of the 'relevant tenancy'. The relevant tenancy for these purposes is the continuation tenancy under s24 of the Act.[2]

In practice, this will mean applications can be made up to six months after the new lease comes into effect. If a new lease is not entered into, eg because the tenant serves a notice of discontinuance in the renewal proceedings, then the interim rent application can be made up to six months after the continuation tenancy comes to an end.

Earliest date for making an interim rent application

An interim rent application can be made at any time after service of the section 25 notice or section 26 request (subject to the latest date as set out above).

How is the interim rent application to be made?

Pre-1 June 2004

Interim rent applications could be made in the landlord's acknowledgment of service. If the application needed to be made before the acknowledgment of service was filed (or, indeed, afterwards, if not in the acknowledgment of service) the choice was to make it in a separate, stand alone, CPR Part 8 application or a CPR Part 23 application. The author's view is that a Part 8 application was the better and more appropriate method in these circumstances (especially if the proceedings were subject to a stay under CPR56).

After 1 June 2004

Note: the new Procedure Rules only apply where the section 25 notice was served or the section 26 request made from 1 June 2004.

Where main proceedings are ongoing

Practice Direction 56 paragraph 3.17 provides that where proceedings have been commenced, either for the grant of a new tenancy or termination of an existing tenancy, the claim for interim rent under s24A shall be made in those proceedings by:

- the claim form;
- the acknowledgment of service or defence; or
- an application on notice under Part 23.

---

2 Section 24A(1).

Where there are no main proceedings

Where proceedings have not been commenced for the grant of a new tenancy or termination of an existing tenancy, or where such proceedings have been disposed of, an application for interim rent under s24A must be made under the Part 8 procedure.[3]

In such a Part 8 claim form for interim rent should be included details of:

- the property to which the claim relates;
- the particulars of the relevant tenancy, including:

  (a) date,

  (b) parties,

  (c) duration, and

  (d) the current rent (if not the original rent);

- every notice or request given or made under s25 or s26 of the Act;
- if the relevant tenancy has terminated, the date and mode of termination; and
- if the relevant tenancy has been terminated and the landlord has granted a new tenancy of the property to the tenant:

  (a) particulars of the new tenancy (including date, parties and duration) and the rent; and

  (b) in a case where s24C(2) of the Act applies (ie interim rent is same as rent under new tenancy), but the claimant seeks a different rent under s24C(3) (due to substantial change in the market and/or a change in the terms of the lease which substantially affect the rent), particulars and matters on which the claimant relies as satisfying s24C(3) – see **p125** below for details.

From which date is interim rent payable?

Pre-June 2004

Interim rent was payable in practice from and including the later of:

(a) the date requested for a new tenancy in the tenant's section 26 request

---

3 Practice Direction 56 para 3.19.

or the day after the termination date set out in the landlord's section 25 notice; or

(b) the date of the application for interim rent (s24A(2)).

From 1 June 2004

The new s24B(1) of the Act provides that interim rent will be payable from the 'appropriate date'. This is defined by the new s24B(2) and (3) of the Act as the earliest date which:

(a) could have been specified by the landlord in its section 25 notice as the date of termination of the tenancy; or

(b) could have been specified by the tenant in its section 26 request as the date from which the new tenancy is to begin.

This means the earliest date which could have been put in the actual notice which is served by the landlord or tenant: not a hypothetical notice which could have been served. (If it had meant a hypothetical notice, the date would always have been the end of the contractual term.) The very earliest day it will be possible from which interim rent can be payable is, therefore, immediately after the end of the contractual term date.

The interim rent is backdated to the appropriate date irrespective of which party makes the application and when it is made.

Example 1:
The contractual term expires on 1 March 2005. The tenant serves a section 26 request on 6 January 2005 and gives 6 January 2006 as the date the new tenancy should begin (ie twelve months' notice, applying the corresponding date rule). The earliest date it could have given is 6 July 2005 (ie six months' notice) and that will be the appropriate date. Interim rent will be payable from (and including) 6 July 2005.

Example 2:
Again, the contractual term expires on 1 March 2005. A landlord serves a section 25 notice on 6 January 2005 giving 12 months' notice, ie specifying 6 January 2006 as the termination date. The earliest date which it could have given as the termination date is 6 July 2005 (ie six months' notice). Whilst on a strict interpretation of the Act the interim rent will be payable from and including 6 July 2005, this does not make sense as the tenancy is continued under the section 25 notice until midnight on 6 July. It is the author's view that interim rent would, therefore, be payable, in practice, from and including 7 July 2005.

Example 3:
The contractual term expires on 1 March 2005. The landlord serves a section 25 notice on 1 August 2004 specifying 1 May 2005 as the termination date (ie nine months' notice). The earliest date it could have put for termination was 1 March 2005 (ie seven months'

notice ending on the contractual term date). Interim rent will, therefore, run from and including 2 March 2005.

In effect, the appropriate date will always be six months after service of the section 25 notice or section 26 request, or where later, the contractual term date. This backdating effect will mean that neither party will get any benefit from manipulating the length of the section 25 notice or section 26 request in order to take advantage of a longer period where the passing rent is higher (in the case of landlords) or lower (in the case of tenants) than the market rent. There could be some advantage to a party in delaying service of the notice/request at all so that the deeming provisions do not come into play until a later date. However, if the other party is losing out because of this and is well advised, it will serve its own notice/request to start things off.

How is the amount of interim rent determined?

Pre-June 2004

The court determined an amount which it would be reasonable for the tenant to pay having regard to:

1. the rent payable under the old contractual lease (ie the 'passing rent');

2. s34(1) and (2) of the Act (which contain various assumptions and disregards and set out how the rent under any new tenancy is to be valued);

3. the old contractual tenancy being treated as though it were a yearly tenancy of the whole of the property; and

4. the terms of the yearly tenancy are those of the 'old' tenancy so far as they are consistent with a tenancy from year to year.

If there is a rising market, this method of calculation tends to 'cushion' the tenant from the full impact of the current market rent.

From 1 June 2004

This depends on whether it is likely that the tenant will be able to renew the tenancy. Where there 'is little doubt' that the tenant will be able to renew, the 'new' method of determining interim rent under the new s24C of the Act will apply. The Act sets out three conditions which need to be satisfied for the new method to apply (see **p125**, below). If these conditions do not apply then interim rent will be calculated in accordance with the new s24D of the Act which is, broadly speaking, the same method as before (see **p129**, below).

The 'new' method for calculating interim rent under s24C

What are the conditions for the 'new' method of calculating interim rent under section 24C to apply?

The conditions for calculating interim rent under the 'new' method are set out in the new s24C of the Act under the heading 'Amount of interim rent where new tenancy of whole premises granted and landlord not opposed'.

The conditions are:

1. the landlord's section 25 notice or the tenant's section 26 request must apply to the whole of the property let under the current lease;

2. the tenant must occupy the whole of the property;

3. the landlord must not oppose the grant of a new tenancy;

4. the landlord grants a new tenancy of the whole of the property to the tenant (whether as a result of a court order of otherwise).

What is the amount of interim rent under the new section 24C method?

The new s24C(2) of the Act provides that if the conditions above are met, then the interim rent will (usually) be the same as the rent for the new tenancy.

In effect, this will remove the cushioning effect enjoyed by a tenant in a rising market. The rationale is that where the market is stable and there are no significant changes in the terms of the new tenancy, this method of ascertaining interim rent should produce a rent broadly in line with the open market rent over the period during which interim rent is payable.

Are there any situations where the conditions are met where the interim rent will not be the same as the new rent?

There are situations where the conditions are met but where the interim rent differs from the new rent. This is dealt with in the new subsections (3) to (8) of s24C of the Act. In situations where the conditions are met, the interim rent will be the rent under the new lease unless one of the parties can show to the satisfaction of the court:

1. a substantial change in the market; and/or

2. a change in the terms of the new lease which substantially affect the rent.

What exactly is meant by a substantial change in the market?

The meaning of substantial change in the market is dealt with in s24C(3)(a). To change the interim rent from being the rent under the new tenancy the landlord, or the tenant, will have to show to the satisfaction of the court, that the interim rent (ie the new rent) 'differs substantially' from the 'relevant rent'.

The 'relevant rent' is defined in s24C(4) as being the rent the court would have ordered for the new tenancy if it had started at the date interim rent became payable (ie the earliest date which could have been specified in the section 25 notice/section 26 request).

So, the two valuations which need to be made are:

1. the rent on the terms of the new tenancy in accordance with s34, valued at the date the new tenancy commences (ie the new rent); and

2. the rent on the terms of the new tenancy in accordance with s34, valued at the date interim rent became payable.

The only difference in these valuations is the date of the valuation. This makes sense when what is being looked at is a change in the market from one valuation date to the other.

What will the interim rent be if there is such a change in the market?

If there is a substantial difference in these two valuations, reflecting a substantial change in the market, then the interim rent will be the 'relevant rent', ie valuation 2 above.

Example:

The passing rent is £10,000 pa. The interim rent becomes payable on 1 December 2004. The market is still fairly low at that point. The new tenancy commences on 1 December 2005 by which time the market has risen substantially so that the rent under the new tenancy is £100,000 pa. The tenant can show the court that the rent for the new tenancy would have been £20,000 pa. if it had been granted on 1 December 2004. In anyone's view the difference between £20,000 pa. and £100,000 pa. is a substantial difference, reflecting a substantial change in the market. Therefore, the interim rent will be £20,000 pa.

A landlord will be able to make a similar application if the market had fallen drastically over that period. See comments at **p129**, below, as to what is meant by 'substantial'.

What is meant by a change in the terms of the lease which substantially affects the rent?

Section 24C(3)(b) deals with a change in the terms of the lease which substantially affects the rent. To change the interim rent from being the rent under the new tenancy, the landlord or tenant will have to satisfy the court that the terms of the new tenancy differ from the terms of the 'relevant' tenancy (ie the continuation tenancy, which of course is on the same terms as the old tenancy[4]) to such an extent that the rent for the new tenancy is 'substantially different' to the rent which the court would have ordered under a tenancy, on the terms of the old tenancy commencing on the day the new tenancy begins.

So, the two valuations which need to be made are:

1. the rent on the terms of the new tenancy in accordance with s34, valued at the date the new tenancy commences; and

2. the rent on the terms of the old tenancy in accordance with s34, valued at the date the new tenancy commences.

What will be the interim rent if there is such a change in the terms of the lease?

Section 24C(6) provides that where there is such a change in the terms of the lease, the interim rent will be 'the rent which it is reasonable for the tenant to pay' while the tenancy continues under the Act.

How is any section 24C 'reasonable' rent calculated? – section 24C(7)

This is set out in s24C(7) of the Act. The court will have regard to:

1. the passing rent under the old tenancy;

2. the rent of any subtenancy of part of the property in the old tenancy;

3. s34(1) and (2) of the Act;

4. the tenancy being valued being of the whole of the property in the old tenancy; and

5. the tenancy being valued being of the same duration as new tenancy which is actually granted.

In the author's view, the new provisions do not make it clear whether the terms of the tenancy to be valued to calculate the reasonable rent are those

---

4 Practice Direction 56 para 3.19.

of the 'old' tenancy (other than duration) or those of the new tenancy, nor when the valuation date is. The author considers that the terms of the tenancy to be valued are those of the old tenancy (other than duration) and that the valuation date is the 'appropriate' date, ie the date interim rent becomes payable (ie section 34 passing rent etc).

Example 1:

An old 15-year tenancy contains severe restrictions on alienation and also had a rolling landlord's six-month break clause. The new ten-year tenancy granted to the tenant (by agreement) had more relaxed alienation provisions and did not contain the break clause. As a result the rent agreed was substantially higher than the rent under the old tenancy as the new terms are less onerous to the tenant. The tenant could apply to the court for a determination of what would be a reasonable interim rent for it to pay in accordance with s24C(7).

This would be worked out on the basis of the terms of the old tenancy (ie with the restrictions) but with a duration of ten years (ie as in the new tenancy). The other factors mentioned at **p127**, above, would also be taken into account.

Example 2:

An old tenancy is for a term of 25 years at a rent of £100,000 pa. The new tenancy ordered by the court is for a term of five years and the new rent is £200,000 pa. Assuming that the market has not changed drastically, the uplift in rent can be shown to be due to the fact that in the current market a five-year term is more desirable to a tenant than a 25-year term and so the hypothetical tenant will pay a higher rent for that shorter term. This change in the terms of the lease has substantially affected the rent. If one of the parties makes an application (presumably the tenant in this case) the court would have to consider what is a reasonable rent for the tenant to pay as an interim rent in accordance with s24C(7).

In this case, however, the tenant is unlikely to be helped much by this new valuation. The main factor which has produced a change is the rent is the change in the length of term from 25 years to five years. In calculating the 'reasonable' rent, however, the court has to assume the duration of the new tenancy, ie five years – precisely the factor which has caused the uplift in the rent. Whilst the tenant may still get some cushioning effect from consideration of the passing rent in the calculation of the 'reasonable' rent, this may not be sufficient to warrant the expense of the court application.

What if there is a change in the market and the lease terms?

Where there is a change in the market and the lease terms s24C(6) of the Act provides that the interim rent will be the 'reasonable' rent calculated as set out at **p127**, above, ie in accordance with s24C(7).

How big is 'substantial'?

The Act gives no guidance as to how much is 'substantial'. The ODPM considered that it was not necessary to lay down any hard and fast rules and that the courts will have to consider cases on their merits.

In practice, for either the landlord or the tenant to pursue the alternative valuation, the difference in rents would have to exceed comfortably the inevitable increase in costs associated with a longer trial and further valuation evidence which would be needed to prove that difference. It remains to be seen whether, in practice, this line will be pursued.

What will be the interim rent in cases which are not unopposed renewals of the whole? – section 24D calculation

If the conditions at **p125**, above, are not satisfied, ie where there is some doubt that the tenant will be able to renew, the new formula in s24C does not apply. This would occur, for example if:

- the section 25 notice or section 26 request sought a renewal of part only of the property in the old tenancy;

- the tenant occupied part only of the property; or

- the landlord opposed the renewal (whether or not a new tenancy was actually granted).

The interim rent in these other cases is governed by s24D of the Act which is headed 'Amount of interim rent in any other case'. This provides that the interim rent in these circumstances should be the rent which it is 'reasonable' for the tenant to pay while the tenancy continues.

How is the section 24D 'reasonable' rent calculated? – section 24D(2)

Section 24D(2) of the Act provides that in fixing the reasonable amount of interim rent in section 24D cases the court shall have regard to:

1. the passing rent;

2. the rent of any sub-tenancy of part of the property in the old tenancy;

3. s34(1) and (2) of the Act;

4. the tenancy being valued as a tenancy from year to year; and

5. the tenancy to be valued being of the whole of the property in the old tenancy.

Again, the provisions do not make it clear on which terms the tenancy is being valued and what is the valuation date. The author considers that the terms are those of the 'old' lease (other than rent and duration). The duration will be a yearly tenancy and the passing rent will be taken into account as one of the factors, and that the valuation date is the 'appropriate date', ie the date interim rent becomes payable.

This is basically the same as the method of assessing rent before the changes were introduced on 1 June 2004, apart from the additional requirement to consider the rent of any subtenancy of part.

Charts

A chart showing the calculation of interim rent when the section 25 notice/section 26 request is served before 1 June 2004 is set out below (**Figure 21**).

A chart showing the calculation of interim rent where the section 25 notice/section 26 request is served from and including 1 June 2004 is set out opposite (**Figure 22**).

Special situations

The new s24D(3) of the Act provides that if the court orders a new tenancy of the whole following an unopposed renewal and the interim rent is, accordingly, fixed as the same as the new rent, but either:

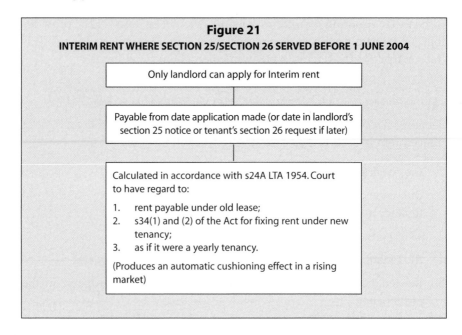

Figure 21

INTERIM RENT WHERE SECTION 25/SECTION 26 SERVED BEFORE 1 JUNE 2004

Only landlord can apply for Interim rent

Payable from date application made (or date in landlord's section 25 notice or tenant's section 26 request if later)

Calculated in accordance with s24A LTA 1954. Court to have regard to:

1. rent payable under old lease;
2. s34(1) and (2) of the Act for fixing rent under new tenancy;
3. as if it were a yearly tenancy.

(Produces an automatic cushioning effect in a rising market)

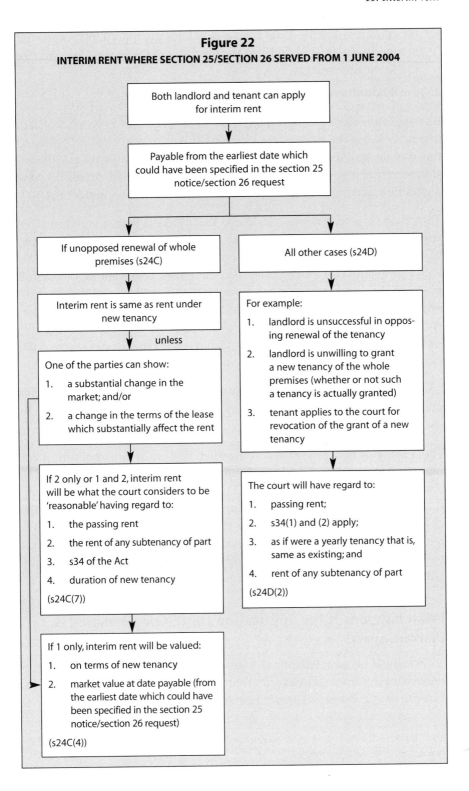

Figure 22
INTERIM RENT WHERE SECTION 25/SECTION 26 SERVED FROM 1 JUNE 2004

Both landlord and tenant can apply for interim rent

Payable from the earliest date which could have been specified in the section 25 notice/section 26 request

If unopposed renewal of whole premises (s24C)

All other cases (s24D)

Interim rent is same as rent under new tenancy

unless

One of the parties can show:

1. a substantial change in the market; and/or

2. a change in the terms of the lease which substantially affect the rent

If 2 only or 1 and 2, interim rent will be what the court considers to be 'reasonable' having regard to:

1. the passing rent
2. the rent of any subtenancy of part
3. s34 of the Act
4. duration of new tenancy

(s24C(7))

If 1 only, interim rent will be valued:

1. on terms of new tenancy
2. market value at date payable (from the earliest date which could have been specified in the section 25 notice/section 26 request)

(s24C(4))

For example:

1. landlord is unsuccessful in opposing renewal of the tenancy

2. landlord is unwilling to grant a new tenancy of the whole premises (whether or not such a tenancy is actually granted)

3. tenant applies to the court for revocation of the grant of a new tenancy

The court will have regard to:

1. passing rent;
2. s34(1) and (2) apply;
3. as if were a yearly tenancy that is, same as existing; and
4. rent of any subtenancy of part

(s24D(2))

1. the court revokes the order for the new tenancy under s36(2) of the Act having been asked to do so by the tenant (ie if the tenant does not like the terms ordered); or

2. the landlord and tenant agree not to act on the order,

then the landlord or tenant can apply for the interim rent to be recalculated. Instead of being the same as the new rent, it will be calculated according to the formula set out at **p129** above under s24D, on the old formula with consideration for rent of sub-tenancy of part. This recalculation will be done without the need for a further application for an interim rent under s24A(1).

The rationale is that it was considered that where a tenant withdraws his application without taking a new lease, an interim rent at the full figure that would have been in the new lease is not appropriate, because the reason for withdrawal could be a recognition that the tenant could not afford the full new rent. This is so, particularly, where the Act gives the tenant the opportunity to revoke the renewal order. The Law Commission considered that in such cases to backdate the new rent as interim rent would be wrong, as it would 'force upon the tenant a rent which it could not afford and which the Act expressly permits it to escape by vacating the property'.

The changes to the Civil Procedure Rules provide that an application under s24D(3) shall be made by an application on notice under Part 23 in the original proceedings.

The proposals for reform recommended that such an application for reassessment of the interim rent should be made within one month of the court ordering interim rent at the full market rate, but the tenancy not subsequently being granted. This time limit has not been transported into the amendments to the Act and there is no specific time limited imposed for making such an application. One view would be that the general rule set out in s24A(3) will apply to such applications, ie they should be made within six months after termination of the tenancy.[5]

What happens if the application for the new tenancy is discontinued?

Obviously, if no new tenancy is granted then, even if it is an unopposed renewal of the whole, the interim rent cannot be the same as the new rent, because the new rent will never be fixed.

---

[5] For the date of termination of the tenancy following a revocation of the court order for a new tenancy, see s36(6) of the Act.

The Act does not specifically provide for what is to happen in these circumstances although it is the author's view it would fall within the 'other cases' in s24D. Even if this is not the case, it is the author's view that the courts will not carry out a hypothetical exercise as to what would have been the new terms and new rent. It is considered that the courts will instead apply the section 24D formula. This would fit in with the logic of the rest of the changes to the interim rent provisions.

How may the interim rent be fixed before the new tenancy is ordered?

There are several reasons why either of the parties may wish to do to have the interim rent fixed before the new tenancy is ordered. If it is going to take a while to sort out the terms of the new tenancy the tenant may have cash flow problems. In a falling market, it may wish to stop paying the higher passing rent as soon as possible.

Conversely, in a rising market, the landlord may want the higher rent paid as soon as possible, if it has cash flow problems or thinks the tenant may have difficulties paying that higher amount. The landlord will not want substantial back payments to accumulate.

Under the pre-June 2004 rules a landlord could have the interim rent calculated separately in advance of the court hearing to determine the terms of the new lease and the new rent. Whilst this rarely happened in practice, it was an option open to the landlord. The Law Commission proposals recommended that applications to fix interim rent should be heard during the course of the main proceedings for determination of the terms of the new tenancy, commenting that this would reduce the parties' legal costs. There are no provisions dealing with this situation in the Act as amended or in the amendments to CPR56. The amendments to CPR56 merely deal with making the application, not when it will be heard.

One view is that if one of the parties wants to fix an interim rent before a new tenancy has been granted, whether by agreement or by order of the court, s24D will apply. This will be the case even if the parties have settled the terms of the new tenancy if it has not yet been granted. The interim rent under s24C (interim rent is new rent) does not apply unless the new tenancy is granted. Therefore, the parties may still have the level of interim rent finalised before the main proceedings are dealt with, but the level will be calculated according to s24D rather than s24C.

The thinking behind the interim rent provisions was that there would be no need to fix interim rents earlier as the renewal process is likely to be shorter than it is now. Therefore, the period for which interim rent is payable will be shorter and renewals will be concluded quicker. The author's views is that, with the parties having the ability to extend indefinitely the issuing of proceedings, it may well turn out that interim rent periods will end up being much longer than pre-June 2004 and parties may actually want the interim rent fixed separately on more occasions than pre-June 2004.

12. TERMS OF A NEW TENANCY ORDERED BY THE COURT

Pre-1 June 2004

The details of the new tenancy to be ordered by the court are dealt with in ss32 to 35 of the Act as follows:

- s32 – property to be comprised in new tenancy;
- s33 – duration of new tenancy;
- s34 – rent under new tenancy; and
- s35 – other terms of new tenancy.

From 1 June 2004

There have been a few minor changes to ss33, 34 and 35 of the Act. There are no changes to s32.

Section 33 – duration of new tenancy

The maximum length of term which the court can order for a new tenancy has been increased from 14 years to 15 years. This change is to make the length of the new lease fit more readily with modern rent review patterns of three or five years.

Section 34 – rent under new tenancy

The amendments to s34 are merely consequential on other amendments made to the Act.

Section 34(2)(a) (dealing with improvements to be disregarded in calculating the new rent) refers to improvements completed 'not more than 21 years before the application to the court'. (The old wording was 'not more than 21 years before the application for the new tenancy'.) This reflects the fact that the initial application to the court after 1 June 2004 may have been by the landlord for a termination order, which was refused by the court.

A new s34(2A) has been added. This refers to the disregard in s34(1)(d) of the value attributable to any licence belonging to 'the tenant' of licensed premises. The new s34(2A) reiterates the changes dealing with ownership and control of businesses set out in Chapter 3 above. It makes it clear that in situations where the Act applies because of these new rules then the reference to 'the tenant' in s34(1)(d) shall be construed on the same basis, ie 'the tenant' will include:

1. a company in which the tenant has a controlling interest; or

2. (where the tenant is a company), a person with a controlling interest in the company.

Section 35 – other terms of the tenancy

Section 35 of the Act has been amended to provide for the apportionment of rent where the reversion is split, ie where different landlords own different parts of the property but the tenant occupies the property under a single lease. The court may order the amount of rent the tenant should pay to each landlord.

13. COMPENSATION

There are two distinct types of compensation dealt with by the Act, namely:

- compensation where a new tenancy is not granted; and
- compensation to a tenant for misrepresentation.

Compensation for refusal of renewal

Compensation where a new tenancy is not granted is dealt with in s37 of the Act. Whether the new compensation rules apply will depend on when the section 25 notice or section 26 request was served.

If the section 25 notice or section 26 request was served pre-1 June 2004 then the old rules will apply. If it was served on or after 1 June 2004, the new provisions will apply.

Compensation where notices served before 1 June 2004

A tenant who was not granted a new tenancy by reason of the opposition by its landlord on one of the following grounds (which involve no fault on behalf of the tenant) was entitled to compensation from its landlord.

The grounds were:

- s30(1)(e) – where there is a sub-tenancy of part and the landlord requires possession so he can let or otherwise dispose of the whole at a higher rent;
- s30(1)(f) – where the landlord requires possession so he can demolish and/or reconstruct the premises or carry out a redevelopment; and
- s30(1)(g) – where the landlord requires possession so he can occupy for his own business (or as his residence).

The tenant was entitled to double the amount of compensation if it (or any predecessors to its business) had been in occupation for 14 years or more.

Where the tenant had been in occupation of part only of the property for more than 14 years it was still entitled to double compensation in relation to the whole property.[1]

Compensation where notices served from 1 June 2004

The basic principle of when compensation is payable remains the same ie if the tenant does not obtain a new tenancy because of the landlord's opposition under grounds (e), (f) or (g) of s30(1) of the Act. However, there are some changes.

Where ground (g) is used

As explained in **Chapter 3**, ground (g) of opposition to a new tenancy, ie the landlord's intention to occupy for his own use, has been extended to cover use for a business carried on by a company under the landlord's control or vice versa. These amendments mean that a tenant will also be entitled to compensation in a case where the extended ground (g) applies.

Proceedings brought by landlord for a termination order

Section 37 is amended to include the provision that compensation will be payable where the landlord has brought proceedings for a termination order on grounds (e), (f) or (g) and the court is precluded from making an order for the grant of a new tenancy.

Compensation where the tenant has occupied part only of the premises for more than 14 years

This is a substantial change to s37. The new provisions in s37(3A) now provide that where parts of the premises have been occupied for different lengths of time, compensation will be calculated for each part separately. Higher rate compensation will apply only to those parts which have been continuously occupied for 14 years.

Example:
The tenant has occupied the first, second and third floors of the premises for 15 years apart from a period, five years ago, when the first floor was sublet for two years. Under the pre-June 2004 compensation rules the tenant would have been entitled to compensation of 2 x rateable value of whole premises. From 1 June 2004, it will be entitled to

---

1 *Edicron Ltd v William Whitely Ltd* [1984] 1 WLR 59

compensation in relation to the ground and second floors of 2 x rateable value, but only of 1 x rateable value for the first floor.

Split reversions

As mentioned in **Chapter 4** above, the reforms have provided that where the ownership of the reversion to a tenancy has been split the owners of the different parts of the property are, for the purposes of the statutory renewal procedure, together to be treated as 'the landlord'. The result of that change would have meant, without more, that where the tenant of several landlords, each owning a different part of the property, was entitled to compensation the tenant could recover the whole sum from any of them. Clearly, this would have been unfair as each landlord would only benefit from obtaining possession of its part of the property.

Accordingly, the new s37(3B) of the Act provides that where a property is split between different landlords, compensation will be determined separately for each part, and the tenant may only claim from the relevant landlord for each part.

Compensation for misrepresentation

Pre-June 2004

Compensation for misrepresentation was dealt with in s55 of the Act which has been repealed. It provided that where the court refused an order for a new tenancy and it later appeared that the decision was induced by a misrepresentation or concealment of material facts, the court could order the landlord to pay the tenant compensation for any resulting damage or loss.

The Law Commission pointed out in its proposals that the compensation provisions did not apply where no application was made to the court and that they did not provide any remedy where the tenant was induced to apply for a consent order that the premises be vacated.[2]

From 1 June 2004

The new provisions extend the right to compensation following misrepresentation to cases where the tenant is induced not to apply to the court for a new tenancy, or withdraws an application because of misrepresentation or concealment of material facts, and then quits the premises.

---

2 *Deeley v Maison AEL Ltd* (1989), unreported, CA.

The compensation provisions are in the new s37A of the Act. Section 37A(1) basically repeals the old provisions. The new provisions are in s37A(2) which states:

> Where –
>
> (a) the tenant has quit the holding –
>
> > (i)   after making but withdrawing an application under s24(1) of this Act [ie an application for a new tenancy]; or
> >
> > (ii) without making such an application; and
>
> (b) it is made to appear to the court that he did so by reason of misrepresentation or the concealment of material facts,
>
> the court may order the landlord to pay to the tenant such sum as appears sufficient as compensation for damage or loss sustained by the tenant as the result of quitting the holding.

The provisions do not state that a section 25 notice or section 26 request must have been served. It could be possible for a tenant to argue that it left at the end of the contractual fixed term without serving any notices as the landlord had stated, for example, that it was going to redevelop and then it did not. This would come down ultimately to a matter of evidence. Clearly, if a spurious ground of opposition had been put in a section 25 notice (or counternotice to a section 26 request) the tenant would be in a stronger position evidentially than if the landlord has merely made oral representations. Tenants who do vacate on the strength of the landlord's claims would do well to obtain something in writing from the landlord on its intentions in order to use it as evidence later if it turns out that these were incorrect.

Transitional provisions

The transitional provision in Art 29 paragraph (5) of the Order provides that the new s37A of the Act (compensation for possession obtained by misrepresentation) does not have effect where the tenant quit the holding before the Order came into force, ie before 1 June 2004.

Appendix 1: Keeling Schedule – Landlord and Tenant Act 1954

Landlord and Tenant Act 1954

PART I

SECURITY OF TENURE FOR RESIDENTIAL TENANTS

Provisions as to possession on termination of a long tenancy

Compensation for possession obtained by misrepresentation

14A. Where an order is made for possession of the property comprised in a tenancy to which section 1 of this Act applies and it is subsequently made to appear to the court that the order was obtained by misrepresentation or the concealment of material facts, the court may order the landlord to pay to the tenant such a sum as appears sufficient as compensation for damage or loss sustained by the tenant as the result of the order.

PART II

SECURITY OF TENURE FOR BUSINESS, PROFESSIONAL AND OTHER TENANTS

Tenancies to which Part II applies

Tenancies to which Part II applies

23-(1) Subject to the provisions of this Act, this Part of this Act applies to any tenancy where the property comprised in the tenancy is or includes premises which are occupied by the tenant and are so occupied for the purposes of a business carried on by him or for those and other purposes.

(1A) Occupation or the carrying on of a business –

(a) by a company in which the tenant has a controlling interest; or

(b) where the tenant is a company, by a person with a controlling interest in the company,

shall be treated for the purposes of this section as equivalent to occupation or, as the case may be, the carrying on of a business by the tenant.

(1B) Accordingly references (however expressed) in this Part of this Act to the business of, or to use, occupation or enjoyment by, the tenant shall be construed as including references to the business of, or to use, occupation or enjoyment by, a company falling within subsection (1A)(a) above or a person falling within subsection (1A)(b) above.

(2) In this Part of this Act the expression 'business' includes a trade, profession or employment and includes any activity carried on by a body of persons, whether corporate or unincorporate.

(3) In the following provisions of this Part of this Act the expression 'the holding,' in relation to a tenancy to which this Part of this Act applies, means the property comprised in the tenancy, there being excluded any part thereof which is occupied neither by the tenant nor by a person employed by the tenant and so employed for the purposes of a business by reason of which the tenancy is one to which this Part of this Act applies.

(4) Where the tenant is carrying on a business, in all or any part of the property comprised in a tenancy, in breach of a prohibition (however expressed) of use for business purposes which subsists under the terms of the tenancy and extends to the whole of that property, this Part of this Act shall not apply to the tenancy unless the immediate landlord or his predecessor in title has consented to the breach or the immediate landlord has acquiesced therein. In this

subsection the reference to a prohibition of use for business purposes does not include a prohibition of use for the purposes of a specified business, or of use for purposes of any but a specified business, but save as aforesaid includes a prohibition of use for the purposes of some one or more only of the classes of business specified in the definition of that expression in subsection (2) of this section.

Continuation and renewal of tenancies

Continuation of tenancies to which Part II applies and grant of new tenancies

24-(1) A tenancy to which this Part of this Act applies shall not come to an end unless terminated in accordance with the provisions of this Part of this Act; and, subject to the ~~provisions of section twenty-nine of this Act, the tenant under such a tenancy may apply to the court for~~ **following provisions of this Act either the tenant or the landlord under such a tenancy may apply to the court for an order for the grant of** a new tenancy –

> (a) if the landlord has given notice under section 25 of this Act to terminate the tenancy, or

> (b) if the tenant has made a request for a new tenancy in accordance with section 26 of this Act.

(2) The last foregoing subsection shall not prevent the coming to an end of a tenancy by notice to quit given by the tenant, by surrender or forfeiture, or by the forfeiture of a superior tenancy unless –

> (a) in the case of a notice to quit, the notice was given before the tenant had been in occupation in right of the tenancy for one month;~~ or~~

> ~~(b) in the case of an instrument of surrender, the instrument was executed before, or was executed in pursuance of an agreement made before, the tenant had been in occupation in right of the tenancy for one month.~~

(2A) Neither the tenant nor the landlord may make an application under subsection (1) above if the other has made such an application and the application has been served.

(2B) Neither the tenant nor the landlord may make such an application if the landlord has made an application under section 29(2) of this Act and the application has been served.

(2C) The landlord may not withdraw an application under subsection (1) above unless the tenant consents to its withdrawal.

(3) Notwithstanding anything in subsection (1) of this section –

> (a) where a tenancy to which this Part of this Act applies ceases to be such a tenancy, it shall not come to an end by reason only of the cesser, but if it was granted for a term of years certain and has been continued by subsection (1) of this section then (without prejudice to the termination thereof in accordance with any terms of the tenancy) it may be terminated by not less than three nor more than six months' notice in writing given by the landlord to the tenant;

> (b) where, at a time when a tenancy is not one to which this Part of this Act applies, the landlord gives notice to quit, the operation of the notice shall not be affected by reason that the tenancy becomes one to which this Part of this Act applies after the giving of the notice.

~~24A (1) The landlord of a tenancy to which this Part of this Act applies may,–~~

> ~~(a) if he has given notice under section 25 of this Act to terminate the tenancy; or~~

> ~~(b) if the tenant has made a request for a new tenancy in accordance with section 26 of this Act,~~

~~apply to the court to determine a rent which it would be reasonable for the tenant to pay while the tenancy continues by virtue of section 24 of this Act, and the court may determine a rent accordingly.~~

~~(2) A rent determined in proceedings under this section shall be deemed to be the rent payable under the tenancy from the date on which the proceedings were commenced or the date specified in the landlord's notice or the tenant's request, whichever is the later.~~

(3) In determining a rent under this section the court shall have regard to the rent payable under the terms of the tenancy, but otherwise subsections (1) and (2) of section 34 of this Act shall apply to the determination as they would apply to the determination of a rent under that section if a new tenancy from year to year of the whole of the property comprised in the tenancy were granted to the tenant by order of the court.

Applications for determination of interim rent while tenancy continues

24A-(1) Subject to subsection (2) below, if –

(a) the landlord of a tenancy to which this Part of this Act applies has given notice under section 25 of this Act to terminate the tenancy; or

(b) the tenant of such a tenancy has made a request for a new tenancy in accordance with section 26 of this Act,

either of them may make an application to the court to determine a rent (an 'interim rent') which the tenant is to pay while the tenancy ('the relevant tenancy') continues by virtue of section 24 of this Act and the court may order payment of an interim rent in accordance with section 24C or 24D of this Act.

(2) Neither the tenant nor the landlord may make an application under subsection (1) above if the other has made such an application and has not withdrawn it.

(3) No application shall be entertained under subsection (1) above if it is made more than six months after the termination of the relevant tenancy.

Date from which interim rent is payable

24B-(1) The interim rent determined on an application under section 24A(1) of this Act shall be payable from the appropriate date.

(2) If an application under section 24A(1) of this Act is made in a case where the landlord has given a notice under section 25 of this Act, the appropriate date is the earliest date of termination that could have been specified in the landlord's notice.

(3) If an application under section 24A(1) of this Act is made in a case where the tenant has made a request for a new tenancy under section 26 of this Act, the appropriate date is the earliest date that could have been specified in the tenant's request as the date from which the new tenancy is to begin.

Amount of interim rent where new tenancy of whole premises granted and landlord not opposed

24C-(1) This section applies where –

(a) the landlord gave a notice under section 25 of this Act at a time when the tenant was in occupation of the whole of the property comprised in the relevant tenancy for purposes such as are mentioned in section 23(1) of this Act and stated in the notice that he was not opposed to the grant of a new tenancy; or

(b) the tenant made a request for a new tenancy under section 26 of this Act at a time when he was in occupation of the whole of that property for such purposes and the landlord did not give notice under subsection (6) of that section,

and the landlord grants a new tenancy of the whole of the property comprised in the relevant tenancy to the tenant (whether as a result of an order for the grant of a new tenancy or otherwise).

(2) Subject to the following provisions of this section, the rent payable under and at the commencement of the new tenancy shall also be the interim rent.

(3) Subsection (2) above does not apply where –

(a) the landlord or the tenant shows to the satisfaction of the court that the interim rent under that subsection differs substantially from the relevant rent; or

(b) the landlord or the tenant shows to the satisfaction of the court that the terms of the new tenancy differ from the terms of the relevant tenancy to such an extent that the interim rent under that subsection is substantially different from the rent which (in default of such agreement) the court would have determined under section 34 of

143

this Act to be payable under a tenancy which commenced on the same day as the new tenancy and whose other terms were the same as the relevant tenancy.

(4) In this section 'the relevant rent' means the rent which (in default of agreement between the landlord and the tenant) the court would have determined under section 34 of this Act to be payable under the new tenancy if the new tenancy had commenced on the appropriate date (within the meaning of section 24B of this Act).

(5) The interim rent in a case where subsection (2) above does not apply by virtue only of subsection (3)(a) above is the relevant rent.

(6) The interim rent in a case where subsection (2) above does not apply by virtue only of subsection (3)(b) above, or by virtue of subsection (3)(a) and (b) above, is the rent which it is reasonable for the tenant to pay while the relevant tenancy continues by virtue of section 24 of this Act.

(7) In determining the interim rent under subsection (6) above the court shall have regard –

(a) to the rent payable under the terms of the relevant tenancy; and

(b) to the rent payable under any sub-tenancy of part of the property comprised in the relevant tenancy,

but otherwise subsections (1) and (2) of section 34 of this Act shall apply to the determination as they would apply to the determination of a rent under that section if a new tenancy of the whole of the property comprised in the relevant tenancy were granted to the tenant by order of the court and the duration of that new tenancy were the same as the duration of the new tenancy which is actually granted to the tenant.

(8) In this section and section 24D of this Act 'the relevant tenancy' has the same meaning as in section 24A of this Act.

Amount of interim rent in any other case

24D-(1) The interim rent in a case where section 24C of this Act does not apply is the rent which it is reasonable for the tenant to pay while the relevant tenancy continues by virtue of section 24 of this Act.

(2) In determining the interim rent under subsection (1) above the court shall have regard –

(a) to the rent payable under the terms of the relevant tenancy; and

(b) to the rent payable under any sub-tenancy of part of the property comprised in the relevant tenancy,

but otherwise subsections (1) and (2) of section 34 of this Act shall apply to the determination as they would apply to the determination of a rent under that section if a new tenancy from year to year of the whole of the property comprised in the relevant tenancy were granted to the tenant by order of the court.

(3) If the court –

(a) has made an order for the grant of a new tenancy and has ordered payment of interim rent in accordance with section 24C of this Act, but

(b) either –

(i) it subsequently revokes under section 36(2) of this Act the order for the grant of a new tenancy; or

(ii) the landlord and tenant agree not to act on the order,

the court on the application of the landlord or the tenant shall determine a new interim rent in accordance with subsections (1) and (2) above without a further application under section 24A(1) of this Act.

Termination of tenancy by the landlord

25-(1) The landlord may terminate a tenancy to which this Part of this Act applies by a notice given to the tenant in the prescribed form specifying the date at which the tenancy is to come to an end (hereinafter referred to as 'the date of termination'):

Provided that this subsection has effect subject to **the provisions of section 29B(4) of this Act and** Part IV of this Act as to the interim continuation of tenancies pending the disposal of applications to the court.

(2) Subject to the provisions of the next following subsection, a notice under this section shall not have effect unless it is given not more than twelve nor less than six months before the date of termination specified therein.

(3) In the case of a tenancy which apart from this Act could have been brought to an end by notice to quit given by the landlord –

(a) the date of termination specified in a notice under this section shall not be earlier than the earliest date on which apart from this Part of this Act the tenancy could have been brought to an end by notice to quit given by the landlord on the date of the giving of the notice under this section; and

(b) where apart from this Part of this Act more than six months' notice to quit would have been required to bring the tenancy to an end, the last foregoing subsection shall have effect with the substitution for twelve months of a period six months longer than the length of notice to quit which would have been required as aforesaid.

(4) In the case of any other tenancy, a notice under this section shall not specify a date of termination earlier than the date on which apart from this Part of this Act the tenancy would have come to an end by effluxion of time.

(5) A notice under this section shall not have effect unless it requires the tenant, within two months after the giving of the notice, to notify the landlord in writing whether or not, at the date of termination, the tenant will be willing to give up possession of the property comprised in the tenancy.

(6) A notice under this section shall not have effect unless it states whether the landlord would oppose an application to the court under this Part of this Act for the grant of a new tenancy and, if so, also states on which of the grounds mentioned in section 30 of this Act he would do so.

(6) A notice under this section shall not have effect unless it states whether the landlord is opposed to the grant of a new tenancy to the tenant.

(7) A notice under this section which states that the landlord is opposed to the grant of a new tenancy to the tenant shall not have effect unless it also specifies one or more of the grounds specified in section 30(1) of this Act as the ground or grounds for his opposition.

(8) A notice under this section which states that the landlord is not opposed to the grant of a new tenancy to the tenant shall not have effect unless it sets out the landlord's proposals as to –

(a) the property to be comprised in the new tenancy (being either the whole or part of the property comprised in the current tenancy);

(b) the rent to be payable under the new tenancy; and

(c) the other terms of the new tenancy.

Tenant's request for a new tenancy

26-(1) A tenant's request for a new tenancy may be made where the ~~tenancy under which he holds for the time being (hereinafter referred to as 'the current tenancy)~~ current tenancy is a tenancy granted for a term of years certain exceeding one year, whether or not continued by section 24 of this Act, or granted for a term of years certain and thereafter from year to year.

(2) A tenant's request for a new tenancy shall be for a tenancy beginning with such date, not more than twelve nor less than six months after the making of the request, as may be specified therein;

Provided that the said date shall not be earlier than the date on which apart from this Act the current tenancy would come to an end by effluxion of time or could be brought to an end by notice to quit given by the tenant.

(3) A tenant's request for a new tenancy shall not have effect unless it is made by notice in the prescribed form given to the landlord and sets out the tenant's proposals as to the property

to be comprised in the new tenancy (being either the whole or part of the property comprised in the current tenancy), as to the rent to be payable under the new tenancy and as to the other terms of the new tenancy.

(4) A tenant's request for a new tenancy shall not be made if the landlord has already given notice under the last foregoing section to terminate the current tenancy, or if the tenant has already given notice to quit or notice under the next following section; and no such notice shall be given by the landlord or the tenant after the making by the tenant of a request for a new tenancy.

(5) Where the tenant makes a request for a new tenancy in accordance with the foregoing provisions of this section, the current tenancy shall, subject to the provisions of ~~subsection (2) of section thirty-six~~ **sections 29B(4) and 36(2)** of this Act and the provisions of Part IV of this Act as to the interim continuation of tenancies, terminate immediately before the date specified in the request for the beginning of the new tenancy.

(6) Within two months of the making of a tenant's request for a new tenancy the landlord may give notice to the tenant that he will oppose an application to the court for the grant of a new tenancy, and any such notice shall state on which of the grounds mentioned in section 30 of this Act the landlord will oppose the application.

Termination by tenant of tenancy for fixed term

27-(1) Where the tenant under a tenancy to which this Part of this Act applies, being a tenancy granted for a term of years certain, gives to the immediate landlord, not later than three months before the date on which apart from this Act the tenancy would come to an end by effluxion of time, a notice in writing that the tenant does not desire the tenancy to be continued, section 24 of this Act shall not have effect in relation to the tenancy, unless the notice is given before the tenant has been in occupation in right of the tenancy for one month.

(1A) Section 24 of this Act shall not have effect in relation to a tenancy for a term of years certain where the tenant is not in occupation of the property comprised in the tenancy at the time when, apart from this Act, the tenancy would come to an end by effluxion of time.

(2) A tenancy granted for a term of years certain which is continuing by virtue of section 24 of this Act **shall not come to an end by reason only of the tenant ceasing to occupy the property comprised in the tenancy but** may be brought to an end on any ~~quarter~~ day by not less than three months' notice in writing given by the tenant to the immediate landlord, whether the notice is given after the date on which apart from this Act the tenancy would have come to an end or before that date, but not before the tenant has been in occupation in right of the tenancy for one month.

(3) Where a tenancy is terminated under subsection (2) above, any rent payable in respect of a period which begins before, and ends after, the tenancy is terminated shall be apportioned, and any rent paid by the tenant in excess of the amount apportioned to the period before termination shall be recoverable by him.

Renewal of tenancies by agreement

28 Where the landlord and tenant agree for the grant to the tenant of a future tenancy of the holding, or of the holding with other land, on terms and from a date specified in the agreement, the current tenancy shall continue until that date but no longer, and shall not be a tenancy to which this Part of this Act applies.

~~*Application to court for new tenancies*~~

Order by court for grant of a new tenancy

~~29-(1) Subject to the provisions of this Act, on an application under subsection (1) of section 24 of this Act for a new tenancy the court shall make an order for the grant of a tenancy comprising such property, at such rent and on such other terms, as are hereinafter provided.~~

~~(2) Where such an application is made in consequence of a notice given by the landlord under section 25 of this Act, it shall not be entertained unless the tenant has duly notified the landlord that he will not be willing at the date of termination to give up possession of the property comprised in the tenancy.~~

~~(3) No application under subsection (1) of section 24 of this Act shall be entertained unless it is made not less than two nor more than four months after the giving of the landlord's notice~~

~~under section 25 of this Act or, as the case may be, after the making of the tenant's request for a new tenancy.~~

Applications to court

Order by court for grant of new tenancy or termination of current tenancy

29-(1) Subject to the provisions of this Act, on an application under section 24(1) of this Act, the court shall make an order for the grant of a new tenancy and accordingly for the termination of the current tenancy immediately before the commencement of the new tenancy.

(2) Subject to the following provisions of this Act, a landlord may apply to the court for an order for the termination of a tenancy to which this Part of this Act applies without the grant of a new tenancy –

(a) if he has given notice under section 25 of this Act that he is opposed to the grant of a new tenancy to the tenant; or

(b) if the tenant has made a request for a new tenancy in accordance with section 26 of this Act and the landlord has given notice under subsection (6) of that section.

(3) The landlord may not make an application under subsection (2) above if either the tenant or the landlord has made an application under section 24(1) of this Act.

(4) Subject to the provisions of this Act, where the landlord makes an application under subsection (2) above –

(a) if he establishes, to the satisfaction of the court, any of the grounds on which he is entitled to make the application in accordance with section 30 of this Act, the court shall make an order for the termination of the current tenancy <u>in accordance with section 64 of this Act</u> without the grant of a new tenancy; and

(b) if not, it shall make an order for the grant of a new tenancy and accordingly for the termination of the current tenancy immediately before the commencement of the new tenancy.

(5) The court shall dismiss an application by the landlord under section 24(1) of this Act if the tenant informs the court that he does not want a new tenancy.

(6) The landlord may not withdraw an application under subsection (2) above unless the tenant consents to its withdrawal.

Time limits for applications to court

29A-(1) Subject to section 29B of this Act, the court shall not entertain an application –

(a) by the tenant or the landlord under section 24(1) of this Act; or

(b) by the landlord under section 29(2) of this Act,

if it is made after the end of the statutory period.

(2) In this section and section 29B of this Act 'the statutory period' means a period ending –

(a) where the landlord gave a notice under section 25 of this Act, on the date specified in his notice; and

(b) where the tenant made a request for a new tenancy under section 26 of this Act, immediately before the date specified in his request.

(3) Where the tenant has made a request for a new tenancy under section 26 of this Act, the court shall not entertain an application under section 24(1) of this Act which is made before the end of the period of two months beginning with the date of the making of the request, unless the application is made after the landlord has given a notice under section 26(6) of this Act.

Agreements extending time limits

29B-(1) After the landlord has given a notice under section 25 of this Act, or the tenant has made a request under section 26 of this Act, but before the end of the statutory period, the landlord and tenant may agree that an application such as is mentioned in section 29A(1) of this Act may be made before the end of a period specified in the agreement which will expire after the end of the statutory period.

(2) The landlord and tenant may from time to time by agreement further extend the period for making such an application, but any such agreement must be made before the end of the period specified in the current agreement.

(3) Where an agreement is made under this section, the court may entertain an application such as is mentioned in section 29A(1) of this Act if it is made before the end of the period specified in the agreement.

(4) Where an agreement is made under this section, or two or more agreements are made under this section, the landlord's notice under section 25 of this Act or tenant's request under section 26 of this Act shall be treated as terminating the tenancy at the end of the period specified in the agreement or, as the case may be, at the end of the period specified in the last of those agreements.

Opposition by landlord to application for new tenancy

30-(1) The grounds on which a landlord may oppose an application under ~~subsection (1) of section twenty-four of this Act~~ **section 24(1) of this Act, or make an application under section 29(2) of this Act,** are such of the following grounds as may be stated in the landlord's notice under section 25 of this Act or, as the case may be, under subsection (6) of section 26 thereof, that is to say –

(a) where under the current tenancy the tenant has any obligations as respects the repair and maintenance of the holding, that the tenant ought not to be granted a new tenancy in view of the state of repair of the holding, being a state resulting from the tenant's failure to comply with the said obligations;

(b) that the tenant ought not to be granted a new tenancy in view of his persistent delay in paying rent which has become due;

(c) that the tenant ought not to be granted a new tenancy in view of other substantial breaches by him of his obligations under the current tenancy, or for any other reason connected with the tenant's use or management of the holding;

(d) that the landlord has offered and is willing to provide or secure the provision of alternative accommodation for the tenant, that the terms on which the alternative accommodation is available are reasonable having regard to the terms of the current tenancy and to all other relevant circumstances, and that the accommodation and the time at which it will be available are suitable for the tenant's requirements (including the requirement to preserve goodwill) having regard to the nature and class of his business and to the situation and extent of, and facilities afforded by, the holding;

(e) where the current tenancy was created by the sub-letting of part only of the property comprised in a superior tenancy and the landlord is the owner of an interest in reversion expectant on the termination of that superior tenancy, that the aggregate of the rents reasonably obtainable on separate lettings of the holding and the remainder of that property would be substantially less than the rent reasonably obtainable on a letting of that property as a whole, that on the termination of the current tenancy the landlord requires possession of the holding for the purpose of letting or otherwise disposing of the said property as a whole, and that in view thereof the tenant ought not to be granted a new tenancy;

(f) that on the termination of the current tenancy the landlord intends to demolish or reconstruct the premises comprised in the holding or a substantial part of those premises or to carry out substantial work of construction on the holding or part thereof and that he could not reasonably do so without obtaining possession of the holding;

(g) subject as hereinafter provided, that on the termination of the current tenancy the landlord intends to occupy the holding for the purposes, or partly for the purposes, of a business to be carried on by him therein, or as his residence.

(1A) Where the landlord has a controlling interest in a company, the reference in subsection (1)(g) above to the landlord shall be construed as a reference to the landlord or that company.

(1B) Subject to subsection (2A) below, where the landlord is a company and a person has a controlling interest in the company, the reference in subsection (1)(g) above to the landlord shall be construed as a reference to the landlord or that person.

(2) The landlord shall not be entitled to oppose an application under **section 24(1) of this Act, or make an application under section 29(2) of this Act**, on the ground specified in paragraph (g) of the last foregoing subsection if the interest of the landlord, or an interest which has merged in that interest and but for the merger would be the interest of the landlord, was purchased or created after the beginning of the period of five years which ends with the termination of the current tenancy, and at all times since the purchase or creation thereof the holding has been comprised in a tenancy or successive tenancies of the description specified in subsection (1) of section 23 of this Act.

(2A) Subsection (1B) above shall not apply if the controlling interest was acquired after the beginning of the period of five years which ends with the termination of the current tenancy, and at all times since the acquisition of the controlling interest the holding has been comprised in a tenancy or successive tenancies of the description specified in section 23(1) of this Act.

~~(3) Where the landlord has a controlling interest in a company any business to be carried on by the company shall be treated for the purposes of subsection (1) (g) of this section as a business to be carried on by him.~~

~~For the purposes of this subsection, a person has a controlling interest in a company if and only if either –~~

~~a) he is a member of it and able, without the consent of any other person, to appoint or remove the holders of at least a majority of the directorships; or~~

~~(b) he holds more than one half of its equity share capital, there being disregarded any shares held by him in a fiduciary capacity or as nominee for another person;~~

~~and in this subsection 'company' and 'share' have the meanings assigned to them by section 455(1) of the Companies Act 1948 and 'equity share capital' the meaning assigned to it by section 154(5) of that Act.~~

Dismissal of application for new tenancy where landlord successfully opposes

31-(1) If the landlord opposes an application under subsection (1) of section 24 of this Act on grounds on which he is entitled to oppose it in accordance with the last foregoing section and establishes any of those grounds to the satisfaction of the court, the court shall not make an order for the grant of a new tenancy.

(2) **Where the landlord opposes an application under section 24(1) of this Act, or makes an application under section 29(2) of this Act, on one or more of the grounds specified in section 30(1)(d) to (f) of this Act but establishes none of those grounds, and none of the other grounds specified in section 30(1) of this Act, to the satisfaction of the court, then if the court would have been satisfied on any of the grounds specified in section 30(1)(d) to (f) of this Act** ~~Where in a case not falling within the last foregoing subsection the landlord opposes an application under the said subsection (1) on one or more of the grounds specified in paragraphs (d), (e) and (f) of subsection (1) of the last foregoing section but establishes none of those grounds to the satisfaction of the court, then if the court would have been satisfied of any of those grounds~~ if the date of termination specified in the landlord's notice or, as the case may be, the date specified in the tenant's request for a new tenancy as the date from which the new tenancy is to begin, had been such later date as the court may determine, being a date not more than one year later than the date so specified, –

(a) the court shall make a declaration to that effect, stating of which of the said grounds the court would have been satisfied as aforesaid and specifying the date determined by the court as aforesaid, but shall not make an order for the grant of a new tenancy;

(b) if, within fourteen days after the making of the declaration, the tenant so requires the court shall make an order substituting the said date for the date specified in the said landlord's notice or tenant's request, and thereupon that notice or request shall have effect accordingly.

Grant of new tenancy in some cases where section 30(1)(f) applies

31A-(1) Where the landlord opposes an application under section 24(1) of this Act on the ground specified in paragraph (f) of section 30(1) of this Act, **or makes an application under section 29(2) of this Act on that ground,** the court shall not hold that the landlord could not reasonably carry out the demolition, reconstruction or work of construction intended without obtaining possession of the holding if –

(a) the tenant agrees to the inclusion in the terms of the new tenancy of terms giving the landlord access and other facilities for carrying out the work intended and, given that access and those facilities, the landlord could reasonably carry out the work without obtaining possession of the holding and without interfering to a substantial extent or for a substantial time with the use of the holding for the purposes of the business carried on by the tenant; or

(b) the tenant is willing to accept a tenancy of an economically separable part of the holding and either paragraph (a) of this section is satisfied with respect to that part or possession of the remainder of the holding would be reasonably sufficient to enable the landlord to carry out the intended work.

(2) For the purposes of subsection (1) (b) of this section a part of a holding shall be deemed to be an economically separate part if, and only if, the aggregate of the rents which, after the completion' of the intended work, would be reasonably obtainable on separate lettings of that part and the remainder of the premises affected by or resulting from the work would not be substantially less than the rent which would then be reasonably obtainable on a letting of those premises as a whole.

Property to be comprised in new tenancy

32-(1) Subject to the following provisions of this section, an order under section 29 of this Act for the grant of a new tenancy shall be an order for the grant of a new tenancy of the holding; and in the absence of agreement between the landlord and the tenant as to the property which constitutes the holding the court shall in the order designate that property by reference to the circumstances existing at the date of the order.

(1A) Where the court, by virtue of paragraph (b) of section 31A(1) of this Act, makes an order under section 29 of this Act for the grant of a new tenancy in a case where the tenant is willing to accept a tenancy of part of the holding, the order shall be an order for the grant of a new tenancy of that part only.

(2) The foregoing provisions of this section shall not apply in a case where the property comprised in the current tenancy includes other property besides the holding and the landlord requires any new tenancy ordered to be granted under section 29 of this Act to be a tenancy of the whole of the property comprised in the current tenancy; but in any such case –

(a) any order under the said section 29 for the grant of a new tenancy shall be an order for the grant of a new tenancy of the whole of the property comprised in the current tenancy, and

(b) references in the following provisions of this Part of this Act to the holding shall be construed as references to the whole of that property.

(3) Where the current tenancy includes rights enjoyed by the tenant in connection with the holding, those rights shall be included in a tenancy ordered to be granted under section 29 of this Act, except as otherwise agreed between the landlord and the tenant or, in default of such agreement, determined by the court.

Duration of new tenancy

33. Where on an application under this Part of this Act the court makes an order for the grant of a new tenancy, the new tenancy shall be such tenancy as may be agreed between the landlord and the tenant, or, in default of such an agreement, shall be such a tenancy as may be determined by the court to be reasonable in all the circumstances, being, if it is a tenancy for a term of years certain, a tenancy for a term not exceeding ~~fourteen~~ **fifteen** years, and shall begin on the coming to an end of the current tenancy.

Rent under new tenancy

34-(1) The rent payable under a tenancy granted by order of the court under this Part of this Act shall be such as may be agreed between the landlord and the tenant or as, in default of such agreement, may be determined by the court to be that at which, having regard to the terms of the tenancy (other than those relating to rent), the holding might reasonably be expected to be let in the open market by a willing lessor, there being disregarded –

(a) any effect on rent of the fact that the tenant has or his predecessors in title have been in occupation of the holding,

(b) any goodwill attached to the holding by reason of the carrying on thereat of the business of the tenant (whether by him or by a predecessor of his in that business),

(c) any effect on rent of an improvement to which this paragraph applies,

(d) in the case of a holding comprising licensed premises, any addition to its value attributable to the licence, if it appears to the court that having regard to the terms of the current tenancy and any other relevant circumstances the benefit of the licence belongs to the tenant.

(2) Paragraph (c) of the foregoing subsection applies to any improvement carried out by a person who at the time it was carried out was the tenant, but only if it was carried out otherwise than in pursuance of an obligation to his immediate landlord, and either it was carried out during the current tenancy or the following conditions are satisfied, that is to say –

(a) that it was completed not more than twenty-one years before the application ~~for the new tenancy~~ **to the court** was made; and

(b) that the holding or any part of it affected by the improvement has at all times since the completion of the improvement been comprised in tenancies of the description specified in section 23(1) of this Act; and

(c) that at the termination of each of those tenancies the tenant did not quit.

(2A) If this Part of this Act applies by virtue of section 23(1A) of this Act, the reference in subsection (1)(d) above to the tenant shall be construed as including –

(a) a company in which the tenant has a controlling interest, or

(b) where the tenant is a company, a person with a controlling interest in the company.

(3) Where the rent is determined by the court the court may, if it thinks fit, further determine that the terms of the tenancy shall include such provision for varying the rent as may be specified in the determination.

(4) It is hereby declared that the matters which are to be taken into account by the court in determining the rent include any effect on rent of the operation of the provisions of the Landlord and Tenant (Covenants) Act 1995.

Other terms of new tenancy

35-(1) The terms of a tenancy granted by order of the court under this Part of this Act (other than terms as to the duration thereof and as to the rent payable thereunder), **including, where different persons own interests which fulfil the conditions specified in section 44(1) of this Act in different parts of it, terms as to the apportionment of the rent,** shall be such as may be agreed between the landlord and the tenant or as, in default of such agreement, may be determined by the court; and in determining those terms the court shall have regard to the terms of the current tenancy and to all relevant circumstances.

(2) In subsection (1) of this section the reference to all relevant circumstances includes (without prejudice to the generality of that reference) a reference to the operation of the provisions of the Landlord and Tenant (Covenants) Act 1995.

Carrying out of order for new tenancy

36-(1) Where under this Part of this Act the court makes an order for the grant of a new tenancy, then, unless the order is revoked under the next following subsection or the landlord and the tenant agree not to act upon the order, the landlord shall be bound to execute or make in favour of the tenant, and the tenant shall be bound to accept, a lease or agreement for a tenancy of the holding embodying the terms agreed between the landlord and the tenant or determined by the court in accordance with the foregoing provisions of this Part of this Act; and

where the landlord executes or makes such a lease or agreement the tenant shall be bound, if so required by the landlord, to execute a counterpart or duplicate thereof.

(2) If the tenant, within fourteen days after the making of an order under this Part of this Act for the grant of a new tenancy, applies to the court for the revocation of the order the court shall revoke the order; and where the order is so revoked, then, if it is so agreed between the landlord and the tenant or determined by the court, the current tenancy shall continue, beyond the date at which it would have come to an end apart from this subsection, for such period as may be so agreed or determined to be necessary to afford to the landlord a reasonable opportunity for reletting or otherwise disposing of the premises which would have been comprised in the new tenancy; and while the current tenancy continues by virtue of this subsection it shall not be a tenancy to which this Part of this Act applies.

(3) Where an order is revoked under the last foregoing subsection any provision thereof as to payment of costs shall not cease to have effect by reason only of the revocation; but the court may, if it thinks fit, revoke or vary any such provision or, where no costs have been awarded in the proceedings for the revoked order, award such costs.

(4) A lease executed or agreement made under this section, in a case where the interest of the lessor is subject to a mortgage, shall be deemed to be one authorised by section 99 of the Law of Property Act 1925 (which confers certain powers of leasing on mortgagors in possession), and subsection (13) of that section (which allows those powers to be restricted or excluded by agreement) shall not have effect in relation to such a lease or agreement.

Compensation where order for new tenancy precluded on certain grounds

~~37-(1) Where on the making of an application under section 24 of this Act the court is precluded (whether by subsection (1) or subsection (2) of section 31 of this Act) from making an order for the grant of a new tenancy by reason of any of the grounds specified in paragraphs (e), (f) and (g) of subsection (1) of section 30 of this Act and not of any grounds specified in any other paragraph of that subsection, or where no other ground is specified in the landlord's notice under section 25 of this Act or, as the case may be, under section 26(6) thereof, than those specified in the said paragraphs (e), (f) and (g) and either no application under the said section 24 is made or such an application is withdrawn, then, subject to the provisions of this Act, the tenant shall be entitled on quitting the holding to recover from the landlord by way of compensation an amount determined in accordance with the following provisions of this section.~~

37-(1) Subject to the provisions of this Act, in a case specified in subsection (1A), (1B) or (1C) below (a 'compensation case') the tenant shall be entitled on quitting the holding to recover from the landlord by way of compensation an amount determined in accordance with this section.

(1A) The first compensation case is where on the making of an application by the tenant under section 24(1) of this Act the court is precluded (whether by subsection (1) or subsection (2) of section 31 of this Act) from making an order for the grant of a new tenancy by reason of any of the grounds specified in paragraphs (e), (f) and (g) of section 30(1) of this Act (the 'compensation grounds') and not of any grounds specified in any other paragraph of section 30(1).

(1B) The second compensation case is where on the making of an application under section 29(2) of this Act the court is precluded (whether by section 29(4)(a) or section 31(2) of this Act) from making an order for the grant of a new tenancy by reason of any of the compensation grounds and not of any other grounds specified in section 30(1) of this Act.

(1C) The third compensation case is where –

(a) the landlord's notice under section 25 of this Act or, as the case may be, under section 26(6) of this Act, states his opposition to the grant of a new tenancy on any of the compensation grounds and not on any other grounds specified in section 30(1) of this Act; and

(b) either –

(i) no application is made by the tenant under section 24(1) of this Act or by the landlord under section 29(2) of this Act; or

(ii) such an application is made but is subsequently withdrawn.

(2) Subject to ~~subsections (5A) to (5E) of this section the said amount~~ **the following provisions of this section, compensation under this section** shall be as follows, that is to say –

(a) where the conditions specified in the next following subsection are satisfied **in relation to the whole of the holding** it shall be the product of the appropriate multiplier and twice the rateable value of the holding,

(b) in any other case it shall be the product of the appropriate multiplier and the rateable value of the holding.

(3) The said conditions are –

(a) that, during the whole of the fourteen years immediately preceding the termination of the current tenancy, premises being or comprised in the holding have been occupied for the purposes of a business carried on by the occupier or for those and other purposes;

(b) that, if during those fourteen years there was a change in the occupier of the premises, the person who was the occupier immediately after the change was the successor to the business carried on by the person who was the occupier immediately before the change.

(3A) If the conditions specified in subsection (3) above are satisfied in relation to part of the holding but not in relation to the other part, the amount of compensation shall be the aggregate of sums calculated separately as compensation in respect of each part, and accordingly, for the purpose of calculating compensation in respect of a part any reference in this section to the holding shall be construed as a reference to that part.

(3B) Where section 44(1A) of this Act applies, the compensation shall be determined separately for each part and compensation determined for any part shall be recoverable only from the person who is the owner of an interest in that part which fulfils the conditions specified in section 44(1) of this Act.

(4) Where the court is precluded from making an order for the grant of a new tenancy under this Part of this Act in ~~the circumstances mentioned in subsection (1) of this section~~ a **compensation case**, the court shall on the application of the tenant certify that fact.

(5) For the purposes of subsection (2) of this section the rateable value of the holding shall be determined as follows –

(a) where in the valuation list in force at the date on which the landlord's notice under section 25 or, as the case may be, subsection (6) of section 26 of this Act is given a value is then shown as the annual value (as hereinafter defined) of the holding, the rateable value of the holding shall be taken to be that value;

(b) where no such value is so shown with respect to the holding but such a value or such values is or are so shown with respect to premises comprised in or comprising the holding or part of it, the rateable value of the holding shall be taken to be such value as is found by a proper apportionment or aggregation of the value or values so shown;

(c) where the rateable value of the holding cannot be ascertained in accordance with the foregoing paragraphs of this subsection, it shall be taken to be the value which, apart from any exemption from assessment to rates, would on a proper assessment be the value to be entered in the said valuation list as the annual value of the holding;

and any dispute arising, whether in proceedings before the court or otherwise, as to the determination for those purposes of the rateable value of the holding shall be referred to the Commissioners of Inland Revenue for decision by the valuation officer.

An appeal shall lie to the Lands Tribunal from any decision of a valuation officer under this subsection, but subject thereto any such decision shall be final.

(5A) If part of the holding is domestic property, as defined in section 66 of the Local Government Finance Act 1988 –

(a) the domestic property shall be disregarded in determining the rateable value of the holding under subsection (5) of this section; and

(b) if, on the date specified in subsection (5) (a) of this section, the tenant occupied the whole or any part of the domestic property, the amount of compensation to which he is entitled under subsection (1) of this section shall be increased by the addition of a sum equal to his reasonable expenses in removing from the domestic property.

(5B) Any question as to the amount of the sum referred to in paragraph (b) of subsection (5A) of this section shall be determined by agreement between the landlord and the tenant or, in default of agreement, by the court.

(5C) If the whole of the holding is domestic property, as defined in section 66 of the Local Government Finance Act 1988, for the purposes of subsection (2) of this section the rateable value of the holding shall be taken to be an amount equal to the rent at which it is estimated the holding might reasonably be expected to let from year to year if the tenant undertook to pay all usual tenant's rates and taxes and to bear the cost of the repairs and insurance and the other expenses (if any) necessary to maintain the holding in a state to command that rent.

(5D) The following provisions shall have effect as regards a determination of an amount mentioned in subsection (5C) of this section-(

(a) the date by reference to which such a determination is to be made is the date on which the landlord's notice under section 25 or, as the case may be, subsection (6) of section 26 of this Act is given;

(b) any dispute arising, whether in proceedings before the court or otherwise, as to such a determination shall be referred to the Commissioners of Inland Revenue for decision by a valuation officer;

(c) an appeal shall lie to the Lands Tribunal from such a decision, but subject to that, such a decision shall be final.

(5E) Any deduction made under paragraph 2A of Schedule 6 to the Local Government Finance Act 1988 (deduction from valuation of hereditaments used for breeding horses etc) shall be disregarded, to the extent that it relates to the holding, in determining the rateable value of the holding under subsection (5) of this section.

(6) The Commissioners of Inland Revenue may by statutory instrument make rules prescribing the procedure in connection with references under this section.

(7) In this section –

the reference to the termination of the current tenancy is a reference to the date of termination specified in the landlord's notice under section 25 of this Act or, as the case may be, the date specified in the tenant's request for a new tenancy as the date from which the new tenancy is to begin;

the expression 'annual value' means rateable value except that where the rateable value differs from the net annual value the said expression means net annual value;

the expression 'valuation officer' means any officer of the Commissioners of Inland Revenue for the time being authorised by a certificate of the Commissioners to act in relation to a valuation list.

(8) In subsection (2) of this section 'the appropriate multiplier' means such multiplier as the Secretary of State may by order made by statutory instrument prescribe and different multipliers may be so prescribed in relation to different cases.

(9) A statutory instrument containing an order under subsection (8) of this section shall be subject to annulment in pursuance of a resolution of either House of Parliament.

Compensation for possession obtained by misrepresentation

37A-(1) Where the court –

(a) makes an order for the termination of the current tenancy but does not make an order for the grant of a new tenancy, or

(b) refuses an order for the grant of a new tenancy,

and it is subsequently made to appear to the court that the order was obtained, or the court was induced to refuse the grant, by misrepresentation or the concealment of material facts, the court may order the landlord to pay to the tenant such sum as appears sufficient as compensation for damage or loss sustained by the tenant as the result of the order or refusal.

(2) Where –

(a) the tenant has quit the holding –

(i) after making but withdrawing an application under section 24(1) of this Act; or

(ii) without making such an application; and

(b) it is made to appear to the court that he did so by reason of misrepresentation or the concealment of material facts,

the court may order the landlord to pay to the tenant such sum as appears sufficient as compensation for damage or loss sustained by the tenant as the result of quitting the holding.

Restriction on agreements excluding provisions of Part II

38-(1) Any agreement relating to a tenancy to which this Part of this Act applies (whether contained in the instrument creating the tenancy or not) shall be void (except as provided by ~~subsection (4) of this section~~ **section 38A of this Act**) in so far as it purports to preclude the tenant from making an application or request under this Part of this Act or provides for the termination or the surrender of the tenancy in the event of his making such an application or request or for the imposition of any penalty or disability on the tenant in that event.

(2) Where –

(a) during the whole of the five years immediately preceding the date on which the tenant under a tenancy to which this Part of this Act applies is to quit the holding, premises being or comprised in the holding have been occupied for the purposes of a business carried on by the occupier or for those and other purposes, and

(b) if during those five years there was a change in the occupier of the premises, the person who was the occupier immediately after the change was the successor to the business carried on by the person who was the occupier immediately before the change,

any agreement (whether contained in the instrument creating the tenancy or not and whether made before or after the termination of that tenancy) which purports to exclude or reduce compensation under ~~the last foregoing section~~ **section 37 of this Act** shall to that extent be void, so however that this subsection shall not affect any agreement as to the amount of any such compensation which is made after the right to compensation has accrued.

(3) In a case not falling within the last foregoing subsection the right to compensation conferred by ~~the last foregoing section~~ **section 37 of this Act** may be excluded or modified by agreement.

~~(4) The court may –~~

~~(a) on the joint application of the persons who will be the landlord and the tenant in relation to a tenancy to be granted for a term of years certain which will be a tenancy to which this Part of this Act applies, authorise an agreement excluding in relation to that tenancy the provisions of sections 24 to 28 of this Act; and~~

~~(b) on the joint application of the persons who are the landlord and the tenant in relation to a tenancy to which this Part of this Act applies, authorise an agreement for the surrender of the tenancy on such date or in such circumstances as may be specified in the agreement and on such terms (if any) as may be so specified;~~

~~if the agreement is contained in or endorsed on the instrument creating the tenancy or such other instrument as the court may specify; and an agreement contained in or endorsed on an instrument in pursuance of an authorisation given under this subsection shall be valid notwithstanding anything in the preceding provisions of this section.~~

Agreements to exclude provisions of Part II

38A-(1) The persons who will be the landlord and the tenant in relation to a tenancy to be granted for a term of years certain which will be a tenancy to which this Part of this Act applies may agree that the provisions of sections 24 to 28 of this Act shall be excluded in relation to that tenancy.

(2) The persons who are the landlord and the tenant in relation to a tenancy to which this Part of this Act applies may agree that the tenancy shall be surrendered on such date or in such circumstances as may be specified in the agreement and on such terms (if any) as may be so specified.

(3) An agreement under subsection (1) above shall be void unless –

(a) the landlord has served on the tenant a notice in the form, or substantially in the form, set out in Schedule 1 to the Regulatory Reform (Business Tenancies) (England and Wales) Order 2003 ('the 2003 Order'); and

(b) the requirements specified in Schedule 2 to that Order are met.

(4) An agreement under subsection (2) above shall be void unless-(

(a) the landlord has served on the tenant a notice in the form, or substantially in the form, set out in Schedule 3 to the 2003 Order; and

(b) the requirements specified in Schedule 4 to that Order are met.'

General and supplementary provisions

Saving for compulsory acquisitions

39-(1) [Repealed]

(2) If the amount of the compensation which would have been payable under section 37 of this Act if the tenancy had come to an end in circumstances giving rise to compensation under that section and the date at which the acquiring authority obtained possession had been the termination of the current tenancy exceeds the amount of the compensation payable under section 121 of the Lands Clauses Consolidation Act 1845, or section 20 of the Compulsory Purchase Act 1965, in the case of a tenancy to which this Part of this Act applies, that compensation shall be increased by the amount of the excess.

(3) Nothing in section 24 of this Act shall affect the operation of the said section 121.

Duty of tenants and landlords of business premises to give information to each other

~~40-(1) Where any person having an interest in any business premises, being an interest in reversion expectant (whether immediately or not) on a tenancy of those premises, serves on the tenant a notice in the prescribed form requiring him to do so, it shall be the duty of the tenant to notify that person in writing within one month of the service of the notice –~~

~~(a) whether he occupies the premises or any part thereof wholly or partly for the purposes of a business carried on him, and~~

~~(b) whether his tenancy has effect subject to any sub-tenancy on which his tenancy is immediately expectant and, if so, what premises are comprised in the sub-tenancy, for what term it has effect (or, if it is terminable by notice, by what notice it can be terminated), what is the rent payable thereunder, who is the sub-tenant, and (to the best of his knowledge and belief) whether the sub-tenant is in occupation of the premises or of part of the premises comprised in the sub-tenancy and, if not, what is the sub-tenant's address.~~

~~(2) Where the tenant of any business premises, being a tenant under such a tenancy as is mentioned in subsection (1) of section 26 of this Act, service on any persons mentioned in the next following subsection a notice in the prescribed form requiring him to do so, it shall be the duty of that person to notify the tenant in writing within one month after the service of the notice –~~

~~(a) whether he is the owner of the fee simple in respect of those premises or any part thereof or the mortgagee in possession of such an owner and, if not,~~

~~(b) (to the best of his knowledge and belief) the name and address of the person who is his or, as the case may be, his mortgagor's immediate landlord in respect of those premises or of the part in respect of which he or his mortgagor is not the owner in fee simple, for what term his or his mortgagor's tenancy thereof has effect and what is the earliest date (if any) at which that tenancy is terminable by notice to quit given by the landlord.~~

~~(3) The persons referred to in the last foregoing subsection are, in relation to the tenant of any business premises –~~

~~(a) any person having an interest in the premises, being an interest in reversion expectant (whether immediately or not) on the tenant's, and~~

~~(b) any person being a mortgagee in possession in respect of such an interest in reversion as is mentioned in paragraph (a) of this subsection;~~

~~and the information which any such person as is mentioned in paragraph (a) of this sub-section is required to give under the last foregoing subsection shall include information whether there is a mortgagee in possession of his interest in the premises and, if so, what is the name and address of the mortgagee.~~

~~(4) The foregoing provisions of this section shall not apply to a notice served by or on the tenant more than two years before the date on which apart from this Act his tenancy would come to an end by effluxion of time or could be brought to an end by notice to quit given by the landlord.~~

~~(5) In this section –~~

~~the expression 'business premises' means premises used wholly or partly for the purposes of a business;~~

~~the expression 'mortgagee in possession' includes a receiver appointed by the mortgagee or by the court who is in receipt of the rents and profits, and the expression 'his mortgagor' shall be construed accordingly;~~

~~the expression 'sub-tenant' includes a person retaining possession of any premises by virtue of the Rent Act 1977 after the coming to an end of a sub-tenancy, and the expression 'sub-tenancy' includes a right so to retain possession.~~

40-(1) Where a person who is an owner of an interest in reversion expectant (whether immediately or not) on a tenancy of any business premises has served on the tenant a notice in the prescribed form requiring him to do so, it shall be the duty of the tenant to give the appropriate person in writing the information specified in subsection (2) below.

(2) That information is –

(a) whether the tenant occupies the premises or any part of them wholly or partly for the purposes of a business carried on by him;

(b) whether his tenancy has effect subject to any sub-tenancy on which his tenancy is immediately expectant and, if so –

(i) what premises are comprised in the sub-tenancy;

(ii) for what term it has effect (or, if it is terminable by notice, by what notice it can be terminated);

(iii) what is the rent payable under it;

(iv) who is the sub-tenant;

(v) (to the best of his knowledge and belief) whether the sub-tenant is in occupation of the premises or of part of the premises comprised in the sub-tenancy and, if not, what is the sub-tenant's address;

(vi) whether an agreement is in force excluding in relation to the sub-tenancy the provisions of sections 24 to 28 of this Act; and

(vii) whether a notice has been given under section 25 or 26(6) of this Act, or a request has been made under section 26 of this Act, in relation to the sub-tenancy and, if so, details of the notice or request; and

(c) (to the best of his knowledge and belief) the name and address of any other person who owns an interest in reversion in any part of the premises.

(3) Where the tenant of any business premises who is a tenant under such a tenancy as is mentioned in section 26(1) of this Act has served on a reversioner or a reversioner's mortgagee in possession a notice in the prescribed form requiring him to do so, it shall be the duty of the person on whom the notice is served to give the appropriate person in writing the information specified in subsection (4) below.

(4) That information is –

(a) whether he is the owner of the fee simple in respect of the premises or any part of them or the mortgagee in possession of such an owner,

(b) if he is not, then (to the best of his knowledge and belief) –

(i) the name and address of the person who is his or, as the case may be, his mortgagor's immediate landlord in respect of those premises or of the part in respect of which he or his mortgagor is not the owner in fee simple;

(ii) for what term his or his mortgagor's tenancy has effect and what is the earliest date (if any) at which that tenancy is terminable by notice to quit given by the landlord; and

(iii) whether a notice has been given under section 25 or 26(6) of this Act, or a request has been made under section 26 of this Act, in relation to the tenancy and, if so, details of the notice or request;

(c) (to the best of his knowledge and belief) the name and address of any other person who owns an interest in reversion in any part of the premises; and

(d) if he is a reversioner, whether there is a mortgagee in possession of his interest in the premises and, if so, (to the best of his knowledge and belief) what is the name and address of the mortgagee.

(5) A duty imposed on a person by this section is a duty –

(a) to give the information concerned within the period of one month beginning with the date of service of the notice; and

(b) if within the period of six months beginning with the date of service of the notice that person becomes aware that any information which has been given in pursuance of the notice is not, or is no longer, correct, to give the appropriate person correct information within the period of one month beginning with the date on which he becomes aware.

(6) This section shall not apply to a notice served by or on the tenant more than two years before the date on which apart from this Act his tenancy would come to an end by effluxion of time or could be brought to an end by notice to quit given by the landlord.

(7) Except as provided by section 40A of this Act, the appropriate person for the purposes of this section and section 40A(1) of this Act is the person who served the notice under subsection (1) or (3) above.

(8) In this section –

'business premises' means premises used wholly or partly for the purposes of a business;

'mortgagee in possession' includes a receiver appointed by the mortgagee or by the court who is in receipt of the rents and profits, and 'his mortgagor' shall be construed accordingly;

'reversioner' means any person having an interest in the premises, being an interest in reversion expectant (whether immediately or not) on the tenancy;

'reversioner's mortgagee in possession' means any person being a mortgagee in possession in respect of such an interest; and

'sub-tenant' includes a person retaining possession of any premises by virtue of the Rent (Agriculture) Act 1976 or the Rent Act 1977 after the coming to an end of a sub-tenancy, and 'sub-tenancy' includes a right so to retain possession.'.

Duties in transfer cases

40A-(1) If a person on whom a notice under section 40(1) or (3) of this Act has been served has transferred his interest in the premises or any part of them to some other person and gives the appropriate person notice in writing –

(a) of the transfer of his interest; and

(b) of the name and address of the person to whom he transferred it, on giving the notice he ceases in relation to the premises or (as the case may be) to that part to be under any duty imposed by section 40 of this Act.

(2) If –

(a) the person who served the notice under section 40(1) or (3) of this Act ('the transferor') has transferred his interest in the premises to some other person ('the transferee'); and

(b) the transferor or the transferee has given the person required to give the information notice in writing –

(i) of the transfer; and

(ii) of the transferee's name and address,

the appropriate person for the purposes of section 40 of this Act and subsection (1) above is the transferee.

(3) If –

(a) a transfer such as is mentioned in paragraph (a) of subsection (2) above has taken place; but

(b) neither the transferor nor the transferee has given a notice such as is mentioned in paragraph (b) of that subsection, any duty imposed by section 40 of this Act may be performed by giving the information either to the transferor or to the transferee.

Proceedings for breach of duties to give information

40B A claim that a person has broken any duty imposed by section 40 of this Act may be made the subject of civil proceedings for breach of statutory duty; and in any such proceedings a court may order that person to comply with that duty and may make an award of damages.

Trusts

41-(1) Where a tenancy is held on trust, occupation by all or any of the beneficiaries under the trust, and the carrying on of a business by all or any of the beneficiaries, shall be treated for the purposes of section 23 of this Act as equivalent to occupation or the carrying on of a business by the tenant; and in relation to a tenancy to which this Part of this Act applies by virtue of the foregoing provisions of this subsection –

(a) references (however expressed) in this Part of this Act and in the Ninth Schedule to this Act to the business of, or to carrying on of business, use, occupation or enjoyment by, the tenant shall be construed as including references to the business of, or to carrying on of business, use, occupation or enjoyment by, the beneficiaries or beneficiary;

(b) the reference in paragraph (d) of subsection (1) of section 34 of this Act to the tenant shall be construed as including the beneficiaries or beneficiary; and

(c) a change in the persons of the trustees shall not be treated as a change in the person of the tenant.

(2) Where the landlord's interest is held on trust the references in paragraph (g) of subsection (1) of section 30 of this Act to the landlord shall be construed as including references to the beneficiaries under the trust or any of them; but, except in the case of a trust arising under a will or on the intestacy of any person, the reference in subsection (2) of that section to the creation of the interest therein mentioned shall be construed as including the creation of the trust.

Partnerships

41A-(1) The following provisions of this section shall apply where –

(a) a tenancy is held jointly by two or more persons (in this section referred to as the joint tenants); and

(b) the property comprised in the tenancy is or includes premises occupied for the purposes of a business; and

(c) the business (or some other business) was at some time during the existence of the tenancy carried on in partnership by all the persons who were then the joint tenants or by those and other persons and the joint tenants' interest in the premises was then partnership property; and

(d) the business is carried on (whether alone or in partnership with other persons) by one or some only of the joint tenants and no part of the property comprised in the tenancy is occupied, in right of the tenancy, for the purposes of a business carried on (whether alone or in partnership with other persons) by the other or others.

(2) In the following provisions of this section those of the joint tenants who for the time being carry on the business are referred to as the business tenants and the others as the other joint tenants.

(3) Any notice given by the business tenants which, had it been given by all the joint tenants, would have been –

(a) a tenant's request for a new tenancy made in accordance with section 26 of this Act; or

(b) a notice under subsection (1) or subsection (2) of section 27 of this Act; shall be treated as such if it states that it is given by virtue of this section and sets out the facts by virtue of which the persons giving it are the business tenants;

and references in those sections and in section 24A of this Act to the tenant shall be construed accordingly.

(4) A notice given by the landlord to the business tenants which, had it been given to all the joint tenants, would have been a notice under section 25 of this Act shall be treated as such a notice, and references in that section to the tenant shall be construed accordingly.

(5) An application under section 24(1) of this Act for a new tenancy may, instead of being made by all the joint tenants, be made by the business tenants alone; and where it is so made –

(a) this Part of this Act shall have effect, in relation to it, as if the references therein to the tenant included references to the business tenants alone; and

(b) the business tenants shall be liable, to the exclusion of the other joint tenants, for the payment of rent and the discharge of any other obligation under the current tenancy for any rental period beginning after the date specified in the landlord's notice under section 25 of this Act or, as the case my be, beginning on or after the date specified in their request for a new tenancy.

(6) Where the court makes an order under ~~section 29(1) of this Act for the grant of a new tenancy on an application made by the business tenants it may order the grant to be made to them or to them jointly~~ **section 29 of this Act for the grant of a new tenancy it may order the grant to be made to the business tenants or to them jointly** with the persons carrying on the business in partnership with them, and may order the grant to be made subject to the satisfaction, within a time specified by the order, of such conditions as to guarantors, sureties or otherwise as appear to the court equitable, having regard to the omission of the other joint tenants from the persons who will be the tenants under the new tenancy.

(7) The business tenants shall be entitled to recover any amount payable by way of compensation under section 37 or section 59 of this Act.

Groups of companies

42-(1) For the purposes of this section two bodies corporate shall be taken to be members of a group if and only if one is a subsidiary of the other or both are subsidiaries of the third body corporate **or the same person has a controlling interest in both.**

~~In this subsection 'subsidiary' has the same meaning given by section 736 of the Companies Act 1985.~~

(2) Where a tenancy is held by a member of a group, occupation by another member of the group, and the carrying on of a business by another member of the group, shall be treated for the purposes of section 23 of this Act as equivalent to occupation or the carrying on of a business by the member of the group holding the tenancy; and in relation to a tenancy to which this Part of this Act applies by virtue of the foregoing provisions of this subsection –

(a) references (however expressed) in this Part of this Act and in the Ninth Schedule to this Act to the business of or to use occupation or enjoyment by the tenant shall be construed as including references to the business of or to use occupation or enjoyment by the said other member;

(b) the reference in paragraph (d) of subsection (1) of section 34 of this Act to the tenant shall be construed as including the said other member; and

(c) an assignment of the tenancy from one member of the group to another shall not be treated as a change in the person of the tenant.

(3) Where the landlord's interest is held by a member of a group –

(a) the reference in paragraph (g) of subsection (1) of section 30 of this Act to intended occupation by the landlord for the purposes of a business to be carried on by him shall be construed as including intended occupation by any member of the group for the purposes of a business to be carried on by that member; and

(b) the reference in subsection (2) of that section to the purchase or creation of any interest shall be construed as a reference to a purchaser from or creation by a person other than a member of the group.

Tenancies excluded from Part II

43-(1) This Part of this Act does not apply –

(a) to a tenancy of an agricultural holding which is a tenancy in relation to which the Agricultural Holdings Act 1986 applies or a tenancy which would be a tenancy of an agricultural holding in relation to which that Act applied if subsection (3) of section 2 of that Act did not have effect or, in a case where approval was given under subsection (1) of that section, if that approval had not been given;

(aa) to a farm business tenancy;

(b) to a tenancy created by a mining lease; or

(c) [Repealed]

(d) [Repealed]

(2) This Part of this Act does not apply to a tenancy granted by reason that the tenant was the holder of an office, appointment or employment from the grantor thereof and continuing only so long as the tenant holds the office, appointment or employment, or terminable by the grantor on the tenant's ceasing to hold it, or coming to an end at a time fixed by reference to the time at which the tenant ceases to hold it:

Provided that this subsection shall not have effect in relation to a tenancy granted after the commencement of this Act unless the tenancy was granted by an instrument in writing which expressed the purpose for which the tenancy was granted.

(3) This Part of this Act does not apply to a tenancy granted for a term certain not exceeding six months unless –

(a) the tenancy contains provision for renewing the term or for extending it beyond six months from its beginning; or

(b) the tenant has been in occupation for a period which, together with any period during which any predecessor in the carrying on of the business carried on by the tenant was in occupation, exceeds twelve months.

Jurisdiction of county court to make declaration

43A. Where the rateable value of the holding is such that the jurisdiction conferred on the court by any other provision of this Part of this Act is, by virtue of section 63 of this Act, exercisable by the county court, the county court shall have jurisdiction (but without prejudice to the jurisdiction of the High Court) to make any declaration as to any matter arising under this Part of this Act, whether or not any other relief is sought in the proceedings.

Meaning of 'the landlord', in Part II, and provisions as to mesne landlords, etc

44-(1) Subject to ~~the next following subsection~~ **subsections (1A) and (2) below**, in this Part of this Act the expression 'the landlord' in relation to a tenancy (in this section referred to as 'the relevant tenancy'), means the person (whether or not he is the immediate landlord) who is the owner of that interest in the property comprised in the relevant tenancy which for the time being fulfils the following conditions, that is to say –

(a) that it is an interest in reversion expectant (whether immediately or not) on the termination of the relevant tenancy, and

(b) that it is either the fee simple or a tenancy which will not come to an end within fourteen months by effluxion of time and, if it is such a tenancy, that no notice has been given by virtue of which it will come to an end within fourteen months or any further time by which it may be continued under section 36(2) or section 64 of this Act, and is not itself in reversion expectant (whether immediately or not) on an interest which fulfils those conditions.

(1A) The reference in subsection (1) above to a person who is the owner of an interest such as is mentioned in that subsection is to be construed, where different persons own such interests in different parts of the property, as a reference to all those persons collectively.

(2) References in this Part of this Act to a notice to quit given by the landlord are references to a notice to quit given by the immediate landlord.

(3) The provisions of the Sixth Schedule to this Act shall have effect for the application of this Part of this Act to cases where the immediate landlord of the tenant is not the owner of the fee simple in respect of the holding.

45 [Repealed]

Interpretation of Part II

46-(1) In this Part of this Act:

'business' has the meaning assigned to it by subsection (2) of section 23 of this Act;

~~'current tenancy' has the meaning assigned to it by subsection (1) of section 26 of this Act~~
'current tenancy' means the tenancy under which the tenant holds for the time being;

'date of termination' has the meaning assigned to it by subsection (1) of section 25 of this Act;

subject to the provisions of section 32 of this Act, 'the holding' has the meaning assigned to it by subsection (3) of section 23 of this Act;

'interim rent' has the meaning given by section 24A(1) of this Act;

'mining lease' has the same meaning as in the Landlord and Tenant Act 1927.

(2) For the purposes of this Part of this Act, a person has a controlling interest in a company if, had he been a company, the other company would have been its subsidiary; and in this Part –

'company' has the meaning given by section 735 of the Companies Act 1985; and

'subsidiary' has the meaning given by section 736 of that Act.

PART III

COMPENSATION FOR IMPROVEMENTS

Time for making claims for compensation for improvements

47-(1) Where a tenancy is terminated by notice to quit, whether given by the landlord or by the tenant, or by a notice given by any person under Part I or Part II of this Act, the time for making a claim for compensation at the termination of the tenancy shall be a time falling within the period of three months beginning on the date on which the notice is given:

Provided that where the tenancy is terminated by a tenant's request for a new tenancy under section 26 of this Act, the said time shall be a time falling within the period of three months beginning on the date on which the landlord gives notice, or (if he has not given such a notice) the latest date on which he could have given notice, under subsection (6) of the said section 26 or, as the case may be, paragraph (a) of subsection (4) of section 57 or paragraph (b) of subsection (1) of section 58 of this Act.

(2) Where a tenancy comes to an end by effluxion of time, the time for making such a claim shall be a time not earlier than six nor later than three months before the coming to an end of the tenancy.

(3) Where a tenancy is terminated by forfeiture or re-entry, the time for making such a claim shall be a time falling within the period of three months beginning with the effective date of the order of the court for the recovery of possession of the land comprised in the tenancy or, if the tenancy is terminated by re-entry without such an order, the period of three months beginning with the date of the re-entry.

(4) In the last foregoing subsection the reference to the effective date of an order is a reference to the date on which the order is to take effect according to the terms thereof or the date on which it ceases to be subject to appeal, which ever is the later.

(5) In subsection (1) of section 1 of the Act of 1927, for paragraphs (a) and (b) (which specify the time for making claims for compensation) there shall be substituted the words 'and within the time limited by section 47 of the Landlord and Tenant Act 1954.'

Amendments as to limitations on tenant's right to compensation

48-(1) So much of paragraph (b) of subsection (1) of section 2 of the Act of 1927 as provides that a tenant shall not be entitled to compensation in respect of any improvement made in pursuance of a statutory obligation shall not apply to any improvement begun after the commencement of this Act, but section 3 of the Act of 1927 (which enables a landlord to object to a proposed improvement) shall not have effect in relation to an improvement made in pursuance of a statutory obligation except so much thereof as –

(a) requires the tenant to serve on the landlord notice of his intention to make the improvement together with such a plan and specification as are mentioned in that section and to supply copies of the plan and specification at the request of any superior landlord; and

(b) enables the tenant to obtain at his expense a certificate from the landlord or the tribunal that the improvement has been duly executed.

(2) Paragraph (c) of the said subsection (1) (which provides that a tenant shall not be entitled to compensation in respect of any improvement made less than three years before the termination of the tenancy) shall not apply to any improvement begun after the commencement of this Act.

(3) No notice shall be served after the commencement of this Act under paragraph (d) of the said subsection (1) (which excludes rights to compensation where the landlord serves on the tenant notice offering a renewal of the tenancy on reasonable terms).

Restrictions on contracting out

49 In section 9 of the Act of 1927 (which provides that Part I of that Act shall apply notwithstanding any contract to the contrary made after the date specified in that section) the proviso (which requires effect to be given to such a contract where it appears to the tribunal that the contract was made for adequate consideration) shall cease to have effect except as respects a contract made before the tenth day of December, nineteen hundred and fifty-three.

Interpretation of Part III

50 In this Part of this Act the expression 'Act of 1927' means the Landlord and Tenant Act 1927, the expression 'compensation' means compensation under Part I of that Act in respect of an improvement, and other expressions used in this Part of this Act and in the Act of 1927 have the same meanings in this Part of this Act as in that Act.

[Sections 51 to 54 not reproduced here]

PART IV

MISCELLANEOUS AND SUPPLEMENTARY

~~Compensation for possession obtained by misrepresentation~~

~~55-(1) Where under Part I of this Act an order is made for possession of the property comprised in a tenancy, or under Part II of this Act the court refuses an order for the grant of a new tenancy, and it is subsequently made to appear to the court that the order was obtained, or the court induced to refuse the grant, by misrepresentation or the concealment of material facts, the court may order the landlord to pay to the tenant such sum as appears sufficient as compensation for damage or loss sustained by the tenant as the result of the order or refusal.~~

~~(2) In this section the expression 'the landlord' means the person applying for possession or opposing an application for the grant of a new tenancy and the expression 'the tenant' means the person against whom the order for possession was made or to whom the grant of a new tenancy was refused.~~

Application to Crown

56-(1) Subject to the provisions of this and the four next following sections, Part II of this Act shall apply where there is an interest belonging to Her Majesty in right of the Crown or the Duchy of Lancaster or belonging to the Duchy of Cornwall, or belonging to a Government department or held on behalf of Her Majesty for the purposes of a Government department, in like manner as if that interest were an interest not so belonging or held.

(2) The provisions of the Eighth Schedule to this Act shall have effect as respects the application of Part II of this Act to cases where the interest of the landlord belongs to Her Majesty in right of the Crown or the Duchy of Lancaster or to the Duchy of Cornwall.

(3) Where a tenancy is held by or on behalf of a Government department and the property comprised therein is or includes premises occupied for any purposes of a Government department, the tenancy shall be one to which Part II of this Act applies; and for the purposes of any provision of the said Part II or the Ninth Schedule to this Act which is applicable only if either or both of the following conditions are satisfied, that is to say –

> (a) that any premises have during any period been occupied for the purposes of the tenant's business;

> (b) that on any change of occupier of any premises the new occupier succeeded to the business of the former occupier,

the said conditions shall be deemed to be satisfied respectively, in relation to such a tenancy, if during that period or, as the case may be, immediately before and immediately after the change, the premises were occupied for the purposes of a Government department.

(4) The last foregoing subsection shall apply in relation to any premises provided by a Government department without any rent being payable to the department therefor as if the premises were occupied for the purposes of a Government department.

(5) The provisions of Parts III and IV of this Act, amending any other enactment which binds the Crown or applies to land belonging to Her Majesty in right of the Crown or the Duchy of Lancaster, or land belonging to the Duchy of Cornwall, or to land belonging to any Government department, shall bind the Crown or apply to such land.

(6) Sections 53 and 54 of this Act shall apply where the interest of the landlord, or any other interest in the land in question, belongs to Her Majesty in right of the Crown or the Duchy of Lancaster or to the Duchy of Cornwall, or belongs to a Government department or is held on behalf of Her Majesty for the purposes of a Government department, in like manner as if that interest were an interest not so belonging or held.

(7) Part I of this Act shall apply where –

> (a) there is an interest belonging to Her Majesty in right of the Crown and that interest is under the management of the Crown Estate Commissioners; or

> (b) there is an interest belonging to Her Majesty in right of the Duchy of Lancaster or belonging to the Duchy of Cornwall;

as if it were an interest not so belonging.

Modification on grounds of public interest of rights under Part II

57-(1) Where the interest of the landlord or any superior landlord in the property comprised in any tenancy belongs to or is held for the purposes of a Government department or is held by a local authority, statutory undertakers or a development corporation, the Minister or Board in charge of any Government department may certify that it is requisite for the purposes of the first-mentioned department, or, as the case may be, of the authority, undertakers or corporation, that the use or occupation of the property or a part thereof shall be changed by a specified date.

(2) A certificate under the last foregoing subsection shall not be given unless the owner of the interest belonging or held as mentioned in the last foregoing subsection has given to the tenant a notice stating –

> (a) that the question of the giving of such a certificate is under consideration by the Minister or Board specified in the notice, and

(b) that if within twenty-one days of the giving of the notice the tenant makes to that Minister or Board representations in writing with respect to that question, they will be considered before the question is determined, and if the tenant makes any such representations within the said twenty-one days the Minister or Board shall consider them before determining whether to give the certificate.

(3) Where a certificate has been given under subsection (1) of this section in relation to any tenancy, then –

(a) if a notice given under subsection (1) of section 25 of this Act specifies as the date of termination a date not earlier than the date specified in the certificate and contains a copy of the certificate ~~subsections (5) and~~ **subsection** (6) of that section shall not apply to the notice and no application for a new tenancy shall be made by the tenant under **subsection (1) of** section 24 of this Act;

(b) if such a notice specifies an earlier date as the date of termination and contains a copy of the certificate, then if the court makes an order under Part II of this Act for the grant of a new tenancy the new tenancy shall be for a term expiring not later than the date specified in the certificate and shall not be a tenancy to which Part II of this Act applies.

(4) Where a tenant makes a request for a new tenancy under section 26 of this Act, and the interest of the landlord or any superior landlord in the property comprised in the current tenancy belongs or is held as mentioned in subsection (1) of this section, the following provisions shall have effect:

(a) if a certificate has been given under the said subsection (1) in relation to the current tenancy, and within two months after the making of the request the landlord gives notice to the tenant that the certificate has been given and the notice contains a copy of the certificate, then, –

(i) if the date specified in the certificate is not later than that specified in the tenant's request for a new tenancy, the tenant shall not make an application under section 24 of this Act for the grant of a new tenancy;

(ii) if, in any other case, the court makes an order under Part II of this Act for the grant of a new tenancy the new tenancy shall be for a term expiring not later than the date specified in the certificate and shall not be a tenant to which Part II of this Act applies;

(b) if no such certificate has been given but notice under subsection (2) of this section has been given before the making of the request or within two months thereafter, the request shall not have effect, without prejudice however, to the making of a new request when the Minister or Board has determined whether to give a certificate.

(5) Where application is made to the court under Part II of this Act for the grant of a new tenancy and the landlord's interest in the property comprised in the tenancy belongs or is held as mentioned in subsection (1) of this section, the Minister or Board in charge of any Government department may certify that it is necessary in the public interest that if the landlord makes an application in that behalf the court shall determine as a term of the new tenancy that is shall be terminable by six months' notice to quit given by the landlord.

Subsection (2) of this section shall apply in relation to a certificate under this subsection, and if notice under the said subsection (2) has been given to the tenant –

(a) the court shall not determine the application for the grant of a new tenancy until the Minister or Board has determined whether to give a certificate,

(b) if a certificate is given, the court shall on the application of the landlord determine as a term of the new tenancy that it shall be terminable as aforesaid, and section 25 of this Act shall apply accordingly.

(6) The foregoing provisions of this section shall apply to an interest held by a Health Authority or Special Health Authority as they apply to an interest held by a local authority but with the substitution, for the reference to the purposes of the authority, of a reference to the purposes of the National Health Service Act 1977.

(7) Where the interest of the landlord or any superior landlord in the property comprised in any tenancy belongs to the National Trust the Minister of Works may certify that it is

requisite, for the purpose of securing that the property will as from a specified date be used or occupied in a manner better suited to the nature thereof, that the use or occupation of the property should be changed; and subsections (2) to (4) of this section shall apply in relation to certificates under this subsection, and to cases where the interest of the landlord or any superior landlord belongs to the National Trust, as those subsections apply in relation to certificates under subsection (1) of this section and to cases where the interest of the landlord or any superior landlord belongs or is held as mentioned in that subsection.

(8) In this and the next following section the expression 'Government department' does not include the Commissioners of Crown Lands and the expression 'landlord' has the same meaning as in Part II of this Act; and in the last foregoing subsection the expression 'National Trust' means the National Trust for Places of Historic Interest or Natural Beauty.

Termination on special grounds of tenancies to which Part II applies

58-(1) Where the landlord's interest in the property comprised in any tenancy belongs or is held for the purposes of a Government department, and the Minister or Board in charge of any Government department certifies that for reasons of national security it is necessary that the use or occupation of the property should be discontinued or changed, then –

(a) if the landlord gives a notice under subsection (1) of section 25 of this Act containing a copy of the certificate, subsections (5) and subsection (6) of that section shall not apply to the notice and no application for a new tenancy shall be made by the tenant under subsection (1) of section 24 of this Act;

(b) if (whether before or after the giving of the certificate) the tenant makes a request for a new tenancy under section 26 of this Act, and within two months after the making the request the landlord gives notice to the tenant that the certificate has been given and the notice contains a copy of the certificate –

(i) the tenant shall not make an application under section 24 of this Act for the grant of a new tenancy, and

(ii) if the notice specifies as the date on which the tenancy is to terminate a date earlier than that specified in the tenant's request as the date on which the new tenancy is to begin but neither earlier than six months from the giving of the notice nor earlier than the earliest date at which apart from this Act the tenancy would come to an end or could be brought to an end, the tenancy shall terminate on the date specified in the notice instead of that specified in the request.

(2) Where the landlord's interest in the property comprised in any tenancy belongs to or is held for the purposes of a Government department, nothing in this Act shall invalidate an agreement to the effect –

(a) that on the giving of such a certificate as is mentioned in the last foregoing subsection the tenancy may be terminated by notice to quit given by the landlord of such length as may be specified in the agreement, if the notice contains a copy of the certificate; and

(b) that after the giving of such a notice containing such a copy the tenancy shall not be one to which Part II of this Act applies.

(3) Where the landlord's interest in the property comprised in any tenancy is held by statutory undertakers, nothing in this Act shall invalidate an agreement to the effect

(a) that where the Minister or Board in charge of a Government department certifies that possession of the property comprised in the tenancy or a part thereof is urgently required for carrying out repairs (whether on that property or elsewhere) which are needed for the proper operation of the landlord's undertaking, the tenancy may be terminated by notice to quit given by the landlord of such length as may be specified in the agreement, if the notice contains a copy of the certificate; and

(b) that after the giving of such a notice containing such a copy, the tenancy shall not be one to which Part II of this Act applies.

(4) Where the court makes an order under Part II of this Act for the grant of a new tenancy and the Minister or Board in charge of any Government department certifies that the public interest requires the tenancy to be subject to such a term as is mentioned in paragraph (a) or (b) of this subsection, as the case may be, then –

(a) if the landlord's interest in the property comprised in the tenancy belongs to or is held for the purposes of a Government department, the court shall on the application of the landlord determine as a term of the new tenancy that such an agreement as is mentioned in subsection (2) of this section and specifying such length of notice as is mentioned in the certificate shall be embodied in the new tenancy;

(b) if the landlord's interest in that property is held by statutory undertakers, the court shall on the application of the landlord determine as a term of the new tenancy that such an agreement as is mentioned in subsection (3) of this section and specifying such length of notice as is mentioned in the certificate shall be embodied in the new tenancy.

Compensation for exercise of powers under sections 57 and 58

59-(1) Where by virtue of any certificate given for the purposes of either of the two last foregoing sections or, subject to subsection (1A) below, section 60A below the tenant is precluded from obtaining an order for the grant of a new tenancy, or of a new tenancy for a term expiring later than a specified date, the tenant shall be entitled on quitting the premises to recover from the owner of the interest by virtue of which the certificate was given an amount by way of compensation, and subsections (2), (3) **to (3B)** and (5) to (7) of section 37 of this Act shall with the necessary modifications apply for the purposes of ascertaining the amount.

(1A) No compensation shall be recoverable under subsection (1) above where the certificate was given under section 60A below and either –

(a) the premises vested in the Welsh Development Agency under section 7 (property of Welsh Industrial Estates Corporation) or 8 (land held under Local Employment Act 1972) of the Welsh Development Agency Act 1975, or

(b) the tenant was not tenant of the premises when the said Agency acquired the interest by virtue of which the certificate was given.

(2) Subsections (2) and (3) of section 38 of this Act shall apply to compensation under this section as they apply to compensation under section 37 of this Act.

Special provisions as to premises in development or intermediate areas

60-(1) Where the property comprised in a tenancy consists of premises of which the Secretary of State or the Urban Regeneration Agency is the landlord, being premises situated in a locality which is either –

(a) a development area; or

(b) an intermediate area;

and the Secretary of State certifies that it is necessary or expedient for achieving the purpose mentioned in section 2(1) of the Local Employment Act 1972 that the use or occupation of the property should be changed, paragraphs (a) and (b) of subsection (1) of section 58 of this Act shall apply as they apply where such a certificate is given as is mentioned in that subsection.

(2) Where the court makes an order under Part II of this Act for the grant of a new tenancy of any such premises as aforesaid, and the Secretary of State certifies that it is necessary or expedient as aforesaid that the tenancy should be subject to a term, specified in the certificate, prohibiting or restricting the tenant from assigning the tenancy or sub-letting, charging or parting with possession of the premises or any part thereof or changing the use of the premises or any part thereof, the court shall determine that the terms of the tenancy shall include the terms specified in the certificate.

(3) In this section 'development area' and 'intermediate area' mean an area for the time being specified as a development area or, as the case may be, as an intermediate area by an order made, or having effect as if made, under section 1 of the Industrial Development Act 1982.

Welsh Development Agency premises

60A-(1) Where property comprised in a tenancy consists of premises of which the Welsh Development Agency is the landlord, and the Secretary of State certifies that it is necessary or expedient, for the purpose of providing employment appropriate to the needs of the area in which the premises are situated, that the use or occupation of the property should be changed, paragraphs (a) and (b) of section 58(1) above shall apply as they apply where such a certificate is given as is mentioned in that sub-section.

(2) Where the court makes an order under Part II of this Act for the grant of a new tenancy of any such premises as aforesaid, and the Secretary of State certifies that it is necessary or expedient as aforesaid that the tenancy should be subject to a term, specified in the certificate, prohibiting or restricting the tenant from assigning the tenancy or subletting, charging or parting with possession of the premises or any part of the premises or changing the use of the premises or any part of the premises, the court shall determine that the terms of the tenancy shall include the terms specified in the certificate.

60B to 62 [Repealed]

Jurisdiction of court for purposes of Parts I and II and of Part I of Landlord and Tenant Act 1927

63-(1) Any jurisdiction conferred on the court by any provision of Part I of this Act shall be exercised by the county court.

(2) Any jurisdiction conferred on the court by any provision of Part II of this Act or conferred on the tribunal by Part I of the Landlord and Tenant Act 1927, shall, subject to the provisions of this section, be exercised, by the High Court or a county court.

(3) [Repealed]

(4) The following provisions shall have effect as respects transfer of proceedings from or to the High Court or the county court, that is to say –

(a) where an application is made to the one but by virtue of an Order under section 1 of the Courts and Legal Services Act 1990, cannot be entertained except by the other, the application shall not be treated as improperly made but any proceedings thereon shall be transferred to the other court;

(b) any proceedings under the provisions of Part II of this Act or of Part I of the Landlord and Tenant Act 1927, which are pending before one of those courts may by order of that court made on the application of any person interested be transferred to the other court, if it appears to the court making the order that it is desirable that the proceedings and any proceedings before the other court should both be entertained by the other court.

(5) In any proceedings where in accordance with the foregoing provisions of this section the county court exercises jurisdiction the powers of the judge of summoning one or more assessors under subsection (1) of section 63 (1) of the County Courts Act 1984, may be exercised notwithstanding that no application is made in that behalf by any party to the proceedings.

(6) Where in any such proceedings an assessor is summoned by a judge under the said subsection (1),-(

(a) he may, if so directed by the judge, inspect the land to which the proceedings relate without the judge and report to the judge in writing thereon;

(b) the judge may on consideration of the report and any observations of the parties thereon give such judgment or make such order in the proceedings as may be just;

(c) the remuneration of the assessor shall beat such rate as maybe determined by the Lord Chancellor with the approval of the Treasury and shall be defrayed out of moneys provided by Parliament.

(7) In this section the expression 'the holding' –

(a) in relation to proceedings under Part II of this Act, has the meaning assigned to it by subsection (3) of section 23 of this Act,

(b) in relation to proceedings under Part I of the Landlord and Tenant Act 1927, has the same meaning as in the said Part I.

(9) Nothing in this section shall prejudice the operation of section 41 of the County Courts Act 1984 (which relates to the removal into the High Court of proceedings commenced in a county court).

(10) In accordance with the foregoing provisions of this section, for section 21 of the Landlord and Tenant Act 1927, there shall be substituted the following section –

'The tribunal

21. The tribunal for the purposes of Part I of this Act shall be the court exercising jurisdiction in accordance with the provisions of section 63 of the Landlord and Tenant Act 1954.'

64-(1) In any case where –

(a) a notice to terminate a tenancy has been given under Part I or Part II of this Act or a request for a new tenancy has been made under Part II thereof, and

(b) an application to the court has been made under the said Part I or ~~the said Part II,~~ **under section 24(1) or 29(2) of this Act** as the case may be, and

(c) apart from this section the effect of the notice or request would be to terminate the tenancy before the expiration of the period of three months beginning with the date on which the application is finally disposed of, the effect of the notice or request shall be to terminate the tenancy at the expiration of the said period of three months and not at any other time.

(2) The reference in paragraph (c) of subsection (1) of this section to the date on which an application is finally disposed of shall be construed as a reference to the earliest date by which the proceedings on the application (including any proceedings on or in consequence of an appeal) have been determined and any time for appealing or further appealing has expired, except that if the application is withdrawn or any appeal is abandoned the reference shall be construed as a reference to the date of the withdrawal or abandonment.

Provisions as to reversions

65-(1) Where by virtue of any provision of this Act a tenancy (in this sub-section referred to as 'the inferior tenancy') is continued for a period such as to extend to or beyond the end of the term of a superior tenancy, the superior tenancy shall, for the purposes of this Act and of any other enactment and of any rule of law, be deemed so long as it subsists to be an interest in reversion expectant upon the termination of the inferior tenancy and, if there is no intermediate tenancy, to be the interest in reversion immediately expectant upon the termination thereof.

(2) In the case of a tenancy continuing by virtue of any provision of this Act after the coming to an end of the interest in reversion immediately expectant upon the termination thereof, subsection (1) of section 139 of the Law of Property Act 1925 (which relates to the effect of the extinguishment of a reversion) shall apply as if references in the said subsection (1) to the surrender or merger of the reversion included references to the coming to an end of the reversion for any reason other than surrender or merger.

(3) Where by virtue of any provision of this Act a tenancy (in this subsection referred to as 'the continuing tenancy') is continued beyond the beginning of a reversionary tenancy which was granted (whether before or after the commencement of this Act) so as to begin on or after the date on which apart from this Act the continuing tenancy would have come to an end, the reversionary tenancy shall have effect as if it had been granted subject to the continuing tenancy.

(4) Where by virtue of any provision of this Act a tenancy (in this subsection referred to as 'the new tenancy') is granted for a period beginning on the same date as a reversionary tenancy or for a period such as to extend beyond the beginning of the term of a reversionary tenancy, whether the reversionary tenancy in question was granted before or after the commencement of this Act, the reversionary tenancy shall have effect as if it had been granted subject to the new tenancy.

Provisions as to notices

66-(1) Any form of notice required by this Act to be prescribed shall be prescribed by regulations made by the Secretary of State by statutory instrument.

(2) Where the form of a notice to be served on persons of any description is to be prescribed for any of the purposes of this Act, the form to be prescribed shall include such an explanation of the relevant provisions of this Act as appears to the Secretary of State requisite for informing persons of that description of their rights and obligations under those provisions.

(3) Different forms of notice may be prescribed for the purposes of the operation of any provision of this Act in relation to different cases.

(4) Section 23 of the Landlord and Tenant Act 1927 (which relates to the service of notices) shall apply for the purposes of this Act.

(5) Any statutory instrument under this section shall be subject to annulment in pursuance of a resolution of either House of Parliament.

Provisions as to mortgagees in possession

67 Anything authorised or required by the provisions of this Act, other than subsection ~~(2) or~~ (3) of section 40, to be done at any time by, to or with the landlord, or a landlord of a specified description, shall, if at that time the interest of the landlord in question is subject to a mortgage and the mortgagee is in possession or a receiver appointed by the mortgagee or by the courts is in receipt of the rents and profits, be deemed to be authorised or required to be done by, to or with the mortgagee instead of that landlord.

68 [Not reproduced here]

Interpretation

69-(1) In this Act, the following expressions have the meanings hereby assigned to them respectively, that is to say –

'agricultural holding' has the same meaning as in the Agricultural Holdings Act 1986;

'development corporation' has the same meaning as in the New Towns Act 1946;

'farm business tenancy' has the same meaning as in the Agricultural Tenancies Act 1995;

'local authority' means any local authority within the meaning of the Town and Country Planning Act 1990, any National Park Authority, the Broads Authority or joint authority established by Part 4 of the Local Government Act 1985;

'mortgage' includes a charge or lien and 'mortgagor' and 'mortgagee' shall be construed accordingly;

'notice to quit' means a notice to terminate a tenancy (whether a periodical tenancy or a tenancy for a term of years certain) given in accordance with the provisions (whether express or implied) of that tenancy;

'repairs' includes any work of maintenance, decoration or restoration, and references to repairing, to keeping or yielding up in repair and to state of repair shall be construed accordingly;

'statutory undertakers' has the same meaning as in the Town and Country Planning Act 1990;

'tenancy' means a tenancy created either immediately or derivatively out of the freehold, whether by a lease or underlease, by an agreement for a lease or underlease or by a tenancy agreement or in pursuance of any enactment (including this Act), but does not include a mortgage term or any interest arising in favour of a mortgagor by his attorning tenant to his mortgagee, and references to the granting of a tenancy and to demised property shall be construed accordingly;

'terms', in relation to a tenancy, includes conditions.

(2) References in this Act to an agreement between the landlord and the tenant (except in section 17 and subsections (1) and (2) of section 38 thereof) shall be construed as references to an agreement in writing between them.

(3) Reference in this Act to an action for any relief shall be construed as including references to a claim for that relief by way of counterclaim in any proceedings.

Short title and citation, commencement and extent

70-(1) This Act may be cited as the Landlord and Tenant Act, 1954, and the Landlord and Tenant Act, 1927, and this Act may be cited together as the Landlord and Tenant Acts, 1927 and 1954.

(2) This Act shall come into operation on the first day of October, nineteen hundred and fifty-four.

(3) This Act shall not extend to Scotland or to Northern Ireland.

Appendix 2: The Regulatory Reform (Business Tenancies) (England and Wales) Order 2003, Schedules 1-4

SCHEDULE 1   **Article 22(2)**

FORM OF NOTICE THAT SECTIONS 24 TO 28 OF THE LANDLORD AND TENANT ACT 1954 ARE NOT TO APPLY TO A BUSINESS TENANCY

To:

....

....

....*[Name and address of tenant]*

From:

....

....

....*[Name and address of landlord]*

IMPORTANT NOTICE

<u>You are being offered a lease without security of tenure. Do not commit yourself to the lease unless you have read this message carefully and have discussed it with a professional adviser.</u>

Business tenants normally have security of tenure – the right to stay in their business premises when the lease ends.

<u>If you commit yourself to the lease you will be giving up these important legal rights.</u>

• You will have **no right** to stay in the premises when the lease ends.

• Unless the landlord chooses to offer you another lease, you will need to leave the premises.

• You will be unable to claim compensation for the loss of your business premises, unless the lease specifically gives you this right.

• If the landlord offers you another lease, you will have no right to ask the court to fix the rent.

It is therefore important to get professional advice – from a qualified surveyor, lawyer or accountant – before agreeing to give up these rights.

If you want to ensure that you can stay in the same business premises when the lease ends, you should consult your adviser about another form of lease that does not exclude the protection of the Landlord and Tenant Act 1954.

If you receive this notice at least 14 days before committing yourself to the lease, you will need to sign a simple declaration that you have received this notice and have accepted its consequences, before signing the lease.

<u>But if you do not receive at least 14 days' notice, you will need to sign a 'statutory' declaration. To do so, you will need to visit an independent solicitor (or someone else empowered to administer oaths).</u>

Unless there is a special reason for committing yourself to the lease sooner, you may want to ask the landlord to let you have at least 14 days to consider whether you wish to give up your statutory rights. If you then decided to go ahead with the agreement to exclude the protection of the Landlord and Tenant Act 1954, you would only need to make a simple declaration, and so you would not need to make a separate visit to an independent solicitor.

SCHEDULE 2   Article 22(2)

REQUIREMENTS FOR A VALID AGREEMENT THAT SECTIONS 24 TO 28 OF THE LANDLORD AND TENANT ACT 1954 ARE NOT TO APPLY TO A BUSINESS TENANCY

1. The following are the requirements referred to in section 38A(3)(b) of the Act.

2. Subject to paragraph 4, the notice referred to in section 38A(3)(a) of the Act must be served on the tenant not less than 14 days before the tenant enters into the tenancy to which it applies, or (if earlier) becomes contractually bound to do so.

3. If the requirement in paragraph 2 is met, the tenant, or a person duly authorised by him to do so, must, before the tenant enters into the tenancy to which the notice applies, or (if earlier) becomes contractually bound to do so, make a declaration in the form, or substantially in the form, set out in paragraph 7.

4. If the requirement in paragraph 2 is not met, the notice referred to in section 38A(3)(a) of the Act must be served on the tenant before the tenant enters into the tenancy to which it applies, or (if earlier) becomes contractually bound to do so, and the tenant, or a person duly authorised by him to do so, must before that time make a statutory declaration in the form, or substantially in the form, set out in paragraph 8.

5. A reference to the notice and, where paragraph 3 applies, the declaration or, where paragraph 4 applies, the statutory declaration must be contained in or endorsed on the instrument creating the tenancy.

6. The agreement under section 38A(1) of the Act, or a reference to the agreement, must be contained in or endorsed upon the instrument creating the tenancy.

7. The form of declaration referred to in paragraph 3 is as follows: –

I ....(*name of declarant*) of............................(*address*) declare that –

1. I/...............................(*name of tenant*) propose(s) to enter into a tenancy of premises at ....(*address of premises*) for a term commencing on ....

2. I/The tenant propose(s) to enter into an agreement with .... (*name of landlord*) that the provisions of sections 24 to 28 of the Landlord and Tenant Act 1954 (security of tenure) shall be excluded in relation to the tenancy.

3. The landlord has, not less than 14 days before I/the tenant enter(s) into the tenancy, or (if earlier) become(s) contractually bound to do so served on me/the tenant a notice in the form, or substantially in the form, set out in Schedule 1 to the Regulatory Reform (Business Tenancies) (England and Wales) Order 2003. The form of notice set out in that Schedule is reproduced below.

4. I have/The tenant has read the notice referred to in paragraph 3 above and accept(s) the consequences of entering into the agreement referred to in paragraph 2 above.

5. (*as appropriate*) I am duly authorised by the tenant to make this declaration.

DECLARED this ....day of...

To:

....

....

....[*Name and address of tenant*]

From:

....

....

....[*Name and address of landlord*]

IMPORTANT NOTICE

<u>You are being offered a lease without security of tenure. Do not commit yourself to the lease unless you have read this message carefully and have discussed it with a professional adviser.</u>

Business tenants normally have security of tenure – the right to stay in their business premises when the lease ends.

If you commit yourself to the lease you will be giving up these important legal rights.

- You will have **no right** to stay in the premises when the lease ends.

- Unless the landlord chooses to offer you another lease, you will need to leave the premises.

- You will be unable to claim compensation for the loss of your business premises, unless the lease specifically gives you this right.

- If the landlord offers you another lease, you will have no right to ask the court to fix the rent.

It is therefore important to get professional advice – from a qualified surveyor, lawyer or accountant – before agreeing to give up these rights.

If you want to ensure that you can stay in the same business premises when the lease ends, you should consult your adviser about another form of lease that does not exclude the protection of the Landlord and Tenant Act 1954.

If you receive this notice at least 14 days before committing yourself to the lease, you will need to sign a simple declaration that you have received this notice and have accepted its consequences, before signing the lease.

But if you do not receive at least 14 days' notice, you will need to sign a 'statutory' declaration. To do so, you will need to visit an independent solicitor (or someone else empowered to administer oaths).

Unless there is a special reason for committing yourself to the lease sooner, you may want to ask the landlord to let you have at least 14 days to consider whether you wish to give up your statutory rights. If you then decided to go ahead with the agreement to exclude the protection of the Landlord and Tenant Act 1954, you would only need to make a simple declaration, and so you would not need to make a separate visit to an independent solicitor.

8. The form of statutory declaration referred to in paragraph 4 is as follows: –

I ....(*name of declarant*) of..............................(*address*) do solemnly and sincerely declare that –

1. I/..............................(*name of tenant*) propose(s) to enter into a tenancy of premises at ....(*address of premises*) for a term commencing on ....

2. I/The tenant propose(s) to enter into an agreement with (*name of landlord*) that the provisions of sections 24 to 28 of the Landlord and Tenant Act 1954 (security of tenure) shall be excluded in relation to the tenancy.

3. The landlord has served on me/the tenant a notice in the form, or substantially in the form, set out in Schedule 1 to the Regulatory Reform (Business Tenancies) (England and Wales) Order 2003. The form of notice set out in that Schedule is reproduced below.

4. I have/The tenant has read the notice referred to in paragraph 3 above and accept(s) the consequences of entering into the agreement referred to in paragraph 2 above.

5. (*as appropriate*) I am duly authorised by the tenant to make this declaration.

To:

....
....
....[*Name and address of tenant*]

From:

....
....
....[*Name and address of landlord*]

IMPORTANT NOTICE

You are being offered a lease without security of tenure. Do not commit yourself to the lease unless you have read this message carefully and have discussed it with a professional adviser.

Business tenants normally have security of tenure – the right to stay in their business premises when the lease ends.

If you commit yourself to the lease you will be giving up these important legal rights.

- You will have **no right** to stay in the premises when the lease ends.

- Unless the landlord chooses to offer you another lease, you will need to leave the premises.

- You will be unable to claim compensation for the loss of your business premises, unless the lease specifically gives you this right.

- If the landlord offers you another lease, you will have no right to ask the court to fix the rent.

It is therefore important to get professional advice – from a qualified surveyor, lawyer or accountant – before agreeing to give up these rights.

If you want to ensure that you can stay in the same business premises when the lease ends, you should consult your adviser about another form of lease that does not exclude the protection of the Landlord and Tenant Act 1954.

If you receive this notice at least 14 days before committing yourself to the lease, you will need to sign a simple declaration that you have received this notice and have accepted its consequences, before signing the lease.

But if you do not receive at least 14 days' notice, you will need to sign a 'statutory' declaration. To do so, you will need to visit an independent solicitor (or someone else empowered to administer oaths).

Unless there is a special reason for committing yourself to the lease sooner, you may want to ask the landlord to let you have at least 14 days to consider whether you wish to give up your statutory rights. If you then decided to go ahead with the agreement to exclude the protection of the Landlord and Tenant Act 1954, you would only need to make a simple declaration, and so you would not need to make a separate visit to an independent solicitor.

AND I make this solemn declaration conscientiously believing the same to be true and by virtue of the Statutory Declaration Act 1835.

DECLARED at ....this ....day of ....

Before me

(*signature of person before whom declaration is made*)

A commissioner for oaths *or* A solicitor empowered to administer oaths or (*as appropriate*)

SCHEDULE 3   **Article 22(2)**

FORM OF NOTICE THAT AN AGREEMENT TO SURRENDER A BUSINESS TENANCY IS TO BE MADE

To:

....

....

....[*Name and address of tenant*]

From:

....

....

....[*Name and address of landlord*]

IMPORTANT NOTICE FOR TENANT

Do not commit yourself to any agreement to surrender your lease unless you have read this message carefully and discussed it with a professional adviser.

Normally, you have the right to renew your lease when it expires. By committing yourself to an agreement to surrender, **you will be giving up this important statutory right**.

- You will not be able to continue occupying the premises beyond the date provided for under the agreement for surrender, unless the landlord chooses to offer you a further term (in which case you would lose the right to ask the court to determine the new rent). You will need to leave the premises.

- You will be unable to claim compensation for the loss of your premises, unless the lease or agreement for surrender gives you this right.

A qualified surveyor, lawyer or accountant would be able to offer you professional advice on your options.

You do not have to commit yourself to the agreement to surrender your lease unless you want to.

If you receive this notice at least 14 days before committing yourself to the agreement to surrender, you will need to sign a simple declaration that you have received this notice and have accepted its consequences, before signing the agreement to surrender.

But if you do not receive at least 14 days' notice, you will need to sign a 'statutory' declaration. To do so, you will need to visit an independent solicitor (or someone else empowered to administer oaths).

Unless there is a special reason for committing yourself to the agreement to surrender sooner, you may want to ask the landlord to let you have at least 14 days to consider whether you wish to give up your statutory rights. If you then decided to go ahead with the agreement to end your lease, you would only need to make a simple declaration, and so you would not need to make a separate visit to an independent solicitor.

SCHEDULE 4   **Article 22(2)**

REQUIREMENTS FOR A VALID AGREEMENT TO SURRENDER A BUSINESS TENANCY

1. The following are the requirements referred to in section 38A(4)(b) of the Act.

2. Subject to paragraph 4, the notice referred to in section 38A(4)(a) of the Act must be served on the tenant not less than 14 days before the tenant enters into the agreement under section 38A(2) of the Act, or (if earlier) becomes contractually bound to do so.

3. If the requirement in paragraph 2 is met, the tenant or a person duly authorised by him to do so, must, before the tenant enters into the agreement under section 38A(2) of the Act, or (if earlier) becomes contractually bound to do so, make a declaration in the form, or substantially in the form, set out in paragraph 6.

4. If the requirement in paragraph 2 is not met, the notice referred to in section 38A(4)(a) of the Act must be served on the tenant before the tenant enters into the agreement under section 38A(2) of the Act, or (if earlier) becomes contractually bound to do so, and the tenant, or a person duly authorised by him to do so, must before that time make a statutory declaration in the form, or substantially in the form, set out in paragraph 7.

5. A reference to the notice and, where paragraph 3 applies, the declaration or, where paragraph 4 applies, the statutory declaration must be contained in or endorsed on the instrument creating the agreement under section 38A(2).

6. The form of declaration referred to in paragraph 3 is as follows: -

I ....(*name of declarant*) of............................(*address*) declare that –

1. I have/ ....(*name of tenant*) has a tenancy of premises at ....(*address of premises*) for a term commencing on ....

2. I/The tenant propose(s) to enter into an agreement with .... (*name of landlord*) to surrender the tenancy on a date or in circumstances specified in the agreement.

3. The landlord has not less than 14 days before I/the tenant enter(s) into the agreement referred to in paragraph 2 above, or (if earlier) become(s) contractually bound to do so, served on me/the tenant a notice in the form, or substantially in the form, set out in Schedule 3 to Regulatory Reform (Business Tenancies) (England and Wales) Order 2003. The form of notice set out in that Schedule is reproduced below.

4. I have/The tenant has read the notice referred to in paragraph 3 above and accept(s) the consequences of entering into the agreement referred to in paragraph 2 above.

5. (as appropriate) I am duly authorised by the tenant to make this declaration.

DECLARED this ....day of...

To:

....
....
....*[Name and address of tenant]*

From:

....
....
....*[Name and address of landlord]*

IMPORTANT NOTICE FOR TENANT

Do not commit yourself to any agreement to surrender your lease unless you have read this message carefully and discussed it with a professional adviser.

Normally, you have the right to renew your lease when it expires. By committing yourself to an agreement to surrender, **you will be giving up this important statutory right**.

* You will not be able to continue occupying the premises beyond the date provided for under the agreement for surrender, **unless** the landlord chooses to offer you a further term (in which case you would lose the right to ask the court to determine the new rent). You will need to leave the premises.

* You will be unable to claim compensation for the loss of your premises, unless the lease or agreement for surrender gives you this right.

A qualified surveyor, lawyer or accountant would be able to offer you professional advice on your options.

You do not have to commit yourself to the agreement to surrender your lease unless you want to.

If you receive this notice at least 14 days before committing yourself to the agreement to surrender, you will need to sign a simple declaration that you have received this notice and have accepted its consequences, before signing the agreement to surrender.

But if you do not receive at least 14 days' notice, you will need to sign a 'statutory' declaration. To do so, you will need to visit an independent solicitor (or someone else empowered to administer oaths).

Unless there is a special reason for committing yourself to the agreement to surrender sooner, you may want to ask the landlord to let you have at least 14 days to consider whether you wish to give up your statutory rights. If you then decided to go ahead with the agreement to end your lease, you would only need to make a simple declaration, and so you would not need to make a separate visit to an independent solicitor.

7. The form of statutory declaration referred to in paragraph 4 is as follows: –

I ....*(name of declarant)* of.............................*(address)* do solemnly and sincerely declare that –

1. I have/ ....*(name of tenant)* has a tenancy of premises at ....*(address of premises)* for a term commencing on ....

2. I/The tenant propose(s) to enter into an agreement with ....
(name of landlord) to surrender the tenancy on a date or in circumstances specified in the agreement.

3. The landlord has served on me/the tenant a notice in the form, or substantially in the form, set out in Schedule 3 to the Regulatory Reform (Business Tenancies) (England and Wales) Order 2003. The form of notice set out in that Schedule is reproduced below.

4. I have/The tenant has read the notice referred to in paragraph 3 above and accept(s) the consequences of entering into the agreement referred to in paragraph 2 above.

5. (*as appropriate*) I am duly authorised by the tenant to make this declaration.

To:

....
....
....*[Name and address of tenant]*

From:

....
....
....*[Name and address of landlord]*

IMPORTANT NOTICE FOR TENANT

Do not commit yourself to any agreement to surrender your lease unless you have read this message carefully and discussed it with a professional adviser.

Normally, you have the right to renew your lease when it expires. By committing yourself to an agreement to surrender, **you will be giving up this important statutory right**.

- You will **not** be able to continue occupying the premises beyond the date provided for under the agreement for surrender, **unless** the landlord chooses to offer you a further term (in which case you would lose the right to ask the court to determine the new rent). You will need to leave the premises.

- You will be unable to claim compensation for the loss of your premises, unless the lease or agreement for surrender gives you this right.

A qualified surveyor, lawyer or accountant would be able to offer you professional advice on your options.

You do not have to commit yourself to the agreement to surrender your lease unless you want to.

If you receive this notice at least 14 days before committing yourself to the agreement to surrender, you will need to sign a simple declaration that you have received this notice and have accepted its consequences, before signing the agreement to surrender.

But if you do not receive at least 14 days' notice, you will need to sign a 'statutory' declaration. To do so, you will need to visit an independent solicitor (or someone else empowered to administer oaths).

Unless there is a special reason for committing yourself to the agreement to surrender sooner, you may want to ask the landlord to let you have at least 14 days to consider whether you wish to give up your statutory rights. If you then decided to go ahead with the agreement to end your lease, you would only need to make a simple declaration, and so you would not need to make a separate visit to an independent solicitor.

AND I make this solemn declaration conscientiously believing the same to be true and by virtue of the Statutory Declarations Act 1835

DECLARED at ....this ....day of ....

Before me

(*signature of person before whom declaration is made*)

A commissioner for oaths *or* A solicitor empowered to administer oaths or (*as appropriate*)

APPENDIX 3: THE REGULATORY REFORM (BUSINESS TENANCIES) (ENGLAND AND WALES) ORDER 2003, ARTICLE 29

Transitional provisions

29-(1) Where, before this Order came into force –

    (a) the landlord gave the tenant notice under section 25 of the Act; or

    (b) the tenant made a request for a new tenancy in accordance with section 26 of the Act,

nothing in this Order has effect in relation to the notice or request or anything done in consequence of it.

(2) Nothing in this Order has effect in relation –

    (a) to an agreement –

        (i) for the surrender of a tenancy which was made before this Order came into force and which fell within section 24(2)(b) of the Act; or

        (ii) which was authorised by the court under section 38(4) of the Act before this Order came into force; or

    (b) to a notice under section 27(2) of the Act which was given by the tenant to the immediate landlord before this Order came into force.

(3) Any provision in a tenancy which requires an order under section 38(4) of the Act to be obtained in respect of any sub-tenancy shall, so far as is necessary after the coming into force of this Order, be construed as if it required the procedure mentioned in section 38A of the Act to be followed, and any related requirement shall be construed accordingly.

(4) If a person has, before the coming into force of this Order, entered into an agreement to take a tenancy, any provision in that agreement which requires an order under section 38(4) of the Act to be obtained in respect of the tenancy shall continue to be effective, notwithstanding the repeal of that provision by Article 21(2) of this Order, and the court shall retain jurisdiction to make such an order.

(5) Article 20 above does not have effect where the tenant quit the holding before this Order came into force.

(6) Nothing in Articles 23 and 24 above applies to a notice under section 40 of the Act served before this Order came into force.

Appendix 4: The Landlord and Tenant Act 1954 Part II (Notices) Regulations 2004, Schedule 1

SCHEDULE 1   Regulations 2(2) and 3

PRESCRIBED FORMS, AND PURPOSES FOR WHICH THEY ARE TO BE USED

(1) Form number	(2) Purpose for which to be used
1	Ending a tenancy to which Part 2 of the Act applies, where the landlord is not opposed to the grant of a new tenancy (notice under section 25 of the Act).
2	Ending a tenancy to which Part 2 of the Act applies, where - (a) the landlord is opposed to the grant of a new tenancy (notice under section 25 of the Act); and (b) the tenant is not entitled under the 1967 Act to buy the freehold or an extended lease.
3	Tenant's request for a new tenancy of premises where Part 2 of the Act applies (notice under section 26 of the Act).
4	Landlord's notice activating tenant's duty under section 40(1) of the Act to give information as to his or her occupation of the premises and as to any sub-tenancies.
5	Tenant's notice activating duty under section 40(3) of the Act of reversioner or reversioner's mortgagee in possession to give information about his or her interest in the premises.
6	Withdrawal of notice given under section 25 of the Act ending a tenancy to which Part 2 of the Act applies (notice under section 44 of, and paragraph 6 of Schedule 6 to, the Act).
7	Ending a tenancy to which Part 2 of the Act applies, where the landlord is opposed to the grant of a new tenancy but where the tenant may be entitled under the 1967 Act to buy the freehold or an extended lease (notice under section 25 of the Act and paragraph 10 of Schedule 3 to the 1967 Act).
8	Ending a tenancy to which Part 2 of the Act applies, where: (a) the notice under section 25 of the Act contains a copy of a certificate given under section 57 of the Act that the use or occupation of the property or part of it is to be changed by a specified date; (b) the date of termination of the tenancy specified in the notice is not earlier than the date specified in the certificate; and (c) the tenant is not entitled under the 1967 Act to buy the freehold or an extended lease.
9	Ending a tenancy to which Part 2 of the Act applies, where: (a) the notice under section 25 of the Act contains a copy of a certificate given under section 57 of the Act that the use or occupation of the property or part of it is to be changed at a future date; (b) the date of termination of the tenancy specified in the notice is earlier than the date specified in the certificate; (c) the landlord opposes the grant of a new tenancy; and (d) the tenant is not entitled under the 1967 Act to buy the freehold or an extended lease.

10	Ending a tenancy to which Part 2 of the Act applies, where:
	(a) the notice under section 25 of the Act contains a copy of a certificate given under section 57 of the Act that the use or occupation of the property or part of it is to be changed at a future date; (b) the date of termination of the tenancy specified in the notice is earlier than the date specified in the certificate; (c) the landlord does not oppose the grant of a new tenancy; and (d) the tenant is not entitled under the 1967 Act to buy the freehold or an extended lease.
11	Ending a tenancy to which Part 2 of the Act applies, where the notice under section 25 of the Act contains a copy of a certificate given under section 58 of the Act that for reasons of national security it is necessary that the use or occupation of the property should be discontinued or changed.
12	Ending a tenancy to which Part 2 of the Act applies, where -
	(a) the notice under section 25 of the Act contains a copy of a certificate given under section 58 of the Act (as applied by section 60 of the Act) that it is necessary or expedient for achieving the purpose mentioned in section 2(1) of the Local Employment Act 1972[6] that the use or occupation of the property should be changed; and (b) the tenant is not entitled under the 1967 Act to buy the freehold or an extended lease.
13	Ending a tenancy to which Part 2 of the Act applies, where:
	(a) the notice under section 25 of the Act contains a copy of a certificate given under section 57 of the Act that the use or occupation of the property or part of it is to be changed by a specified date; and (b) the date of termination of the tenancy specified in the notice is not earlier than the date specified in the certificate; and (c) the tenant may be entitled under the 1967 Act to buy the freehold or an extended lease.
14	Ending a tenancy to which Part 2 of the Act applies, where:
	(a) the notice under section 25 of the Act contains a copy of a certificate given under section 57 of the Act that the use or occupation of the property or part of it is to be changed at a future date; (b) the date of termination of the tenancy specified in the notice is earlier than the date specified in the certificate; and (c) the tenant may be entitled under the 1967 Act to buy the freehold or an extended lease the landlord opposes the grant of a new tenancy.
15	Ending a tenancy to which Part 2 of the Act applies, where:
	(a) the notice under section 25 of the Act contains a copy of a certificate given under section 58 of the Act (as applied by section 60 of the Act) that it is necessary or expedient for achieving the purpose mentioned in section 2(1) of the Local Employment Act 1972[7] that the use or occupation of the property should be changed; and (b) the tenant may be entitled under the 1967 Act to buy the freehold or an extended lease the landlord opposes the grant of a new tenancy.
16	Ending a tenancy of Welsh Development Agency premises where -
	(a) the notice under section 25 of the Act contains a copy of a certificate given under section 58 of the Act (as applied by section 60A of the Act) that it is necessary or expedient, for the purposes of providing employment appropriate to the needs of the area in which the premises are situated, that the use or occupation of the property should be changed; and (b) the tenant is not entitled under the 1967 Act to buy the freehold or an extended lease.
17	Ending a tenancy of Welsh Development Agency premises where:
	(a) the notice under section 25 of the Act contains a copy of a certificate given under section 58 of the Act (as applied by section 60A of the Act) that it is necessary or expedient, for the purposes of providing employment appropriate to the needs of the area in which the premises are situated, that the use or occupation of the property should be changed; and (b) the tenant may be entitled under the 1967 Act to buy the freehold or an extended lease.

Appendix 5: CPR Part 56 and PD56 (Paragraphs 1.1-4.2) as amended

PART 56

LANDLORD AND TENANT CLAIMS AND MISCELLANEOUS PROVISIONS ABOUT LAND

I LANDLORD AND TENANT CLAIMS

Scope and interpretation

56.1-(1) In this Section of this Part 'landlord and tenant claim' means a claim under –

(a) the Landlord and Tenant Act 1927[1];

(b) the Leasehold Property (Repairs) Act 1938[2];

(c) the Landlord and Tenant Act 1954[3];

(d) the Landlord and Tenant Act 1985[4]; or

(e) the Landlord and Tenant Act 1987[5].

(2) A practice direction may set out special provisions with regard to any particular category of landlord and tenant claim.

Starting the claim

56.2-(1) The claim must be started in the county court for the district in which the land is situated unless **paragraph (2) applies** or an enactment provides otherwise.

(2) The claim may be started in the High Court if the claimant files with his claim form a certificate stating the reasons for bringing the claim in that court verified by a statement of truth in accordance with rule 22.1(1).

(3) The practice direction refers to circumstances which may justify starting the claim in the High Court.

(4) A joint claim by a landlord and tenant to authorise an agreement under section 38(4) of the Landlord and Tenant Act 1954 may be started in the High Court or any county court.

Claims for a new tenancy under section 24 and for the termination of a tenancy under section 29(2) of the Landlord and Tenant Act 1954[6]

56.3-(1) This rule applies to a claim for a new tenancy under section 24 and to a claim for the termination of a tenancy under section 29(2) of the 1954 Act.

(2) In this rule –

---

1 1927 c 36.

2 1938 c 34.

3 1954 c 56.

4 1985 c 70.

5 1987 c 31.

6 1954 c.56. Section 24 was amended by article 3 of SI2003/3096. Section 29(2) was substituted by article 5 of SI 2003/3096. 1954 c 56; section 24 was amended by the Law of Property Act 1969 (c 59).

(a) 'the 1954 Act' means the Landlord and Tenant Act 1954;

(b) 'an unopposed claim' means a claim for a new tenancy under section 24 of the 1954 Act in circumstances where the grant of a new tenancy is not opposed;

(c) 'an opposed claim' means a claim for –

(i) a new tenancy under section 24 of the 1954 Act in circumstances where the grant of a new tenancy is opposed; or

(ii) the termination of a tenancy under section 29(2) of the 1954 Act.

(3) Where the claim is an unopposed claim –

(a) the claimant must use the Part 8 procedure, but the following rules do not apply –

(i) rule 8.5; and

(ii) rule 8.6;

(b) the claim form must be served within 2 months after the date of issue and rules 7.5 and 7.6 are modified accordingly; and

(c) the court will give directions about the future management of the claim following receipt of the acknowledgment of service.

(4) Where the claim is an opposed claim –

(a) the claimant must use the Part 7 procedure; but

(b) the claim form must be served within 2 months after the date of issue, and rules 7.5 and 7.6 are modified accordingly.

(The practice direction to this Part contains provisions about evidence, including expert evidence in opposed claims)

(5) Where the defendant files and serves a notice in accordance with paragraph (4)(a), the claim will be stayed for 3 months.

(6) Any party may file and serve a notice requesting the stay to be lifted.

(7) Where a party files a notice in accordance with paragraph (6) the court –

(a) will lift the stay; and

(b) may give directions about the future management of the claim.

(8) Unless the court otherwise orders where –

(a) the stay expires; and

(b) the defendant intends to contest the claim,

he must file and serve his acknowledgment of service within 14 days after the day on which the stay expires.

(9) Unless the court otherwise orders where –

(a) the stay is lifted; and

(b) the defendant intends to contest the claim,

he must file and serve his acknowledgment of service within 14 days after he is served with notification that the stay has been lifted.

(10) The claimant must file and serve any written evidence on which he intends to rely within 14 days of service on him of the acknowledgment of service.

(11) The defendant must file and serve any written evidence on which he intends to rely within 14 days of service on him of the claimant's evidence.

(12) The court will give directions about the future management of the claim –

(a) when it receives the written evidence of the defendant; or

(b) where the defendant fails to file any written evidence within the period set out in paragraph (11), after that period has expired.

(13) No written evidence may be relied on at the hearing of the claim unless –

(a) it has been served in accordance with paragraphs (10) or (11) (as the case may be); or

(b) the court gives permission.

II MISCELLANEOUS PROVISIONS ABOUT LAND

Scope

56.4 A practice direction may set out special provisions with regard to claims under the following enactments –

(a) the Chancel Repairs Act 1932[7];

(b) the Leasehold Reform Act 1967[8];

(c) the Access to Neighbouring Land Act 1992[9];

(d) the Leasehold Reform, Housing and Urban Development Act 1993[10]; and

(e) the Commonhold and Leasehold Reform Act 2002[11].

PRACTICE DIRECTION – LANDLORD AND TENANT CLAIMS AND MISCELLANEOUS PROVISIONS ABOUT LAND

THIS PRACTICE DIRECTION SUPPLEMENTS PART 56

SECTION I – LANDLORD AND TENANT CLAIMS

1.1 In this section of this practice direction –

(1) 'the 1927 Act' means the Landlord and Tenant Act 1927;

(2) 'the 1954 Act' means the Landlord and Tenant Act 1954;

(3) 'the 1985 Act' means the Landlord and Tenant Act 1985; and

(4) 'the 1987 Act' means the Landlord and Tenant Act 1987.

56.2 – STARTING THE CLAIM

2.1 **Subject to paragraph 2.1A, the** claimant in a landlord and tenant claim must use the Part 8 procedure as modified by Part 56 and this practice direction.

2.1A Where the landlord and tenant claim is a claim for –

(1) a new tenancy under section 24 of the 1954 Act in circumstances where the grant of a new tenancy is opposed; or

(2) the termination of a tenancy under section 29(2) of the 1954 Act,

the claimant must use the Part 7 procedure as modified by Part 56 and this practice direction.

2.2 Except where the county court does not have jurisdiction or rule 56.2(4) applies, landlord and tenant claims should normally be brought in the county court. Only exceptional circumstances justify starting a claim in the High Court.

2.3 If a claimant starts a claim in the High Court and the court decides that it should have been started in the county court, the court will normally either strike the claim out or transfer it to the county court on its own initiative. This is likely to result in delay and the court will normally disallow the costs of starting the claim in the High Court and of any transfer.

2.4 Circumstances which may, in an appropriate case, justify starting a claim in the High Court are if –

(1) there are complicated disputes of fact; or

---

7 1932 c 20.

8 1967 c 88.

9 1992 c 23.

10 1993 c 28.

11 2002 c 15.

(2) there are points of law of general importance.

2.5 The value of the property and the amount of any financial claim may be relevant circumstances, but these factors alone will not normally justify starting the claim in the High Court.

2.6 A landlord and tenant claim started in the High Court must be brought in the Chancery Division.

~~CLAIM FOR NEW TENANCY UNDER SECTION 24 OF THE 1954 ACT~~

~~3.1 This paragraph applies to a claim for a new tenancy under section 24 of the 1954 Act.~~

~~Claim form~~

~~3.2 The claim form must include details of:~~

~~(1) the property to which the claim relates;~~

~~(2) the nature of the business carried on at the property;~~

~~(3) the particulars of the current tenancy (including date, parties and duration), the current rent (if not the original rent) and the date and method of termination;~~

~~(4) whether any, and if so what, part of the property comprised in the tenancy is occupied neither by the tenant nor by a person employed by the tenant for the purposes of his business;~~

~~(5) particulars of every notice or request given or made under sections 25 or 26 of the 1954 Act;~~

~~(6) the claimant's proposed terms of the new tenancy;~~

~~(7) the name and address of anyone known to the claimant who –~~

~~(a) has an interest in the reversion in the property (whether immediate or in not more than 14 years) on the termination of the claimant's current tenancy; and~~

~~(b) who is likely to be affected by the grant of a new tenancy (other than a person whose only interest is a freeholder).~~

~~3.3 The claim form must be served on the persons referred to in paragraph 3.2(7).~~

~~Defendant~~

~~3.4 The person who, in relation to the claimant's current tenancy, is the landlord as defined by section 44 of the 1954 Act must be a defendant.~~

~~Notice requesting stay~~

~~3.5 The notice referred to in rule 56.3(4)(a) may be given by letter to the court.~~

~~Acknowledgment of service~~

~~3.6 The acknowledgment of service must state with particulars:~~

~~(1) whether the defendant opposes the grant of a new tenancy and, if so, on what grounds;~~

~~(2) whether, if a new tenancy is granted, the defendant objects to any of the terms proposed by the claimant and, if so, the terms to which he objects and the terms which he proposes in so far as they differ from those proposed by the claimant;~~

~~(3) whether the defendant is a tenant under a lease having less than 14 years unexpired at the date of the termination of the claimant's current tenancy and, if so, the name and address of any person who, to the knowledge of the defendant, has an interest in reversion in the property expectant (whether immediately or in not more than 14 years from that date) on the termination of the defendant's tenancy;~~

~~(4) the name and address of any person having an interest in the property other than a freehold interest or tenancy who is likely to be affected by the grant of a new tenancy;~~

~~(5) if the claimant's current tenancy is one to which section 32(2) of the 1954 Act applies, whether the defendant requires that any new tenancy shall be a tenancy of the whole of the property comprised in the claimant's current tenancy.~~

~~3.7 The acknowledgment of service may include or be accompanied by an application by the defendant for an order that the claimant pay an interim rent under section 24A of the 1954 Act.~~

~~Evidence~~

~~3.8 The evidence required to be served under rule 56.3(10) or (11) is that supporting the parties' positions so that the court can identify the issues and give appropriate further directions which may include directions about –~~

~~(1) the trial of any preliminary issues;~~

~~(2) the service of –~~

~~(a) further witness statements; and~~

~~(b) any expert evidence.~~

CLAIMS FOR A NEW TENANCY UNDER SECTION 24 AND TERMINATION OF A TENANCY UNDER SECTION 29(2) OF THE 1954 ACT

3.1 This paragraph applies to a claim for a new tenancy under section 24 and termination of a tenancy under section 29(2) of the 1954 Act where rule 56.3 applies and in this paragraph –

(1) 'an unopposed claim' means a claim for a new tenancy under section 24 of the 1954 Act in circumstances where the grant of a new tenancy is not opposed;

(2) 'an opposed claim' means a claim for –

(a) a new tenancy under section 24 of the 1954 Act in circumstances where the grant of a new tenancy is opposed; or

(b) the termination of a tenancy under section 29(2) of the 1954 Act; and

(3) 'grounds of opposition' means –

(a) the grounds specified in section 30(1) of the 1954 Act on which a landlord may oppose an application for a new tenancy under section 24(1) of the 1954 Act or make an application under section 29(2) of the 1954 Act; or

(b) any other basis on which the landlord asserts that a new tenancy ought not to be granted.

Precedence of claim forms where there is more than one application to the court under section 24(1) or section 29(2) of the 1954 Act

3.2 Where more than one application to the court under section 24(1) or section 29(2) of the 1954 Act is made, the following provisions shall apply –

(1) once an application to the court under section 24(1) of the 1954 Act has been served on a defendant, no further application to the court in respect of the same tenancy whether under section 24(1) or section 29(2) of the 1954 Act may be served by that defendant without the permission of the court;

(2) if more than one application to the court under section 24(1) of the 1954 Act in respect of the same tenancy is served on the same day, any landlord's application shall stand stayed until further order of the court;

(3) if applications to the court under both section 24(1) and section 29(2) of the 1954 Act in respect of the same tenancy are served on the same day, any tenant's application shall stand stayed until further order of the court; and

(4) if a defendant is served with an application under section 29(2) of the 1954 Act ('the section 29(2) application') which was issued at a time when an application to the court had already been made by that defendant in respect of the same tenancy under section 24(1) of the 1954 Act ('the section 24(1) application'), the service of the section 29(2) application shall be deemed to be a notice under rule 7.7 requiring service or discontinuance of the section 24(1) application within a period of 14 days after the service of the section 29(2) application.

Defendant where the claimant is the tenant making a claim for a new tenancy under section 24 of the 1954 Act

3.3 Where a claim for a new tenancy under section 24 of the 1954 Act is made by a tenant, the person who, in relation to the claimant's current tenancy, is the landlord as defined in section 44 of the 1954 Act must be a defendant.

Contents of the claim form in all cases

3.4 The claim form must contain details of –

(1) the property to which the claim relates;

(2) the particulars of the current tenancy (including date, parties and duration), the current rent (if not the original rent) and the date and method of termination;

(3) every notice or request given or made under sections 25 or 26 of the 1954 Act; and

(4) the expiry date of –

(a) the statutory period under section 29A(2) of the 1954 Act; or

(b) any agreed extended period made under section 29B(1) or 29B(2) of the 1954 Act.

Claim form where the claimant is the tenant making a claim for a new tenancy under section 24 of the 1954 Act

3.5 Where the claimant is the tenant making a claim for a new tenancy under section 24 of the 1954 Act, in addition to the details specified in paragraph 3.4, the claim form must contain details of –

(1) the nature of the business carried on at the property;

(2) whether the claimant relies on section 23(1A), 41 or 42 of the 1954 Act and, if so, the basis on which he does so;

(3) whether the claimant relies on section 31A of the 1954 Act and, if so, the basis on which he does so;

(4) whether any, and if so what part, of the property comprised in the tenancy is occupied neither by the claimant nor by a person employed by the claimant for the purpose of the claimant's business;

(5) the claimant's proposed terms of the new tenancy; and

(6) the name and address of –

(a) anyone known to the claimant who has an interest in the reversion in the property (whether immediate or in not more than 15 years) on the termination of the claimant's current tenancy and who is likely to be affected by the grant of a new tenancy; or

(b) if the claimant does not know of anyone specified by sub-paragraph (6)(a), anyone who has a freehold interest in the property.

3.6 The claim form must be served on the persons referred to in paragraph 3.5(6)(a) or (b) as appropriate.

Claim form where the claimant is the landlord making a claim for a new tenancy under section 24 of the 1954 Act

3.7 Where the claimant is the landlord making a claim for a new tenancy under section 24 of the 1954 Act, in addition to the details specified in paragraph 3.4, the claim form must contain details of –

(1) the claimant's proposed terms of the new tenancy;

(2) whether the claimant is aware that the defendant's tenancy is one to which section 32(2) of the 1954 Act applies and, if so, whether the claimant requires that any new tenancy shall be a tenancy of the whole of the property comprised in the defendant's current tenancy or just of the holding as defined by section 23(3) of the 1954 Act; and

(3) the name and address of –

(a) anyone known to the claimant who has an interest in the reversion in the property (whether immediate or in not more than 15 years) on the termination of the claimant's current tenancy and who is likely to be affected by the grant of a new tenancy; or

(b) if the claimant does not know of anyone specified by sub-paragraph (3)(a), anyone who has a freehold interest in the property.

3.8 The claim form must be served on the persons referred to in paragraph 3.7(3)(a) or (b) as appropriate.

Claim form where the claimant is the landlord making an application for the termination of a tenancy under section 29(2) of the 1954 Act

3.9 Where the claimant is the landlord making an application for the termination of a tenancy under section 29(2) of the 1954 Act, in addition to the details specified in paragraph 3.4, the claim form must contain –

(1) the claimant's grounds of opposition;

(2) full details of those grounds of opposition; and

(3) the terms of a new tenancy that the claimant proposes in the event that his claim fails.

Acknowledgment of service where the claim is an unopposed claim and where the claimant is the tenant

3.10 Where the claim is an unopposed claim and the claimant is the tenant, the acknowledgment of service is to be in form N210 and must state with particulars –

(1) whether, if a new tenancy is granted, the defendant objects to any of the terms proposed by the claimant and if so –

(a) the terms to which he objects; and

(b) the terms that he proposes in so far as they differ from those proposed by the claimant;

(2) whether the defendant is a tenant under a lease having less than 15 years unexpired at the date of the termination of the claimant's current tenancy and, if so, the name and address of any person who, to the knowledge of the defendant, has an interest in the reversion in the property expectant (whether immediate or in not more than 15 years from that date) on the termination of the defendant's tenancy;

(3) the name and address of any person having an interest in the property who is likely to be affected by the grant of a new tenancy; and

(4) if the claimant's current tenancy is one to which section 32(2) of the 1954 Act applies, whether the defendant requires that any new tenancy shall be a tenancy of the whole of the property comprised in the claimant's current tenancy.

Acknowledgment of service where the claim is an unopposed claim and the claimant is the landlord

3.11 Where the claim is an unopposed claim and the claimant is the landlord, the acknowledgment of service is to be in form N210 and must state with particulars –

(1) the nature of the business carried on at the property;

(2) if the defendant relies on section 23(1A), 41 or 42 of the 1954 Act, the basis on which he does so;

(3) whether any, and if so what part, of the property comprised in the tenancy is occupied neither by the defendant nor by a person employed by the defendant for the purpose of the defendant's business;

(4) the name and address of –

(a) anyone known to the defendant who has an interest in the reversion in the property (whether immediate or in not more than 15 years) on the termination of the defendant's current tenancy and who is likely to be affected by the grant of a new tenancy; or

(b) if the defendant does not know of anyone specified by sub-paragraph (4)(a), anyone who has a freehold interest in the property; and

(5) whether, if a new tenancy is granted, the defendant objects to any of the terms proposed by the claimant and, if so –

(a) the terms to which he objects; and

(b) the terms that he proposes in so far as they differ from those proposed by the claimant.

Acknowledgment of service and defence where the claim is an opposed claim and where the claimant is the tenant

3.12 Where the claim is an opposed claim and the claimant is the tenant –

(1) the acknowledgment of service is to be in form N9; and

(2) in his defence the defendant must state with particulars –

(a) the defendant's grounds of opposition;

(b) full details of those grounds of opposition;

(c) whether, if a new tenancy is granted, the defendant objects to any of the terms proposed by the claimant and if so –

(i) the terms to which he objects; and

(ii) the terms that he proposes in so far as they differ from those proposed by the claimant;

(d) whether the defendant is a tenant under a lease having less than 15 years unexpired at the date of the termination of the claimant's current tenancy and, if so, the name and address of any person who, to the knowledge of the defendant, has an interest in the reversion in the property expectant (whether immediately or in not more than 15 years from that date) on the termination of the defendant's tenancy;

(e) the name and address of any person having an interest in the property who is likely to be affected by the grant of a new tenancy; and

(f) if the claimant's current tenancy is one to which section 32(2) of the 1954 Act applies, whether the defendant requires that any new tenancy shall be a tenancy of the whole of the property comprised in the claimant's current tenancy.

Acknowledgment of service and defence where the claimant is the landlord making an application for the termination of a tenancy under section 29(2) of the 1954 Act

3.13 Where the claim is an opposed claim and the claimant is the landlord –

(1) the acknowledgment of service is to be in form N9; and

(2) in his defence the defendant must state with particulars –

(a) whether the defendant relies on section 23(1A), 41 or 42 of the 1954 Act and, if so, the basis on which he does so;

(b) whether the defendant relies on section 31A of the 1954 Act and, if so, the basis on which he does so; and

(c) the terms of the new tenancy that the defendant would propose in the event that the claimant's claim to terminate the current tenancy fails.

Evidence in an unopposed claim

3.14 Where the claim is an unopposed claim, no evidence need be filed unless and until the court directs it to be filed.

Evidence in an opposed claim

3.15 Where the claim is an opposed claim, evidence (including expert evidence) must be filed by the parties as the court directs and the landlord shall be required to file his evidence first.

Grounds of opposition to be tried as a preliminary issue

3.16 Unless in the circumstances of the case it is unreasonable to do so, any grounds of opposition shall be tried as a preliminary issue.

Applications for interim rent under section 24A to 24D of the 1954 Act

3.17 Where proceedings have already been commenced for the grant of a new tenancy or the termination of an existing tenancy, the claim for interim rent under section 24A of the 1954 Act shall be made in those proceedings by –

(1) the claim form;

(2) the acknowledgment of service or defence; or

(3) an application on notice under Part 23.

3.18 Any application under section 24D(3) of the 1954 Act shall be made by an application on notice under Part 23 in the original proceedings.

3.19 Where no other proceedings have been commenced for the grant of a new tenancy or termination of an existing tenancy or where such proceedings have been disposed of, an application for interim rent under section 24A of the 1954 Act shall be made under the procedure in Part 8 and the claim form shall include details of –

(1) the property to which the claim relates;

(2) the particulars of the relevant tenancy (including date, parties and duration) and the current rent (if not the original rent);

(3) every notice or request given or made under sections 25 or 26 of the 1954 Act;

(4) if the relevant tenancy has terminated, the date and mode of termination; and

(5) if the relevant tenancy has been terminated and the landlord has granted a new tenancy of the property to the tenant –

(a) particulars of the new tenancy (including date, parties and duration) and the rent; and

(b) in a case where section 24C(2) of the 1954 Act applies but the claimant seeks a different rent under section 24C(3) of that Act, particulars and matters on which the claimant relies as satisfying section 24C(3).

OTHER CLAIMS UNDER PART II OF THE 1954 ACT

4.1 The mesne landlord to whose consent a claim for the determination of any question arising under paragraph 4(3) of Schedule 6 to the 1954 Act shall be made a defendant to the claim.

4.2 If any dispute as to the rateable value of any holding has been referred under section 37(5) of the 1954 Act to the Commissioners of Inland Revenue for decision by a valuation officer, any document purporting to be a statement of the valuation officer of his decision is admissible as evidence of the matters contained in it.

APPENDIX 6: THE COMPANIES ACT 1985, SECTIONS 735-736

735 'Company' etc

(1) In this Act –

    (a) 'company' means a company formed and registered under this Act, or an existing company;

    (b) 'existing company' means a company formed and registered under the former Companies Acts, but does not include a company registered under the Joint Stock Companies Acts, the Companies Act 1862 or the Companies (Consolidation) Act 1908 in what was then Ireland;

    (c) 'the former Companies Acts' means the Joint Stock Companies Acts, the Companies Act 1862, the Companies (Consolidation) Act 1908, the Companies Act 1929 and the Companies Acts 1948 to 1983.

(2) 'Public company' and 'private company' have the meanings given by section 1(3).

(3) 'The Joint Stock Companies Acts' means the Joint Stock Companies Act 1856, the Joint Stock Companies Acts 1856, 1857, the Joint Stock Banking Companies Act 1857 and the Act to enable Joint Stock Banking Companies to be formed on the principle of limited liability, or any one or more of those Acts (as the case may require), but does not include the Joint Stock Companies Act 1844.

(4) The definitions in this section apply unless the contrary intention appears.

736 'Subsidiary', 'holding company' and 'wholly owned subsidiary'

(1) A company is a 'subsidiary' of another company, its 'holding company', if that other company –

    (a) holds a majority of the voting rights in it, or

    (b) is a member of it and has the right to appoint or remove a majority of its board of directors, or

    (c) is a member of it and controls alone, pursuant to an agreement with other shareholders or members, a majority of the voting rights in it,

or if it is a subsidiary of a company which is itself a subsidiary of that other company.

(2) A company is a 'wholly owned subsidiary' of another company if it has no members except that other and that other's wholly owned subsidiaries or persons acting on behalf of that other or its wholly owned subsidiaries.

(3) In this section 'company' includes any body corporate.

Appendix 7: The Property Litigation Association's Post-action Protocol

PART II LANDLORD AND TENANT ACT 1954

Introduction

1. Business tenancy renewals are governed by Part II of the Landlord and Tenant Act 1954 (the '1954 Act') and Part 56 of the CPR (and the Practice Direction). The purpose of this Post-Action Protocol is to provide general guidance to landlords and tenants, concerning the way in which business tenancy proceedings will normally operate and to provide greater consistency of decision making by County Courts. The Post-Action Protocol has no formal status under the CPR but has been adopted by Central London County Court on a trial basis.

2. The Post-Action Protocol recognises that business tenancy renewals are, if not unique, unlike most other litigation. Part II of the 1954 Act sets out a procedure, which is, in effect, compulsory (subject to the parties agreeing to extend time).[1] As matters stand at present[2] a tenant is bound to issue renewal proceedings in order to preserve the right to a new Lease. In an overwhelming number of cases landlords and tenants are able to agree, by a process of negotiation, the terms upon which a new Lease should be granted or upon which the tenant should vacate. It is recognised that active case management may not be required in every case and stays may be needed beyond those for which Part 56 makes special provision.

3. This Post-Action Protocol recognises that lease renewal proceedings can usefully, from the point of view of case management, be categorised in two ways.

(A) **'Standard lease renewal proceedings'** are those in which the landlord is not opposing the grant of a new tenancy, although the terms upon which the new tenancy is to be granted are disputed.

(B) **'Contested lease renewal proceedings'** are those proceedings in which there is an issue about the jurisdiction of the Court under Section 23 of the 1954 Act to grant a new tenancy or the validity of a Section 25 Notice or Section 26 Request is questioned. In addition, or alternatively, the landlord may oppose the grant of a new tenancy on one or more of the grounds under Section 30 of the 1954 Act

4. There are four appendices to this protocol. **Appendix A** provides a menu of directions for standard lease renewal proceedings. **Appendix B** provides directions for contested lease renewal proceedings. **Appendix C** is a the form of directions for lower value disputes. **Appendix D** is a model form of the particulars required in the Acknowledgement of Service.

5. The menus of directions are intended to be helpful. They are not prescriptive. The parties, their representatives and the Court must consider each case carefully when suggesting directions – not all of the suggested directions will be required.

6. In all cases, whether standard lease renewal proceedings or contested lease renewal proceedings, when an Acknowledgment of Service is filed (either under Part 56.3 (4) (b), (8) or (9), the court file will be referred to the District Judge. Unless the parties have, by the time the District Judge considers the file, submitted to the Court a draft of agreed directions which have regard to the menus of directions at Appendices A, B and C, the District Judge will proceed to make an order for directions.

7. The parties are reminded of the specific requirements for the Acknowledgement of Service under paragraph 3.6 of the Practice Directions to Part 56. It must be in Form N210 with the

---

1 *Kammins' Ballroom Co v Zenith Investments (Torquay)* [1971] AC 850
2 The proposed reform of Part II of the 1954 Act is unlikely to take effect until 2003.

particulars contained therein or alternatively annexed thereto. To assist the parties, a model form of the Particulars is annexed to this protocol as Appendix D.

8. When considering expert evidence, the parties will, of course, be mindful of their obligation to conduct the litigation in a reasonable manner and to avoid unnecessary costs. Their surveyors should, therefore, make every attempt to reach agreement or to narrow issues before they are required to draft and exchange their reports which, of course, should comply with Part 35 and, among other things, include the range of opinions that a reasonable expert might reach. If it transpires that the parties surveyors have not taken such steps, then the Court may make an order that they do so and, in appropriate cases, impose sanctions. Where an expert relies on comparables, consideration should be given to whether or not they need to be proved and, if so, to what extent. In the case of opposed lease renewals, although Appendix B sets out some suggestions for directions, it will be remembered that expert evidence may not be required. For example, ground (g) cases will mainly concern issues of fact.

Standard lease renewal proceedings

9. These proceedings will range from those in which both landlord and tenant agree that no steps are required from the moment the tenant's proceedings have been served to the time when the terms of the new Lease are agreed, to those at the other end of the spectrum in which the terms of the new Lease are hotly contested and directions will be required from an early stage. However, in the majority of cases it is likely that both landlord and tenant will wish to have an opportunity to negotiate and the landlord will apply for a 3 month stay under Part 56.3.

10. The Court has a general discretion to continue such a stay. Where both landlord and tenant wish to continue negotiations, the Court will generally order that a stay is continued on the application of both parties by letter, provided the Court is given sufficient information which confirms that the parties are genuinely making efforts to negotiate the terms for a new Lease. The amount of information which the Court will require for succeeding three month periods will increase and it is unlikely that a stay in aggregate exceeding 9 months will be granted unless there are exceptional circumstances. If the Court is not satisfied that a stay should be ordered on the basis of the information which has been provided, a directions hearing will be fixed.

11. In all cases the parties are encouraged to consider the use of **PACT**[3] or mediation (whether court-based or otherwise) as alternative post-action procedures.

12. Where the parties are not agreed that the proceedings (whether multi-track or fast track) should be stayed, the provisions of Part 56.3 as modified by this protocol will apply and directions given under it.. Where the parties are able to agree a timetable for directions which follows Appendix A or C (adapting such directions as may be necessary), an Order will normally be made by consent without the need for the parties to attend a hearing.

13. If the landlord is directed to supply a draft Lease and the tenant responds to the draft, the parties may at that stage apply to the Court for a stay not exceeding three months in order to pursue negotiations if they both consent and apply to the Court by letter. Such an application for a stay will generally be granted provided the Court is satisfied that it is for the purposes of bona fide negotiations.

14. As a general rule, the Court will not order disclosure of documents in standard lease renewal proceedings. Nonetheless, the parties are reminded of the duty to disclose and specifically Part 31.6 CPR. If a party has no document to disclose, he should say so at the earliest opportunity.

15. The Court will not normally make an order providing for a single expert witness in relation to rent (and interim rent) unless the amount in dispute is relatively low. Each Court will, in its discretion, resolve upon a suitable figure. For the Central London County Court, the appropriate figure will be a difference of £10,000 per annum between the rent proposed by each of the parties. Where such difference is £10,000 or less, the Court will probably make an order for a single expert witness but retains a discretion not to do so if either party objects. In such lower value cases, the alternative simpler form of directions at Appendix C, will apply.

Contested lease renewal proceedings

16. A challenge to the jurisdiction of the Court will arise where;

---

3 Details of the PACT scheme can be obtained from the RICS or the Law Society.

16.1 the landlord, or the tenant, does not accept that a valid Section 25 Notice, or Section 26 Request, has been served, or;

16.2 the landlord asserts that the tenant did not serve a counternotice under Section 29(2) or that any such counternotice was served too early or too late, or;

16.3 the landlord asserts that the tenant's application to court was made too early or too late, or;

16.4 the landlord puts the tenant to proof of the requirements in Section 23 that the tenant is in occupation of the premises carrying on a business.

17. Where the tenant applies to the Court for a new tenancy, but challenges the validity of the Section 25 Notice served by the landlord, the basis upon which the validity of the Section 25 Notice is challenged should be set out briefly in the application to the Court.

18. Where the landlord challenges the validity of the tenant's Section 26 Request, the grounds of challenge should be set out briefly in the Acknowledgement of Service. If the landlord puts the tenant to proof that the tenant occupies the premises for the purposes of a business carried on by him, this challenge should normally be made in the Acknowledgement of Service and brief details provided.

19. The usual order will be that the challenge to jurisdiction or entitlement to a new tenancy is to be dealt with as a preliminary issue prior to the consideration of the terms upon which a new Lease will be granted. Subsequent directions will relate to the trial of the preliminary issue only and directions for the determination for the terms of the lease will be addressed, if necessary, after the preliminary issue has been resolved.

20. Where a landlord relies on one of the grounds in Section 30 (1) of the 1954 Act (whether or not in addition to a challenge to jurisdiction or entitlement) the landlord's written evidence should include particulars of the basis upon which the ground is relied upon. These particulars will frequently include the following:

Ground (a) A Schedule of Dilapidations showing the condition of the premises, the work required to remedy it and the covenant of which the tenant is allegedly in breach;

Ground (b) A schedule showing the payment history in respect of rent;

Ground (c) A schedule showing the covenants in respect of which the tenant has been in breach and the breach or breaches complained of;

Ground (d) A description of the alternative accommodation which the landlord intends to provide;

Ground (e) The level of the rent which the Landlord maintains is obtainable on a letting of the whole and of the individual parts together with an explanation showing when the landlord will obtain vacant possession of the remainder of the building;

Ground (f)

(i) A description, in summary, of the works which the landlord intends to undertake;

(ii) if consents are required whether they have been obtained and, if not, when they are expected to be obtained;

(iii) the time when the landlord intends to commence such works

(iv) if relevant, an explanation showing when the landlord will obtain vacant possession of the remainder of the building to be developed

(v) evidence of the landlord's financial ability to carry out the work may sometimes be required.

Ground (g) A description of the business which the landlord intends to carry on at the premises.

21. Appendix B comprises a menu of directions which may be used in contested lease renewal proceedings. Consideration may be given in the case of grounds (a) and (c) whether or not a single joint expert, or a Court appointed expert, would be appropriate. In the case of ground (f) the Court will normally direct that each party is permitted to call one expert.

22 If the preliminary issue is decided in the tenant's favour and the Court confirms the tenant's entitlement to a new lease, then paragraphs 9 - 15 will apply.

23. Some cases will be suitable for management/trial or both in the Central London County Court's Chancery List. Although the resident judges at Central London all have considerable experience of 1954 Act cases, there are cases which may be helped by being dealt with by a Chancery/Landlord and Tenant specialist. These would include difficult valuation disputes, complex issues of conveyancing/drafting and others of a similar type. If the parties consider that the case ought to be in the Chancery List and they say so at the outset, the papers can be put before a Chancery circuit judge or one of the two Chancery district judges for consideration and immediate transfer. Alternatively, an order for transfer can be sought at the case management conference. Generally, if such an order is made in this type of case, the Chancery judges will keep the case in the Chancery List unless it appears then (or later) that this would be unsuitable.

PROPERTY LITIGATION ASSOCIATION

2002

APPENDIX A

Standard Directions for unopposed Lease Renewals

1. Allocation

The case is allocated to the multi-track/fast track.

[*Note: Although Part 56 claims are automatically allocated to multi-track being within Part 8, in low rent cases the Court will consider whether to re-allocate the case to fast track.*]

2. Part 56

The Court gives permission for written evidence produced in accordance with these directions to be relied on at the hearing of this case and directs that the Claimant and Defendant are not also required to comply with the provisions of Rule 56.3(10) and (11).

3. [Transfer to the Chancery List

This case be transferred to this court's Chancery List and continue under Chancery number…]

[*Note: The parties and the court should consider whether the issues in dispute are such that the case is appropriate for transfer to the Chancery List. Even if the parties consider the matter should be transferred to the Chancery List, they should still seek to agree the other directions in case the court considers that transfer is not appropriate and/or to assist the [Chancery] judge with directions to be given.*]

4. Stay of proceedings

If at any time the Claimant and Defendant jointly notify the Court that they wish the proceedings to be stayed for a fixed period (not exceeding three months) to enable the parties to attempt to negotiate a settlement, the periods of time for compliance with these directions shall be adjusted by such period provided that such stay shall not affect the date fixed for the trial of this case. Prior to the fixing of a date for trial, the parties may jointly apply for the trial window to be adjusted to take into account the agreed period of the stay.

5. Professional Arbitration on Court Terms (PACT) and ADR [optional]

[*Note: The parties should consider a stay to enable the matter to be determined under the PACT scheme. If a reference to the PACT scheme is appropriate, in place of the directions set out below, the parties should use the appropriate form of PACT order – see the PACT booklet published jointly by the Law Society and the Royal Institution of Chartered Surveyors. Alternatively, the parties should consider a stay to enable mediation to take place*]

6. Draft Lease

The Defendant shall serve on the Claimant [, either by e-mail or on computer disc, an electronic copy of] a draft lease by no later than 4.00pm on [insert date].

The Claimant shall serve on the Defendant its proposed amendments/counter-proposals to the lease [, either by e-mail or on computer disc, marked in *italics* or <u>underlined</u> (if the draft lease was submitted electronically) or marked in red or by schedule (if the draft lease was submitted in paper form)], by no later than 4.00pm on [insert date].

The Defendant shall by no later than 4.00pm on [insert date] notify the Claimant which amendments, if any, are disputed and specify the Defendant's additional amendments, [, either by e-mail or on computer disc, marked in *italics* or <u>underlined</u> (if the draft lease was submitted electronically) or marked in green (if the Claimant's amendments were marked in red) or by counter-schedule (if the Claimant's amendments were by schedule)].

7. Disclosure [optional]

Each party [the Claimant/the Defendant] shall give standard disclosure of documents to every other party [to the Defendant/the Claimant] by list by 4.00pm on [insert date].

The last date for service of any request to inspect or for a copy of any document is 4.00pm on [insert date].

8. Witness Statements of Fact [optional]

Each party shall serve on the other party the witness statements of all witnesses of fact on whom it intends to rely.

There shall be simultaneous exchange of such statements by no later than 4.00pm on [insert date].

9. [Disputed Lease Terms [optional]

The parties/solicitors for the parties are to meet/speak by 4.00pm on [insert date] on a without prejudice basis with a view to narrowing the issues between the parties on the lease terms.

The parties do, by no later than 4.00pm on [insert date], prepare and serve a schedule setting out such terms of the draft lease as are not agreed. In each case, the party seeking materially to depart from the terms of the current lease of the premises must set out its reasons for so doing.]

10. Expert Evidence

If the terms of the new lease are not agreed between the parties, experts reports are to be exchanged no later than 4.00pm on [insert date] and agreed if possible, and if not agreed such expert evidence to be limited to one conveyancing expert for such party.

[*Note: Since in many cases only rent and interim rent are in issue, permission for a conveyancing expert will only rarely be appropriate.*]

If the rent [and interim rent] for the new lease is not agreed between the parties, each party is to be at liberty to call one expert valuation witness at the hearing of the Claimant's application for a new tenancy. Their reports, including lists of comparables and photographic evidence (if any) relating to the rent payable under the new lease to be exchanged by no later than 4.00pm on [insert date]. Such reports are to be agreed if possible.

[The respective experts are to meet/speak by 4.00pm on [insert date] on a without prejudice basis with a view to narrowing the issues between the parties.] The experts [the parties] are to agree a joint statement indicating those parts of the experts evidence with which they are/are not in agreement (including as to facts, the description of the premises, any plans and photographs and the comparables (and any plans and photographs relating to them)) with reasons, such statement to be served on all parties by no later than 4.00pm on [insert date].

11. Questions to Experts [optional]

The time for service on another party of any question addressed to an expert instructed by that party is no later than [insert number] days after service of that expert's report.

Any such question is to be answered within [insert number] days of service of the question(s).

12. Request for Information etc [optional]

Each party shall serve any request for clarification or further information based on any document disclosed or statement served by another party no later than [insert number] days after disclosure or service.

Any such request shall be dealt with within [insert number] days of service of the request.

13. Dates for filing Pre-Trial Checklists and Trial

Each party must file a completed Pre-Trial Checklist by no later than 4pm on [insert date] with experts reports, statements of issues by experts[, replies to any questions to experts] and witness statements.

This case [including the Defendant's claim for interim rent] is to be tried as a fixture before a Circuit Judge in the period commencing on [insert date] and ending on [insert date] with a provisional time estimate of [insert estimate of length of hearing].

[*Note: While the court will endeavour to fix the trial window requested by the parties, it will very much depend on the availability of court time. The dates suggested by the parties will be taken as an indication of their assessment of when they will be ready for trial.*]

Either

[The trial date is to be fixed by [a Listing Officer] [the Specialist Jurisdiction manager] at a listing appointment at [insert time] on [insert date] at [13/14] [26] Park Crescent London W1 at which the parties are to attend and to have available all dates to avoid. The parties are to inform each other forthwith of the details of the listing appointment to ensure attendance at that appointment, so that it shall be effective.

If a party does not attend at the listing appointment or does not then provide dates to avoid, the trial date will be fixed for such date as the Listing Officer/Specialist Jurisdiction Manager may decide, and any date so fixed shall only be varied upon an application to a judge.]

Or (which must be used where both solicitors are on e-mail)

[On Thursday   at 12 noon each party must email the Diary Manager at clondctyla@ courtservice.gsi.gov.uk with dates to avoid for parties, witnesses and advocates. The parties are encouraged to agree a list of such dates, in which case one party may email on behalf of all, provided he certifies that all others have agreed.

On receipt of the required information the court will email all parties with the hearing date. If the required information is not received by the time stated the court will proceed to list and email all parties accordingly. In either case a formal notice of hearing will also be sent by post or DX. Thereafter the hearing date will not be altered except on application on notice to a circuit judge.

No email sent to clondctyla@courtservice.gsi.gov.uk will be acknowledged or otherwise dealt with unless it is providing information as directed by the court. Any abuse of this facility will be reported to the senior judge.]

14. Miscellaneous

The Claimant shall lodge at the court and with the Defendant an indexed bundle of documents contained in a ring binder and with each page clearly numbered no more than seven days and not less than three days before the start of the trial.

Skeleton arguments on behalf of both parties are to be lodged no later than three days before the start of the trial.

The parties shall seek to agree the contents of the trial bundle and the case summary.

Each party must inform the court immediately if the claim is settled, whether or not it is then possible to file a draft consent order to give effect to their agreement.

Costs in the case.

APPENDIX B

Standard Directions for opposed Lease Renewals

1. Allocation

The case is allocated to the multi-track/fast track.

[*Note: Although Part 56 claims are automatically allocated to multi-track being within Part 8, in low rent cases the Court will consider whether to re-allocate the case to fast track.*]

2. Preliminary Issue

The trial of the issue(s) as to whether the Defendant satisfies the ground of opposition contained in Section 30(1) [a-b-c-d-e-f-g] be tried as [a] preliminary issue(s).

[The trial of the issue of whether the Court has jurisdiction to make an order granting the Claimant a new lease of [the Premises] be tried as a preliminary issue.]

The directions referred to below shall apply to the preliminary issue(s) only, and all further proceedings herein (save in relation to the preliminary issue(s)) shall be stayed until the determination of the preliminary issue(s) or further order in the meantime.

3. Part 56

The Court gives permission for written evidence produced in accordance with these directions to be relied on at the trial of the preliminary issue(s) and directs that the Claimant and Defendant are not also required to comply with the provisions of Rule 56.3(10) and (11).

4. [Transfer to the Chancery List

This case be transferred to this court's Chancery List and continue under Chancery number......]

[Note: The parties and the court should consider whether the issues in dispute are such that the case is appropriate for transfer to the Chancery List. Even if the parties consider the matter should be transferred to the Chancery List, they should still seek to agree the other directions in case the court considers that transfer is not appropriate and/or to assist the [Chancery] judge with directions to be given.]

5. Disclosure of Documents

Each party [the Defendant] shall give standard disclosure of documents relating to the preliminary issue(s) to every other party [the Claimant] by list by 4.00pm on [insert date].

The last date for service of any request to inspect or for a copy of any document is 4.00pm on [insert date].

[Note: The parties and the court should consider whether the tenant is in a position to give disclosure in any meaningful way and, if not, the order should be altered, accordingly. Disclosure by the tenant may be relevant where the landlord challenges jurisdiction or the entitlement of the tenant to a new tenancy.]

6. Witness Statements of Fact

Each party shall serve on the other party the witness statements of all witnesses of fact on whom it intends to rely.

There shall be simultaneous exchange of such statements by no later than 4pm on [insert date].

[There shall be consecutive service of such statements. The Defendant shall serve its statements by 4.00pm on [insert date] and the Claimant by 4.00pm on [insert date].

[Note: The parties and the court should consider whether the tenant is in a position to adduce factual evidence in any meaningful way and, if not, the order should be altered, accordingly. Factual evidence from or on behalf of the tenant may be relevant where the landlord challenges jurisdiction or the entitlement of the tenant to a new tenancy.]

7. Expert Evidence

[Party appointed experts will be the normal order]

[The parties shall exchange reports setting out the substance of any expert evidence relating to the preliminary issue(s) on which they intend to rely. Such evidence shall be limited to [number] for each party and the discipline(s) of [insert disciplines].

The exchange shall take place simultaneously no later than 4.00pm on [insert date].

Experts reports shall be agreed if possible no later than [   ] days after service.

[The respective experts are to meet/speak by 4.00pm on [insert date] on a without prejudice basis with a view to narrowing the issues between the parties.] The experts [the parties] are to agree a joint statement indicating those parts of the experts evidence with which they are/are not in agreement (including as to facts, the description of the premises, any plans and photographs and the comparables (and any plans and photographs relating to them)) with reasons, such statement to be served on all parties by no later than 4.00pm on [insert date].

Each party has permission to use an expert witness to give [oral] evidence [in the form of a report] at the trial provided that the substance of the evidence to be given has been disclosed as above and has not been agreed].

OR

[A single expert may be appropriate in respect of particular issues eg the condition of the property in relation to ground (a)]

[On it appearing to the court that expert evidence is necessary on the issue of [   ] and that evidence should be given by the report of a [single] expert [insert profession] [instructed jointly by the parties], the [Claimant/Defendant] shall not later than 4.00pm on [insert date] inform the court in writing whether or not such an expert has been instructed].

OR

[The expert evidence on the issue of [   ] shall be limited to a single expert [insert profession] jointly instructed by the parties.

If the parties cannot agree by 4.00pm on [insert date] who that expert is to be and about the payment of his fees, either party may apply for further directions.

Unless the parties agree in writing or the court orders otherwise, the fees and expenses of such an expert shall be paid to him [by the parties equally] [by the Claimant/Defendant].

The report of the expert shall be served on all parties by no later than 4pm on [insert date]].

8. Questions to Experts [optional]

The time for service on another party of any question addressed to an expert whether instructed by that party or jointly instructed by the parties is not later than [insert number] days after service of that expert's report.

Any such question shall be answered within [insert number] days of service of the question(s).

9. Request for Information etc [optional]

Each party shall serve any request for clarification or further information based on any document disclosed or statement served by another party no later than [insert number] days after disclosure or service.

Any such request shall be dealt with within [insert number] days of service of the request.

10. Dates for filing Pre-Trial Checklists and Trial

Each party must file a completed Pre-Trial Checklist no later than [insert date] with experts reports, statements of issues by experts[, replies to any questions to experts] and witness statements.

The preliminary issue(s) [is/are] to be tried as a fixture before a Circuit Judge in the period commencing on [insert date] and ending on [insert date] with a provisional time estimate of [insert estimate of length of hearing].

[*Note: While the court will endeavour to fix the trial window requested by the parties, it will very much depend on the availability of court time. The dates suggested by the parties will be taken as an indication of their assessment of when they will be ready for trial.*]

Either

[The trial date is to be fixed by [a Listing Officer] [the Specialist Jurisdiction manager] at a listing appointment at [insert time] on [insert date] at [13/14] [26] Park Crescent London W1 at which the parties are to attend and to have available all dates to avoid. The parties are to inform each other forthwith of the details of the listing appointment to ensure attendance at that appointment, so that it shall be effective.

If a party does not attend at the listing appointment or does not then provide dates to avoid, the trial date will be fixed for such date as the Listing Officer/Specialist Jurisdiction Manager may decide, and any date so fixed shall only be varied upon an application to a judge.]

Or (which must be used where both solicitors are on e-mail)

[On Thursday   at 12 noon each party must email the Diary Manager at clondctyla@ courtservice.gsi.gov.uk with dates to avoid for parties, witnesses and advocates. The parties are encouraged to agree a list of such dates, in which case one party may email on behalf of all, provided he certifies that all others have agreed.

On receipt of the required information the court will email all parties with the hearing date. If the required information is not received by the time stated the court will proceed to list and email all parties accordingly. In either case a formal notice of hearing will also be sent by post or DX. Thereafter the hearing date will not be altered except on application on notice to a circuit judge.

No email sent to clondctyla@courtservice.gsi.gov.uk will be acknowledged or otherwise dealt with unless it is providing information as directed by the court. Any abuse of this facility will be reported to the senior judge.]

11. Miscellaneous

The Defendant shall lodge at the court and with the Claimant an indexed bundle of documents contained in a ring binder and with each page clearly numbered no more than seven days and not less than three days before the start of the trial.

Skeleton arguments by both parties shall be lodged with the Court not less than three days before the start of the trial.

The parties shall seek to agree the contents of the trial bundle and the case summary.

Each party must inform the court immediately if the claim is settled, whether or not it is then possible to file a draft consent order to give effect to their agreement.

Costs in the case.

APPENDIX C

This case be allocated to the Fast Track.

1. Part 56

The Court gives permission for written evidence produced in accordance with these directions to be relied on at the hearing of this case and directs that the Claimant and Defendant are not also required to comply with the provisions of Rule 56.3(10) and (11).

2. Stay of proceedings

If at any time the Claimant and Defendant jointly notify the Court that they wish the proceedings to be stayed for a fixed period (not exceeding three months) to enable the parties to attempt to negotiate a settlement, the periods of time for compliance with these directions shall be adjusted by such period provided that such stay shall not affect the date fixed for the trial of this case. Prior to the fixing of a date for trial, the parties may jointly apply for the trial window to be adjusted to take into account the agreed period of the stay.

3. The Lease

The defendant do by no later than 4.00pm [   ] serve upon the claimant a copy of the draft lease which it would be prepared to enter into.

The claimant do by no later than 4.00pm [   ] serve upon the defendant a Schedule identifying the clauses (if any) in the draft lease which are disputed and specifying proposed amendments to the said clauses.

4. Disclosure [optional]

Each party shall give to the other party standard disclosure of documents on Form N265 by 4pm [   ] with inspection within 7 days thereafter.

5. Statements [optional]

The parties shall exchange statements of witnesses of fact by 4pm [   ]. No witness whose statement has not been so exchanged shall give evidence without the permission of the Court.

6. Expert Evidence

The evidence on the question of rent shall be limited to the written report of a single expert (valuer) jointly instructed by the parties. Instructions to be given to the expert by 4.00pm [   ], and his written report shall be served by 4.00 pm [   ].

7. Pre Trial Checklist

Each party do file a completed Pre Trial Checklist [and claimant shall pay Listing Fee] together with the expert's report including replies to any questions served and witness statements by 4.00pm [   ].

8. Trial

The case be listed for hearing before a Circuit Judge in the period from [to   ] with a provisional time estimate of [   ] hours.

9. Miscellaneous

Each party must inform the court immediately if the case is settled.

The defendant shall, not less than 14 days before the hearing/beginning of trial window, notify the claimant of all documents to be included in the court bundle. The claimant shall not more than 7 days, and not less than 3 days, before the trial lodge, with the court 2 copies of a paginated and indexed bundle complying with Paragraphs 3.1 to 3.10 of the Practice Direction to Part 39 and containing copies of all relevant documents including statements of case, witness statements and expert's report (if any).

Costs in case.

Because this Order has been made by the Court without considering representations from the parties, the parties have the right to apply to have the order set aside, varied or stayed. A party wishing to make an application must send or deliver the application to the court (together with any appropriate fee) to arrive within seven days of service of this Order.

APPENDIX D

IN THE CENTRAL LONDON COUNTY COURT   CLAIM NO CL..........

B E T W E E N:

[................................]

Claimant

- and -

[................................]

Defendant

PARTICULARS ANNEXED TO ACKNOWLEDGMENT OF SERVICE PURSUANT TO PART 56.3 CIVIL PROCEDURE RULES AND PARAGRAPH 3.6 TO THE PRACTICE DIRECTION TO PART 56 CIVIL PROCEDURE RULES

---

1. The Defendant [does not oppose/opposes] the grant of a new tenancy under Part II of the Landlord & Tenant Act 1954 (the Act) to the Claimant [on ground(s) [   ] of section 30 (1) of the Act].

2. If a new tenancy is granted to the Claimant, the Defendant objects to [all of the terms proposed by the Claimant] [the following terms proposed by the Claimant: specify]. The following are the Defendant's counter proposals:–

    (i) A term of [   ] years.

    (ii) A commencing rent of £[   ] per year

    (iii) [*Specify other terms sought*]

    (iv) The other terms of the new lease be in the form of a modern commercial lease [including provision for, but not limited to, the inclusion of an authorised guarantee agreement as provided for by the Landlord & Tenant (Covenants) Act 1995].

3. [The Defendant is not a tenant under a lease having less than fourteen years unexpired at the date of the termination of the Claimant's tenancy.]

OR

[The Defendant is a tenant under lease having less that 14 years unexpired at the date of termination of the Claimant's current tenancy and the name and address of the person who, to the knowledge of the Defendant, has an interest in reversion in the property expectant (whether immediately or in not more than 14 years from that date) on the termination of the Defendant's tenancy is as follows: *specify name and address*]

4. [There is no-one likely to be affected by the grant of a new lease other than the Defendant.]

OR

[The name and address of any person having an interest in the property other than a freehold interest or tenancy who is likely to be affected by the grant of a new tenancy is as follows: *specify name and address*]

5. The Defendant requires that a new tenancy shall be a tenancy of the whole of the premises comprised in the Claimants' current tenancy. [*Delete this paragraph if the Defendant only wishes the Claimant to have a new tenancy of that part of the property occupied by it for the purposes of a business carried on by it at the property*]

6. Pursuant to paragraph 3.7 of the Practice Direction to Part 56 of the Civil Procedure Rules, the Defendant hereby applies to the Court under section 24A of the Act to determine a rent which would be reasonable for the Claimants to pay while the tenancy continues by virtue of section 24 of the Act. [*Delete if no interim rent is to be sought*]

APPENDIX 8: THE CHANGES AT A GLANCE

OLD SECTION	PRE 1 JUNE 2004	NEW SECTION	FROM 1 JUNE 2004
Contracting out			
s38(4)(a)	Parties could contract out of security of tenure provisions with approval of the court	s38A(1) and (3) and Sch 1 and 2 to the Order	Parties can contract out of security of tenure provisions by service of a health warning notice by landlord and by making of a simple/statutory declaration by the tenant
Surrenders			
s24(2)(b)	Actual surrenders where tenant has been in occupation for less than one month invalid	repealed	All actual surrenders are valid - no longer a prohibition of surrenders during the first month of the tenancy
s24(2)(b) and s38(1)	Ambiguity between s24(2)(b) which seemed to imply validity of a surrender made pursuant to an agreement reached after tenant had been in occupation for one month and s38(1) which said all agreements to surrender invalid unless obtained court approval	repealed	All agreements to surrender are definitely invalid unless proper procedures followed.
s38(1)	Parties could agree to surrender a tenancy with approval by the court	s38A(2) and (4) and Sch 3 and 4 to the Order	Parties can validate an agreement to surrender the lease by service of a heath warning notice by the landlord and by making of a simple/statutory declaration by the tenant.
To whom does the Act apply			
s23	Caused problems where the property and the business were in separate ownerships	s23(1A)	Makes it clear that in identifying the tenant an individual and any company they control will be treated as equivalent when assessing qualification for the statutory procedures
s30(3)	Ground 30(1)(g) did not apply where a company landlord wanted possession so that a controlling shareholder could trade from the premises	s30(3) repealed New s30(1A)	Makes it clear that when identifying the landlord and its business for the purposes of s30(1)(g) an individual and any company they control will be treated as equivalent.

OLD SECTION	PRE 1 JUNE 2004	NEW SECTION	FROM 1 JUNE 2004
		s30(2A)	Extends the five-year rule – ground (g) will not apply if the controlling interest in the landlord company was acquired five years before the end of the current tenancy
s42	Definition of group of companies only covered companies directly or indirectly owned by a holding company.	s42(1)	Extended to also cover associated companies under the control of one individual, where there are no inter-connecting shareholdings
		s46(2)	The definition of 'control of a company' is in accordance with s735 and s736 of the Companies Act 1985 - whether the company is controlled by an individual or another company
s34(1)(d)	Disregards for licensed premises when court is calculating the rent	s34(2A)	Where the Act applies because of the new rules as to ownership and control of a business the reference to 'the tenant' in s34(1)(d) shall be construed on the same basis
s35(1) and s44	Definition of landlord and terms of the tenancy	s35(1) and s44(1A)	Makes it clear that where there is a split reversion 'the landlord' will comprise all the owners collectively and rent under any new tenancy will be apportioned
Information gathering			
s40	Notices could be served by either party requesting information	s40 repealed new s40	Notices can be served by either party requesting information (more information has to be provided). New prescribed forms
		s40(5)	New duty to update information if changes within 6 months.
		s40A	Duties on transfer of interests.
		s40B	New specific claim for breach of statutory duty.
Landlord's s25 notice			
s25	Landlord indicated whether or not it opposed renewal	s25	There are two separate notices depending on whether or not the landlord is opposing renewal For an unopposed renewal – Form 1 For an opposed renewal – Form 2

OLD SECTION	PRE 1 JUNE 2004	NEW SECTION	FROM 1 JUNE 2004
		s25(8)	In an unopposed renewal the landlord also has to set out its proposals for the new tenancy
Tenant's s26 request			
s26		s26	No changes as to substance but a new prescribed form – Form 3
Counternotices			
By tenant s29(2)	The Court would not entertain the tenant's application for a new tenancy if had not served a counternotice	s29(2) and s25(5) repealed	Tenant is no longer required to serve a counternotice
By landlord s26(6)	Where a landlord wishes to oppose renewal it must serve a counternotice setting out its grounds of opposition	s26(6)	Landlord still has to serve a counternotice if opposing renewal
Applications to the court			
s24(1)	The tenant could apply to court for a new tenancy.	s24(1)	Either the tenant or the landlord may apply to the Court for a new tenancy.
		s24(2A)	Neither party can make an application for a new tenancy if the other has done so and served the application.
		s24(2B)	Neither party can make an application for a new tenancy if the landlord has already made and served an application under s29(2) to terminate the tenancy.
		s24(2C)	Landlord cannot withdraw application for a new tenancy unless tenant consents.
Time limits for renewal proceedings			
Latest time for court applications			
s29(3)	Tenant had to apply to court at least two months, but not later than four months, after	s29(3) repealed s29A	Application to court has to be made before the end of the 'statutory period', ie the period ending:

OLD SECTION	PRE 1 JUNE 2004	NEW SECTION	FROM 1 JUNE 2004
	service of s25 notice/s26 request.		• on the date the landlord's s25 notice as date the tenancy will end; or • immediately before the date in the tenant's s26 request as date new tenancy will begin
		s29B	This time can be extended by agreement in writing No limit on number or length of extensions Tenancy is continued during period of extension
Earliest time for court application			
s.29(3)	At least two months after service of s25 notice/s26 request	s29A(3)	*If s26 request made by tenant:* • If landlord does not oppose renewal tenant or landlord has to wait two months from making of s26 request before issuing application • If landlord does oppose renewal proceedings application can be issued straight after service of landlord's counter notice. *If s25 notice served by landlord:* Application can be made at any time after service of s25 notice (subject to latest time mentioned above). No need to wait two months.
Termination proceedings by a landlord			
	If landlord wished to oppose renewal he had to wait until the tenant made an application to the Court and then oppose that application.	s29(2)	Landlord has a new right to start proceedings simply to terminate the tenancy without renewal.
		s29(2)(a)(b)	Right arises if: • landlord has served a hostile s25 notice; or • landlord has served counternotice opposing renewal.

OLD SECTION	PRE 1 JUNE 2004	NEW SECTION	FROM 1 JUNE 2004
		s29(3)	Application cannot be made if either landlord or tenant has made an application to Court for a new tenancy.
		s29A(1)(b)	*Latest time for application* Application has to be made before end of the 'statutory period' (see above for meaning of this and extension by agreement)
		s26(6)	*Earliest time for application* If tenant has made a s26 request: The landlord still has to serve a counternotice opposing renewal within two months of tenant making the s26 request. Application to court can be any time after service of the counternotice (subject to latest time above) If landlord has served s25 notice: No requirement for tenant to serve counternotice, therefore, landlord can make application to court at any time after service of s25 notice (subject to latest time above)
		s29(4)(a)	If landlord establishes grounds of opposition the court may make an order for termination of the tenancy without renewal
		s29(4)(b)	If landlord does not establish grounds of opposition the Court will make an order for the grant of a new tenancy.

Termination of fixed term tenancies by a tenant – s27 notices

Before end of fixed term

OLD SECTION	PRE 1 JUNE 2004	NEW SECTION	FROM 1 JUNE 2004
s27(1)	Tenant had to give at least three months' notice before end of fixed term Plus *Esselte AB v Pearl Plc*: if vacate before end of fixed term tenancy also ends	s27(1)	Tenant can end tenancy at end of contractual term by: • serving at least three months' notice before end of contractual term; or • not being in occupation at end of contractual term (confirms *Esselte*)
		s27(1A)	

211

OLD SECTION	PRE 1 JUNE 2004	NEW SECTION	FROM 1 JUNE 2004
After end of fixed term			
s27(2)	Tenant could serve three months' notice ending on a quarter day.	s27(2)	Three months' notice can end on any day If tenant just moves out s27(2) makes it clear that alone will not bring the tenancy to an end
		s27(3)	Provides for the appointment of rent if the notice does not end on a quarter day
Interim rent			
s24A(1)	Only the landlord could apply for interim rent	s24A	Either landlord or tenant can apply for interim rent provided the other one has not already done so
s24A(2)	Interim rent application could be made at anytime after service of notice/request	s24A(3)	Application not entertained by the court if made more than six months after the termination of the relevant tenancy ie the continuation tenancy
s24A(2)	Interim rent payable from date of the application (of, if later) the date in the s25 notice or s26 request	s24B(1)	Interim rent is payable from the 'appropriate date' which is the earliest date that could have been specified in the s25 notice/s26 request as date of termination of the tenancy/date from which new tenancy to begin.
Amount of interim rent			
s24(3)	Court determine interim rent having regard to: • passing rent • s34(1) and (2) of the Act • as if yearly tenancy of whole property and 'old' tenancy • on terms of 'old' tenancy	s24C	Where a new tenancy of the whole of the premises is granted and the landlord did not oppose: interim rent is the same as the new rent for the new tenancy. Unless: one of the parties can show to the court: • a substantial change in the market (if so rent will be 'relevant rent' as defined in s24C(4)) • a change in lease terms which substantially affects the rent (if so, rent will be a 'reasonable rent' as defined s24C(7))
		s24D	Other cases: The Court fixes a 'reasonable' rent in accordance with s24D(2).

OLD SECTION	PRE 1 JUNE 2004	NEW SECTION	FROM 1 JUNE 2004
		s24D(3)	If new tenancy is ordered, but court revokes the order under s36(2) or parties agree not to act on the order, then either party can apply for interim rent to be recalculated. Instead of being the new rent, it would be the 'reasonable' rent under s24D
New tenancy			
s33	Maximum duration court could order was 14 years	s33	Maximum duration court can order is 15 years
Compensation			
For disturbance			
s37	Where the tenant has occupied part only of the property for more than 14 years it was entitled to double compensation for the whole *Edicron Ltd v William Whitely Ltd* [1984] 1 WLR 59	s37(3A)	Where part of the premises have been occupied for different lengths of time, compensation will be calculated for each part separately. Double compensation will only apply to those parts which have been continuously occupied for 14 years
For misrepresentation			
s55	Was only payable where the Court refused an order for a new tenancy (and it later appeared that decision was induced by a misrepresentation or concealment of material facts).	s55 repealed s37A	The right to compensation is extended to cases where the tenant is induced not to apply to the Court for a new tenancy, or withdraws an application, because of the misrepresentation or concealment of material facts, and then quits the premises

Index